Questions & Answers

Management Accounting

Questions & Answers

Management Accounting

Tim Dunningham

Financial Training

First published in Great Britain by Financial Training Publications Limited,
Avenue House, 131 Holland Park Avenue, London W11 4UT

ISBN: 0 906322 30 8

Typeset by David John Services, Maidenhead and printed by The Pitman Press, Bath

Contents

Acknowledgements

The author and publishers wish to thank the following professional bodies for their kind permission to include selected past examination questions in this publication:

> The Association of Certified Accountants
> The Institute of Chartered Accountants in England and Wales
> The Institute of Cost and Management Accountants

About the author

Tim Dunningham is a director of Financial Training (London) Ltd. He qualified as a chartered accountant in 1976 and joined Financial Training the following year. He is a senior tutor specialising in Management Accounting and Financial Management.

Introduction

All the questions in this book are of examination standard, though they range from questions which provide a simple test of knowledge of basic techniques and procedures to those, the more numerous, which require a more complex and analytical approach.

The questions will therefore give excellent examination practice to all students of management accounting who are studying for degree courses and professional examinations, particularly

ACCA   Paper 2.4, Management Accounting
ICMA   Papers 15 and 16, Management Accounting 1 and 2
ICAEW   PE2, Management Accounting

The book is divided into 21 chapters, containing a varying number of questions according to the relative importance of each subject for practical and examination purposes. Each chapter is prefaced by an explanation of the type of question and subject area covered, and also suggests specific study requirements necessary before tackling the questions.

Because the scope of management accounting is very wide, it will be found that different examining bodies give different degrees of emphasis to particular facets of the subject. The Institute of Cost and Management Accountants, for example, is unique in including investment appraisal techniques in its two Part III papers on management accounting; and it has hitherto given less emphasis to quantitative techniques than the Association of Certified Accountants (Level 2 Paper 2.4) or the Institute of Chartered Accountants in England and Wales (Professional Examination 2). The management accounting paper of the latter institute incorporates questions on management information systems, which other bodies treat as a separate subject.

The aim of this book is to cover the substantial common ground of all the above examinations and to give a few representative questions on those specialised subjects to which the student may have to devote supplementary attention.

Marks have been allocated to each question as indications both of its relative importance for examination purposes and also of the time within which a candidate should be capable of answering it under examination conditions.

The answers provided illustrate the clear and logical approach which a student should aim to develop. Commentaries have been added where necessary to explain why a particular approach has been adopted or to draw attention to points of difficulty. It is hoped that this will help students in improving their understanding of the subjects covered.

At the end of the book there is a comprehensive index of the topics covered, relating them to the questions and answers in which they appear.

1 Control theory in accounting

Although control theory is potentially an examinable subject, examiners prefer to concentrate on control techniques, often linked with responsibility accounting. Such questions may be related to the development of management information systems or to the operation of budgetary control, which are the subjects of separate chapters in this book.

Apart from such specific applications of control techniques, the two essay-type questions given in this chapter illustrate typical examination requirements.

STUDY REQUIREMENTS

Control theory – feedback; open and closed loop systems
Functions of management
Organisation structures: responsibility accounting

QUESTIONS

1 Describe, and outline the operation of, the principal techniques used in management accounting to assist management in its control function. *(6 marks)*

2 Outline the main features of a responsibility accounting system. *(6 marks)*

ANSWERS

1 You have only ten minutes to answer this question, so start with essentials:

(a) How do managers control? Managers carry out their control function by comparing actual performance against planned or forecast performance; and by taking appropriate action, either to adjust future performance or to modify plans.

(b) Which management accounting techniques help managers to do this? The principal techniques are 'budgetary control' and 'standard costing'. Both require the comparison of actual performance with predetermined targets (budgets) or standards; and both report variances from those plans. It is worth saying that by highlighting deviations from plan, these techniques facilitate 'management by exception'. From this point you could branch out in one, or both, of two directions:

(c) By giving more detail about how each system operates; for example:

    (i) Budgets are set for cost centres and cost classifications, whilst standards are set for individual operations and items of material.

    (ii) Cost allowance under standard costing are functions of actual activity; whilst budget allowances may be fixed or flexed only with some broad measure of activity.

    (iii) Under standard costing a detailed analysis of variances can be obtained through the accounting system, and may give indications of both cause and responsibility − though this will not necessarily be conclusive.

(d) By contrasting management control with physical control systems. In the former, control action is not automatic but is subject to human delay and uncertainty in decision making.

2 Another short question on which it should be easy to gain marks. Start, as always, by defining your terms − in this case what is a 'responsibility accounting' system?

It is a system developed around an organisation's framework of responsibility levels. It provides a service to directors and managers at all levels of responsibility within the organisation, providing them with information for decision making and control. The 'main features' of such a system fall into two categories:

(a) Prerequisites for the system to operate, i.e.

    (i) A clearly defined organisation structure.

    (ii) Terms of reference or statements of responsibilities for the various persons filling positions in that organisation structure.

    (iii) A coding system by which transaction documents can be related to individual responsibilities.

(b) Operating features, i.e.

    (i)   The analysis of costs (and revenues if appropriate) using the relevant organisation coding. This analysis would be made of both budgeted and actual amounts.

    (ii)   Reports to individual managers detailing the budgeted and actual amounts of the transactions for which they were responsible.

Finally, it is worth making the point that responsibility occurs in three ways:

    (i)   Direct responsibility for costs which a manager can control day by day (his 'controllable costs').

    (ii)   Responsibility to the extent that his department benefits from costs controlled by other managers ('attributed', 'apportioned' or 'non-controllable' costs, which should be shown separately on his management reports).

    (iii)   Indirect responsibility for items controlled by departments subordinate to him. This could be illustrated by a 'pyramid' of reports in which detailed at the lowest level of reporting are shown in summary at the next highest level, and so on until the final summarisation at board level.

2 Management accounting survey

Questions occasionally occur which require a general description of the scope, nature or purpose of management accounting; or of the concepts of cost accounting, regarded as one of the main techniques used by the management accountant.

Four such questions are illustrated in this chapter.

STUDY REQUIREMENTS

Revision of cost accounting techniques
The nature of management accounting
Long-range planning: business objectives

QUESTIONS

1 'In the broadest sense all accounting is management accounting. All financial and cost information generated by accountants is of some interest to management. But in practice, where management accounting differs from financial accounting. . '

(from *An Insight into Management Accounting* by John Sizer)

Required:

(a) a brief definition of management accounting; *(5 marks)*

(b) a discussion of the major differences between management and financial accounting. *(15 marks)*

(Total 20 marks)

2 'The diverse uses of routinely recorded cost data give rise to a fundamental danger: information prepared for one purpose can be grossly misleading in another context'.

(from *Management Accounting: a Conceptual Approach* by L.R. Amey and D.A. Egginton)

(a) Discuss to what extent the above statement is valid and explain your conclusions. *(13 marks)*

(b) (i) Provide illustrations of three management accounting reports containing routinely recorded data, specify the primary purpose of the reports and give examples of specific contexts in which the information they contain may be grossly misleading.

(ii) Briefly give reasons why the information is valid for the primary purpose of the report but grossly misleading in the alternative stated context. *(6 marks)*

(Total 25 marks)

3 Cost may be classified into a number of non-mutually exclusive groupings for decision-making purposes.

Required:

Definitions of possible major cost classifications and a discussion of the factors that will affect a decision-maker's classification of a cost into one or more of these groupings. *(20 marks)*

4 A company has been formed to provide a repair service for domestic appliances. It is a labour-intensive organisation employing 200 maintenance engineers but involving a minimum of capital expenditure.

As the management accountant, you are requested to explain:

(a) what you consider to be the key areas for financial control;

(b) the procedures you would adopt to measure corporate effectiveness.

(20 marks)

ANSWERS

1

(a) Management accounting may be defined as the application of accounting techniques to the provision of information designed to assist all levels of management in planning and controlling the activities of the organisation.

The question asks for a 'brief' definition, and there is no point in going into greater detail at this stage. Some elaboration of the definition is implicit in part (b) of the question.

Use whatever definition you can remember, provided you bring in the three essential points that:

(i)   information is provided to *managers*;
(ii) at *all levels*;
(iii) for the *purpose* of helping them carry out their job.

(b) A good approach to this part of the question is to take a piece of working paper and tabulate all the differences between financial accounting and management accounting that come readily into your mind. As you do this, points for discussion will occur to you, and you will find what sequence of points is easiest for you to adopt. There is no reason why you should not divide your answers into paragraphs to help the examiner identify markable points. For example:

— Financial accounting derives from the function of a steward to report to his master on the use he had made of the funds entrusted to him. Management accounting could be regarded as an extension of that function, since it elaborates the information given in the financial accounts. This elaboration however is more precisely the role of 'cost accounting', which is only one aspect of management accounting.

— Arising from the stewardship function, the main purpose of financial accounting is usually considered to be the presentation of reports to the proprietors of the business (in the case of a company, to the equity shareholders); and to other parties (such as lenders) who enter into contractual relations with the business. The purpose of management accounting, on the other hand, is to provide information for the managers of the business, as already stated in part (a).

— Or the protection of outside parties; financial reports have to be based on specified rules of accounting and be presented in a prescribed form containing a specified minimum amount of detail. These regulations derive partly from statute and partly from a generally accepted Statement of Standard Accounting Practice. Management reports, on the other hand, will be in whatever form is most helpful to the manager concerned, and will contain whatever information is relevant to the particular decision he has to make.

— Three consequences flow from this distinction:

(i)   Financial reports deal with historical events (though some element of prediction may be found in the Directors' Report). Management reports for review purposes will be concerned with history, but for decision purposes will be mainly predictive.

(ii)   Financial reports summarise the results and position of the business as a whole (though certain items of information are now required to be sub-divided by main activity or main market). Management reports, though aggregated at board level for example, will deal with particular segments of the main business. At junior manager level they may deal with individual operations or items of material.

(iii)   Financial reports (subject to the convention of materiality) must be accurate, even though this often means that there is some delay between the end of a reporting period and the presentation of the related accounts. Management reports must be timely, so that action may be taken on them, even if this means that some degree of approximation is used.

— Because management accounting is providing information for planning and control purposes, it will need to take account of and interpret legal, social and environmental trends and constraints, and to make use of quantitative techniques for both prediction and interpretation of the data used. Management accounting has been described as an inter-disciplinary science.

2

(a)   The statement is valid, but it is not always the case that information provided for one purpose will be misleading in another. If used with intelligence the information may be extremely useful in other contexts, although the actual cost figure attributed to that information may be quite wrong for that precise alternative context.

The reason for this potential danger with cost information is that there is no such thing as the cost of an item. There are in fact many costs and different 'cost' figures are relevant in different circumstances. Any accounting report or cost is merely a monetary expression of an underlying reality — it is a way of translating into money terms that reality. Consider a machine held by a firm; the monetary expression of the machine may be:

(i)   book value — historic cost less depreciation, e.g. £11,000 less £2,000 depreciation;

(ii)   realisable value — sales value e.g. £6,000;

(iii)   replacement cost — cost of replacing the machine's service potential, e.g. £13,000;

(iv)   value in use — capitalised value of the machine's net production e.g. £12,000.

Each of these figures is a valid money description of the machine for some purpose; but because a figure is useful for one purpose it will not automatically be useful in other contexts. If it is to be decided whether the above machine should be retained or sold then realisable value and value in use are relevant. (These show that the machine should be kept and operated rather than sold.)

If it is to be decided whether to keep the machine in its present use or to utilise it in some other function that decision will require the comparison of its present value in use (£12,000) with that of the alternative (unknown).

For both the above decisions the book value is irrelevant. Yet it is the book value which is recorded and would be utilised in any regular financial statements. Indeed most cost data are themselves based on historic or standard cost. The data bank of cost figures available in a management accounting system may therefore be completely irrelevant for many business decisions.

Even the way the recorded historic cost is calculated can give rise to confusion. A factory producing one type of product may have total annual costs of £1 million and total annual production of one million items. This would not mean that for all purposes it could be validly concluded that each item cost £1; on average it is true, but when deciding the extra costs of additional production only the variable costs would be relevant. Hence the manner in which a cost figure has been derived is as important as the base of the cost figure.

The problem with routinely produced cost data is especially severe if there are some fixed costs which have been allocated to cost centres or production. The basic cost figures given are dependent on the overhead allocation base used, which may be overlooked by a naive user or one uneducated in accounting.

Therefore a management accounting report produced monthly and showing the achieved efficiency of each product or department (with or without comparison with the budget) will produce information which can be directly used only for that purpose. It will also produce information which can be used indirectly for other purposes. That a particular product shows a loss is not of itself a ground for assuming that production of that product should cease. (If the product consistently shows a loss over a period of many months careful consideration may be given to ceasing production.) But though it may suggest (without proving) certain courses of action, the information in the routine report is irrelevant as:

(i)   It is based on past activity when what are relevant are the future incremental costs and revenues.

(ii) It is probably based on costs calculated after allocating fixed overhead costs, which are not incremental to the product and not a decision variable. (The consistent 'loss' could be caused by an unfair overhead apportionment and this product may have consistently produced a positive contribution over the period.)

However, the regularly produced statements will provide much information to an intelligent reader, which will provide prima facie evidence that a particular line of investigation (e.g. product discontinuation) is worthy of detailed, and correct, appraisal. But such information, because it is produced on the wrong base, will never itself justify a current decision.

Hence, as with all data, cost information must be used with caution and only after the base of its calculation has been disclosed. Directly relevant data are use-specific and if use alters so will the data.

(b) (i) Examples of management accounting reports include:

Product profitability statements
Purpose — to indicate the profitability of a product
Misleading context — if used as a base for deciding on expansion or contraction of production of apparently profitable or unprofitable products

Cost centre reports
Purpose — to show costs of a cost centre and to provide a comparison with budgets
Misleading context — if used to decide on efficiency of cost centre management

Product cost reports
Purpose — to indicate the average cost per unit of production
Misleading context — if used to decide costs of meeting demand of an extra contract or if used to calculate holding costs of stocks

(ii) Reasons why information is valid or misleading:

Product profitability statements
Valid — each product has its expenses matched with the revenues it produces. However, the fixed overhead cost which has been allocated to the product is calculated on a basis which is always subject to doubt. Therefore the figures are valid subject to the allocation of the joint overhead cost. Misleading — fixed overhead costs are not proportional to output and the statement is based on historic costs whereas expansion/contraction decisions should be based on future incremental costs and revenues.

Cost centre reports
Valid — the basis of cost measurement and overhead allocation will be the same as used in the budget. Therefore comparison is valid to ascertain deviations from budget.
Misleading — to decide on the efficiency of cost centre management, one needs to compare the actual actions with the actions which would have been taken by an efficient management in the actual circumstances. Costs may be higher than budget but without efficiency the costs would have been even higher — the increase in costs may be due to circumstances not reflected in the budget.

Product cost report
Valid — figures show average cost of production and, subject to valid allocation of overheads, this is a valid calculation for its purpose.
Misleading — only incremental costs need be considered in both cases. Fixed costs allocated must be ignored.

3 The answer to this question falls into three parts:

(a) a statement of possible cost classifications, and definitions of the terms used;
(b) an explanation why these classifications are or are not mutually exclusive;
(c) a survey of the factors to be taken into account in classifying a cost for the purpose of a particular decision.

The main groupings of costs are:

Fixed or variable. Fixed costs are those that tend to remain unchanged for a given period of time within a given range of activity levels. Variable costs are those that tend to vary with some selected measure of activity. (Students for the examinations of the Institute of Cost & Management Accountants should use definitions, here and elsewhere, from the Institute's official terminology (1982).)

Direct or indirect. Indirect costs are those which can not conveniently be identified, at the time they are incurred, with a unit of product or service. Costs which are so identified are direct costs of that cost unit; they include the cost of materials entering into and becoming constituent elements of a product or service, and wages for efforts applied directly to the creation of the product or service.

Period or product. Period costs accrue in relation to the passage of time. Product costs are all other costs.

Controllable or uncontrollable. These terms can be used only in relation to a manager to whose area of responsibility a cost has been attributed. If that manager, by his actions, can alter the total amount of cost incurred, then that item of cost is controllable by him. Otherwise it is uncontrollable by him.

Historic (including current) or forecast. An historic cost is one the amount of which has been or can be determined precisely as a matter of observable fact. Forecast costs can only be estimated.

It will be obvious that within each pair of alternatives, a cost must fall under one or the other. They are mutually exclusive.

As between groupings, however, there is no necessary exclusivity. Any cost in the first three groups can be either historic or forecast, and can be controllable or uncontrollable according to the circumstances. Variable costs would not necessarily be fixed.

We now come to the classification of costs for decision purposes. The first thing to be said is that the decision maker is concerned with costs in the future, after he has taken his decision. He will be using forecast costs. Historical costs will interest him only if he wants to use them as the basis for extrapolating future costs.

Secondly, he is interested only in those costs that will change as the result of his decision. Because that decision will alter existing circumstances, it is likely that the way in which costs have been classified historically may cease to be correct.

Having identified which costs are relevant to the decision, because they are going to be changed, the decision maker will classify them by two criteria:

(i)   What time period will be affected by the decision? In the short run, many costs will be fixed. In the long run, most costs will be variable.

(ii)   What range of outputs is being considered? Over a limited range certain costs may vary proportionately to output. Over a more extended range, changes in the 'cost function' are likely to occur. To summarise, therefore, the classification of costs for cost accounting purposes will seldom be valid decision purposes. The decision maker must consider each cost in relation to its relevance, the time period covered by the decision and the range of outputs under consideration.

4   The main difficulty with this question is distinguishing 'key areas for financial control' from measures of 'corporate effectiveness'. It is suggested that 'effectiveness' means achieving what you set out to achieve, so part (b) will be concerned with planning and variances from plan. Part (a) therefore must be concerned with 'efficiency', i.e. ensuring that financial outlays (in this case mainly on manpower) are not used wastefully.

(a)   The key areas for financial control are:

(i)   Utilisation of manpower. In a repair business this can be a major problem for two reasons. Firstly repair calls will be patchy. At some times many appliances will need servicing urgently, and delay in answering service calls would result in loss of customers. At other times, staff will be standing idle through lack of work.

The following actions could help to alleviate the problem:

— Based on a market survey, to split the company's area of operations into regions which would be staffed initially in proportion to the number of appliances to be serviced in each region.

— To arrange for mobility of staff between adjoining regions so as to deal with peak work loads. These temporary transfers of people from one region to another would probably have to be coordinated through head office. It would probably be necessary to pay expense allowances to people working outside their own region, and these would be best borne as central charges to ensure that individual regions were not discouraged from making use of one another's staff. This type of work should be spread fairly among all staff.

— At the same time to undertake selective advertising campaigns in those regions where the work received appeared to be below the level expected. Alternatively, or supplementary to this, to remunerate regional managers to some extent on the basis of the volume of sales achieved. In doing so, however, regard should be paid to efficiency with which work was performed.

(ii)   Efficiency of employees. It may not be practicable to set detailed work standards, or to control actual times against such standards if they were set; but the following could be done:

– Specify work methods applicable to particular types of appliance. These could be set out in instruction manuals.

– Undertake a training programme to ensure that staff were fully conversant with the best working methods.

– Ensure that work sheets were filled out for each job, showing details of the work done (necessary in any case as the basis for billing); the distance travelled to the call; and the times taken on work and travelling. Representative times for each type of job would eventually emerge from these records, could be checked periodically by mobile inspectors, and could be used to compare the performance of individual workers.

– It is necessary for effective work that adequate tools are available. This might be achieved most easily by kitting out each vehicle; making each vehicle the responsibility of a nominated person; and making that person liable for lost or badly damaged tools.

(iii) Efficient use of spares. The work sheet for each job should include details of spares fitted, which will be charged to the customer. Each van should again be kitted out with small spares in constant use, and the driver could be made responsible for keeping his stock up to date – this could alternatively be done by automatic replacement of spares used each day.

More expensive spares would probably best be held in a regional (or even a central) store, so that money was not tied up in slow-moving stocks. Perpetual inventory records of these should be kept, the storekeeper being responsible for requisitioning replacements as needed. Purchases should be made in bulk by head office.

(iv) Vehicle costs. For each vehicle there should be records of mileage run, running costs and maintenance costs, probably kept under head office scrutiny.

(b) Measures of corporate effectiveness

Business plans must be made, preferably by head office in close collaboration with regional managers, since they will be held responsible for meeting the planned performance.

Initially there must be a strategic plan for types of appliance to be serviced and for stages in market penetration. This should be reviewed annually, when yearly sales, costs and investment budgets will be set. It is likely that regional managers will be technicians, and some training will be necessary to give them a broader company perspective. A scheme of remuneration by results might eventually be introduced.

The annual budget would probably be built up in phased form for three-monthly or seasonal periods; there should be a quarterly review meeting at which the budget targets would be confirmed or revised.

The management accounting system should probably be centralised, based on monthly returns from the regions, and budget-actual reports with variance analyses would be sent to each region.

The key financial indicators would probably be sales growth and rate of profit margin on sales; but for the company as a whole there should be a target rate of return on capital employed, and performance against this target would be measured either annually or half-yearly. Selling prices would in some cases be set by market rates, but in other cases would be at a pre-determined mark-up on direct labour costs.

Note to student. This question is related to the subject of Chapter 10 — Performance Evaluation — but has been included at this point because it provides a fairly broad revision of cost accounting techniques, and also illustrates the point that management accounting is not merely a matter of cost bookkeeping.

3 Management information systems

In Chapter 2 it was said that management accounting provides information to managers for the purposes of planning and control. It was also noted that the information needed by managers is not confined to accounting information. In fact it can be derived from sources both internal and external to the company; it can be made available either on a routine basis or on demand; and it can take various forms, such as original statistical information, information in financial terms, or statistics based on financial reports.

The management accounting system is therefore just one module in the complete management information system.

A management information system comprises all the routines necessary to establish managers' information needs, to collect data, to process them and to present the required information to the managers concerned.

Only the Institute of Chartered Accountants incorporates all these elements in its Management Accounting paper. The other accountancy bodies, however, may set questions on those aspects of the subject, including the use of computers, that have particular reference to the processing of financial data.

STUDY REQUIREMENTS

Integrated accounting systems
The design and implementation of management information systems
Use of computer methods
Presentation of reports to management

QUESTIONS

1

(a) What advantages and limitations can be associated with the integration of the financial accounting and management accounting record keeping systems? *(14 marks)*

(b) Discuss whether integrated or separate systems are of the greater use in the provision of information for decision making. *(6 marks)*

(Total 20 marks)

2   As a management consultant, you have recently been appointed by Reardon Haulage Ltd to advise them on the installation of a management information system. The company was founded about ten years ago by Mr Ray as a haulage and warehousing company serving Welsh clients and carrying goods to British and international destinations. The company has grown successfully to the point where it now has a fleet of 30 trucks of varying size, warehouse space of 26,000 square feet and an annual turnover in excess of £13 million.

Mr Ray, in an effort to develop the company further, has made the following new appointments:

Position	*Responsibilities*
(i) transport manager	Maintenance of company trucks
(ii) fleet manager	Job scheduling
(iii) warehouse manager	Optimisation of warehouse usage
(iv) sales manager	Acquisition of new business
(v) financial manager	Administration

As well as acting as general manager, Mr Ray will retain responsibility for the personnel function.

The company currently operates a manual accounting system with an accounting machine for its debtors and creditors. Management accounts are prepared quarterly. The accounts staff comprises a bookkeeper/cashier, a debtor's clerk and cretitors/payroll clerk.

It is the intention of the financial manager to recruit one more person to deal with the immediate expansion plans.

Prepare a report for presentation to the general manager setting out:

(a) the main information needed by each new manager; *(10 marks)*
(b) how you would propose to accumulate the data on a routine basis for the transport, fleet and sales managers; *(9 marks)*
(c) any consequent changes which you would propose in the company's accounting procedures. *(6 marks)*

(Total 25 marks)

3   Draw a systems flow chart to describe the following clerical procedure for order processing in a mail order firm.

A clerk in the mailing department opens each envelope and dumps the contents on the work table. Cheques and cash are compared with the order to see if the amount agrees with the customer's figure. They are then sent to accounts receivable and will eventually be banked. If payment is not received with an order, a second copy of the order is produced. The copy is sent to customer service and filed in case complaints arise. The original goes to accounts receivable where an invoice is typed. One copy of the invoice is sent to customer service and filed for follow up. The top copy is posted to the customer.

The original order is forwarded to a second clerk in the mailing department who types a mailing label with a carbon copy and paper clips these to the order. Orders are batched in groups of 25 and forwarded to order processing.

The goods are assembled and packed in a carton. The order form is placed on top of the merchandise inside the carton with a mailing label and blank order form. The other label is attached to the outside of the carton which is then sealed and placed on a trolley. The trolley is transported to the mail department where packages are weighed, postage is attached and they await collection by the GPO.

When a customer complaint is received it is sent to customer service where a copy of the invoice is pulled from the file and compared to the customer's tally. A letter is sent to the customer with a refund or an explanation of the invoice if the original invoice is determined to be correct. A copy of such letters is filed in the customer service department.   (16 marks)

4   Explain how the increasing use of computers can both:

(a)   provide a challenge to the practice of management accounting and
(b)   assist it.

Illustrate your answer with references to the planning and budgetary control processes or some alternative example of your choice.   (20 marks)

5   Sampler Ltd offers a book warehousing and distribution service to small publishers. It has recently extended this service by employing 15 representatives to visit bookshops (of which there are about 9,000) to promote their clients' publications. Each salesman has access to the company's computer system through his own terminal. The company operates an on-line real-time (OLRT) sales order processing system.

(a)   Suggest probable reasons why Sampler Ltd find it advantageous to operate an
      OLRT sales order processing system rather than a batch-processing system.
                                                                  (5 marks)

(b)   Present a systems flow chart suitable for Sampler Ltd's sales order processing,
      providing for the printout of any documents and reports which you consider
      appropriate.   (10 marks)

(c)   Indicate the principal control features of an **OLRT** sales order processing system, and compare the problems of control in such a system with those of a batch-processing system.   *(10 marks)*

(Total 25 marks)

1   Both financial and management accounting records are based on the same source documents to the extent that they record transactions with the outside world. To some extent also they rely on the same internally generated documentation, for example in calculations of depreciation, accruals and prepayments and, in some cases, records of stock usage.

The type of analysis to which this data are subjected may, however, differ. Financial accounts often make use merely of a subjective analysis, by the nature of items such as sales, costs, assets and liabilities.

Management accounting will require not only more detailed analysis but also analysis by responsibility (department or costs centre) and objective analysis of costs according to the purposes for which those costs are incurred — an analysis by cost units in their various forms.

The forms of report emerging from the two systems will reflect this underlying analysis.

Some companies meet their management accounting needs by a separate, special purpose analysis of the relevant data inputs; traditionally by the 'cost department'. If this is done, it is necessary to ensure that the costing analysis is complete and correct by making a periodic reconciliation between the financial and management accounting reports.

Under an integrated system, the additional analysis required for management purposes is made as part of the financial accounting system. This probably will mean the suppression of the subjective analysis of costs and the presentation of the profit and loss account in a format that distinguishes direct from indirect costs. There is provision in the Companies Act 1981 for published accounts to be presented in this way.

(a)   The main advantages of an integrated system are:

(i)   Consistency. There is no need to reconcile two separate analyses, because only one analysis is made.

(ii)   Time and cost saving in processing the data.

(iii)   Possibly improved speed in the production of period reports.

Among the limitations of integration are:

(i)   Consistency may not be desired. For example, marginal costing or the use of LIFO stock accounting may be the most informative for management use; but total absorption costing and some alternative stock accounting system will be necessary for annual accounts.

(ii)   Where the business is decentralised, separate segmental costing systems may produce management information more quickly than a centralised integrated system.

(iii)   The transaction coding needed for an integrated system may be cumbersome and give rise to errors in use.

To a large extent these advantages and limitations apply equally to a manual or a computerised system. With a computerised system, however, the cost of hardware and software may differ significantly between integrated and segregated configurations.

(b)   The information required for decision making will not usually be the information emerging from records which evaluate past performance. For decision making one needs information about events that might or might not happen in the future. In general, therefore, neither an integrated system nor a separate management accounting system will produce data relevant for decision making; but it is possible that the separate system might provide information from which extrapolations could be made more easily than could an integrated system.

2

To: General Manager, Reardon Haulage Ltd

From: A Smith, Management Consultant

Subject: Installation of Management Information System   Date: 30. 5. X2

As requested in your letter of 3. 4. X2 I now present my report on the factors to be considered in the installation of a management information system at Reardon Haulage Ltd. The major considerations involved will be discussed under three main headings:

(a)   *The main information needed by each new manager*

(i)   **Transport manager**

—   a daily log sheet showing details of times, destinations, tons carried and miles run for each truck;

—   a fuel and oil report showing quantity and price for each vehicle and the relationship with mileage;

—   vehicle cost sheets (summarising the information in the previous two points);

—   fleet cost sheet (summarising the information from the vehicle cost sheets and distinguishing between fixed and variable expenses);

—   the cost per ton and per mile for each vehicle;

—   reports giving standing details of each truck including make, age, cost and the mileage increase for each truck since the last report;

—   regular repair and maintenance reports for each vehicle;

- analysis of maintenance costs by cause and by detail; consideration of their behaviour patterns over time and over different volume levels.

(ii) **Fleet manager**

- report indicating the utilisation of truck facilities;
- knowledge of customer delivery requirements (weight, capacity, dates, source and destination, distances to be travelled).

(iii) **Warehouse manager**

- the capacity limitations of the warehouse together with any special needs (e.g. security) relating to stock;
- size, weight, value and quantity of each item handled;
- regular reports comparing physical stock with stock records;
- reports on capacity utilisation of warehouse space at various times of the year.

(iv) **Sales manager**

- market conditions and trends;
- activities of the firm's principal competitors;
- average and marginal cost data to provide a basis for charging customers;
- volume of goods handled per customer;
- details of new customers and market share;
- geographical areas where market penetration could be improved;
- details of the most profitable customers to ensure that the firm attracts their custom;
- competitor prices, terms and overall customer service;
- business forecast by area and by customer group;
- the relative importance of different advertising media.

(v) **Financial manager**

- cost relating to each truck (depreciation, insurance, fuel, oil, tyres and servicing);
- wages of drivers and loaders;
- supervisory and administration costs;
- analysis of potential customers to assess their creditworthiness, age analysis of debtors, bad debt experience of the firm;

— budgeted cash flow needs of company.

(b) *Accumulation of data on a routine basis*

(i) **Transport manager**

— Much of the information required (times, destinations, tons carried and miles run for each truck, fuel and oil report) can be obtained from log sheets which the truck drivers should complete daily.

— Every time a truck is inspected an inspection report should be prepared and sent to the transport manager for his approval.

— When maintenance work has to be carried out, any major external maintenance work (i.e. work not carried out in the firm's maintenance workshop) should require the prior approval of the transport manager; a repair and maintenance report should be sent to the manager detailing the cost and the cause of each maintenance job undertaken.

(ii) **Fleet manager**

— A listing of customer orders provided by the sales manager will alert the fleet manager to potential scheduling bottlenecks and give him details of truck requirement, customer delivery dates and distances to be travelled. Thus, it is essential that a report on customer orders be sent from the sales manager to the fleet manager frequently (daily, if required).

— The transport manager should send a memorandum to the fleet manager every time a truck has to be sent for maintenance. The
— estimated time needed to complete the maintenance work should be noted.

— The daily log sheet kept by the drivers and analysed in the accounts department will give the fleet manager data on the utilisation of fleet capacity.

(iii) **Sales manager**

— a monthly report from the accounts department indicating the volume of goods handled per customer;

— a periodic report from the accounts department to indicate to him the relative profitability of different customers;

— road haulage magazines to get an idea of competitors' prices and sales opportunities.

(c) *Proposed changes in accounting procedures*

(i) I would recommend that a financial accountant should be employed to assist the financial controller in the accumulation and analysis of operating data.

(ii) I feel that monthly management accounts are required in view of the current size and likely future expansion of the business.

(iii) At present a manual accounting system is in operation. I feel that in the near future a strong case could be made for the computerisation of the order analysis and job scheduling functions. This would lead to a greater accuracy and would result in more timely information being supplied to the accounts department for analysis.

(iv) The accounting department should become more involved with the analysis of operational information:

- An analysis of log sheets would generate cost per ton and cost per mile data and would provide critical information regarding the utilisation of fleet capacity.

- The volume of goods handled per customer and the relative profitability of different customers could be assessed.

- Data on the level of sales penetration by area could be provided to the sales manager.

- Routine cost reports could be provided to the sales manager to assist in developing pricing policies.

(v) The new financial accountant should be involved in the initiation of a budgetary control system for the transport department and the warehouse. This would provide a further control mechanism for management and it could be supplemented later by the development of cost standards for use in these two departments.

3   See Fig. 3:1 on page 26.

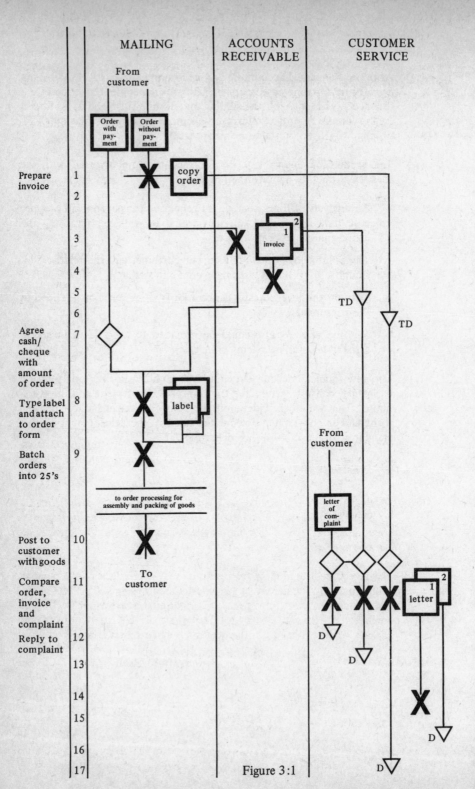

MAILING ACCOUNTS RECEIVABLE CUSTOMER SERVICE

From customer

Order with payment Order without payment

Prepare invoice — 1, 2

copy order

3 — invoice (1, 2)

4

5 — TD

6 — TD

Agree cash/cheque with amount of order — 7

Type label and attach to order form — 8 — label

Batch orders into 25's — 9

to order processing for assembly and packing of goods

From customer

letter of complaint

Post to customer with goods — 10

To customer

Compare order, invoice and complaint — 11 — letter (1, 2)

Reply to complaint — 12

D

13 — D

14

15

16 — D

17 — D

Figure 3:1

26

4   A computer is a device for storing, manipulating and transmitting data at very high speeds. It can be programmed to do whatever the management accountant wants it to do. Computers and their software can be expensive, so it is important that programmes should be designed with care after full investigation of the forms and content of both input and output data.

(a)   Computers provide a challenge to the practice of management accounting in the following ways:

  (i)   The management accountant is obliged to reconsider the content of his management reports, and to investigate precisely what information is needed by the various managers in the business. This must be done without any preconceptions, and might best be handled by someone other than the management accountant.

  One aspect of this investigation will be to ensure that, although a computer may be capable of providing information in greater volume or greater detail than would be available under a manual system, there should be editing of the output to ensure that managers are not subjected to information overload.

  (ii)   The accountant should review the procedures by which data are currently handled, and simplify them if possible. It is not a good use of resources to computerise an existing inefficient system. Systems analysis may be needed.

  (iii)   He should review the source documentation used. Under a manual system, errors in documentation can be identified and corrected before processing is commenced. In a computerised system, incorrect source data may have been processed in various ways before an error is highlighted.

  (iv)   Because computers can be programmed to carry out complex mathematical calculations (see part (b)) not previously used, the management accountant will be obliged to familiarise himself with new techniques, and be able to explain them to his managers.

  (v)   Managers receiving computer printouts may feel a lack of the personal communication inherent in less mechanised systems. The accountant will be under pressure to ensure that personal contacts are reinforced, so that, for example, managers do not feel that their performance against budget is being appraised in a purely automatic way.

(b)   Computers assist the practice of management accounting in the following ways:

  (i)   They ensure accuracy of processing once data have been fed into the system.

  (ii)   They provide rapid feed-out of information, for example on the state of a supplier's account — possibly by way of visual display units.

(iii) They enable individual managers to obtain access to information at the time they need it.

(iv) As mentioned above, they can carry out calculations that would be time-consuming or practically impossible by other means. Examples related to planning and budgetary control are:

- linear programming to establish optimum production levels;

- trend calculations for sales forecasting;

- marginal cost and revenue calculations for profit maximisation;

- probability calculations related to investment evaluation or budgeting;

- complete financial modelling to predict the financial effects of plans or proposals.

- updating of standards under a standard costing system; or of budgets under a system of rolling budgets.

It was suggested earlier that the management accountant would need to understand techniques he would not otherwise have used. He will equally be under challenge to devise data inputs that are relevant to the type of calculation required. A company financial model based only on a simplistic classification of fixed and variable costs could be extremely dangerous.

5

(a) (i) The main advantage of a real time system is the quick response of the system to any transaction. For Sampler Ltd this should shorten the time between receipt of customer orders and delivery.

(ii) The system could access the stock file to confirm availability as an order is placed and the information could then be relayed immediately to the customer.

(iii) The stock file could be updated as the orders were placed and so would always be up to date.

(iv) Assuming all files to be on-line, invoices could be posted to the sales ledger at the same time as the order was processed.

(v) With the sales ledger on-line, the salesman could answer customer enquiries about the status of the customer's account.

(vi) A credit checking process could be incorporated into the order processing routine.

(vii) A sales analysis file could be maintained on-line and updated as orders were placed.

(viii) Stock levels could be checked against reorder levels with each issue from stock and a printed reorder list could be produced as often as required.

(ix)   A copy of each invoice could be transmitted to a terminal in the ware-house if prompt shipment were desired.

(x)   A file of back orders could be held on-line and printed out regularly.

(b)   See Fig. 3:2.

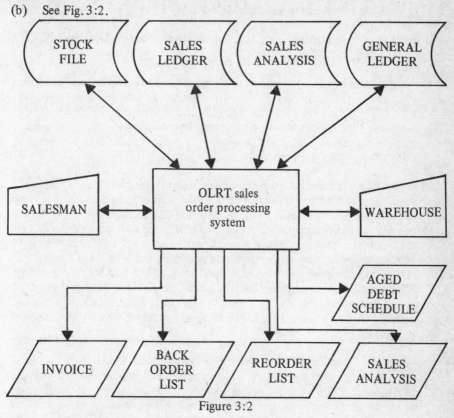

Figure 3:2

(c)   *Control features of OLRT system*

(i)   There is automatic credit checking.

(ii)   Each salesman has a unique user code which is the first item of data to be entered when accessing the system. The system will check the validity of this code before accepting any further data.

(iii)   Each user code should contain an internal code defining the type of transactions this user is allowed to initiate and the files this user is allowed to access.

(iv)   Data entry can be simplified by displaying a form or list of questions on a VDU for the user to fill in. The transaction would not be processed until the data had been entered completely and correctly.

(v)   A data edit (data vet) routine should be programmed into the system to pick up such errors as invalid customer account numbers or invalid stock numbers.

(vi) 'Closed loop' verification can be performed on input. Given only an account number or a stock number, the system could retrieve the customer name or produce description from the files and display these on a VDU for visual verification.

(vii) If the salesman enters prices they can be checked against the list prices on the stock file.

(viii) A transaction log should be maintained by the system to enable the files to be reconstructed if they are accidentally corrupted or destroyed. This transaction log should be maintained on a separate disc unit from any of the files and may be printed out periodically.

Comparison with batch processing

In a batch processing system, entering data into the system requires several steps. First the sales order has to be prepared, approved by the credit controller, used by the warehouse personnel to assemble goods for delivery and finally used as a source document for computer data preparation. Once the data are recorded on a machine readable medium (e.g. punched cards), they must be read in separately for each different file update. These various steps in batch processing create several possibilities for error and the entire process is very time consuming. To improve control, each batch has control totals constructed at the point where the batch is first created. These totals are processed with the batch to check for correctness and completeness at each stage of processing.

A real-time system has a major disadvantage in control of data accuracy: the only point in the system at which accuracy can be controlled is the point of data entry. Since transactions are entered one at a time as they occur, there is no batch of input records or batch total. Responsibility for controlling the accuracy of data input in a real-time system therefore shifts more heavily on to the data vet routines programmed into the system.

4 Inventory management

The title 'inventory management' has been used to cover:

(a) the control of physical inventories;
(b) decisions on procurement timing and quantities;
(c) the costing of inventory holdings and usage.

It does not cover warehouse organisation or procedures other than those listed above.

These three aspects of inventory management are likely to have been studied in connection with earlier examinations, either on cost accounting or on quantitative techniques. They are obviously relevant, however, to the work of the management accountant, and questions are sometimes asked on these subjects.

STUDY REQUIREMENTS

Inventory control: basic economic order quantity (EOQ) and economic batch quantity (EBQ) models.
Basic materials control theory applied to procurement, storage and inventories
Principles of pricing stores issues and stock valuation

QUESTIONS

1   The Spot-On Company manufacture 'dotties'. The bin card for this product states that the maximum stock holding for it is 15,000 and the minimum 5,000.

Four materials are used in the manufacture of dotties and information currently available about these materials is as follows:

Material	Number of kilos required to produce one dottie	Information on bin card (in kilos)		
		on hand	maximum	minimum
Doh	2	3,000	7,000	2,000
Ray	3	3,000	12,000	3,000
Mee	1	5,000	7,000	2,000
Fah	5	20,000	20,000	5,000

Information from various departments within the Spot-On Company about dotties is:

Raw material store

2,000 kilos of Doh and 1,000 kilos of Fah in the store have been reserved for work already in progress.

Finished goods store

The stock of dotties is 5,000 but 1,000 are on order and still have to be withdrawn from the store and sent to the warehouse for despatch.

Production control

2,000 dotties are in the process of manufacture and all the materials necessary to produce these have been either reserved or issued.

Sales department

Orders have just been received for 10,000 dotties which are to be delivered as quickly as possible, but so far the orders concerned have been processed no further than the sales department.

(a)   Prepare statements for management which clearly show working for:

(i)   the size of the production order to be placed to bring stock to a maximum;   *(5 marks)*
(ii)   details of the quantities of material which need to be issued with the production order;   *(2 marks)*
(iii)   information of the purchase order which will have to be placed to bring the stock of raw materials up to the maximum holdings required for each of them.   *(4 marks)*

(b)   In the table showing information on raw materials it can be seen that although twice as much Doh is required in the production of dotties as Mee, the maximum and minimum stock holdings shown on the bin card for these

32

materials is the same. Briefly state the factors that the firm would have taken into consideration when arriving at the maximum and minimum levels of stock holdings shown, and with reference to Doh and Mee explain how these factors may have caused the maximum and minimum stock levels to be the same. *(9 marks)*

(Total 20 marks)

2   Explain briefly the rationale behind economic order quantity (EOQ) models and discuss the extent to which the principles on which they are based can be used by a management accountant to help an organisation to decide the most appropriate levels of service that it should offer its customers. *(20 marks)*

3   Pink Ltd is experiencing some slight problems concerning two stock items sold by the company.

The first of these items is product Exe which is manufactured by Pink. The annual demand for Exe of 4,000 units, which is evenly spread throughout the year, is usually met by production taking place four times per year in batches of 1,000 units. One of the raw material inputs to product Exe is product Dee which is also manufactured by Pink. Product Dee is the firm's major product and is produced in large quantities throughout the year. Production capacity is sufficient to meet in full *all* demands for the production of Dees.

The standard costs of products Exe and Dee are:

STANDARD COST – PER UNIT

	Product	
	Exe	*Dee*
	£	£
Raw materials – purchased from external suppliers	13	8
— Dee standard cost	22	—
Labour – unskilled	7	4
— skilled	9	5
Variable overheads	5	3
Fixed overheads	4	2
Standard cost	£60	£22

Included in the fixed overheads for Exe are the set-up costs for each production run. The costs of each set-up, which apply irrespective of the size of the production run, are:

COSTS PER SET-UP

	£
(i) Labour costs – skilled labour	66
(ii) Machine parts	70
Total	£136

The 'machine parts' relate to the cost of parts required for modifications carried out to the machine on which Exe is produced. The parts can be used for only one run, irrespective of run length, and are destroyed by replacement on reinstatement of the machine. There are no set-up costs associated with Dee.

The cost of financing stocks of Exe is 15 % p.a. Each unit of Exe in stock requires 0.40 square metres of storage space and units *cannot* be stacked on top of one another to reduce costs. Warehouse rent is £20 p.a. per square metre and Pink is required to pay only for storage space actually used.

Pink is not working to full capacity and idle time payments are being made to all grades of labour except unskilled workers. Unskilled labour is not guaranteed a minimum weekly wage and is paid only for work carried out.

The second stock item causing concern is product Wye. Product Wye is purchased by Pink for resale and the 10,000 unit annual demand is again spread evenly throughout the year. Incremental ordering costs are £100 per order and the normal unit cost is £20. However, the suppliers of Wye are now offering quantity discounts for large orders. The details of these are:

Quantity ordered	Unit price
	£
Up to 999	20.00
1,000 to 1,999	19.80
2,000 and over	19.60

The purchasing manager feels that full advantage should be taken of discounts and purchases should be made at £19.60 per unit using orders for 2,000 units or more. Holding costs for Wye are calculated at £8.00 per unit per year and this figure will not be altered by any change in the purchase price per unit.

(a) Show the optimum batch size for the production of Exes. If this differs from the present policy, calculate the annual savings to be made by Pink Ltd from pursuing the optimal policy. Briefly explain the figures incorporated in your calculations. (The time taken to carry out a production run may be ignored.)
(10 marks)

(b) Advise Pink Ltd on the correct size of order for the purchase of Wyes.
(6 marks)

(c) Briefly describe two major limitations, or difficulties inherent in the practical application, of the model used in (a) to determine the optimum batch size.
(4 marks)

(Total 20 marks)

4   While three eccentric sisters, Alice, Betty and Claire, were on holiday in France they obtained the distribution rights for the UK market of a ready-mix flour which was packed in 1 kilo bags for sale to housewives to use to bake French bread.

On 1 January 19X6 the sisters put £1,000 from their savings into a bank account under the name of the Eccentric Sisters' Partnership which they formed to distribute the flour. Initially they commenced operations from the rambling old house in which they lived and in discussion concluded not to charge overheads or to pay themselves a salary but rather to share any profits that the partnership might make equally between them on a six-monthly basis.

Once their capital was in the bank they immediately made a purchase of 10,000 bags of the mix which exactly exhausted their initial capital. Although they understood from the supplier that the price they would have to pay for the flour was likely to fluctuate considerably, as they wanted to be able to offer their own customers a stable price on a six-monthly basis they set their sales price at 15p per bag for their launch period.

During the next six months of the Partnership's trading the following transactions took place:

January	Sold	5,000 bags
February	Bought	5,000 bags @ 12p
	Sold	5,000 bags
March	Bought	10,000 bags @ 10p
April	Sold	10,000 bags
May	Bought	5,000 bags @ 11p
	Sold	5,000 bags
June	Bought	5,000 bags @ 12½p
	Sold	5,000 bags

Early in July 19X6 each of the sisters independently prepared her own version of the partnership's first half-year performance. On 10 July 1976 the sisters held a meeting to decide upon the amount to be distributed as their first profit shares.

Alice was more than happy about the situation saying that each would get more than they originally hoped, and with her share of £450 she would take a trip to North America. Betty said that Alice must have made some mistakes in her calculations because she would get only £408.83 as her third share. Claire could not hold back her growing exasperation at the ineptitude of her sisters at calculating profit and jumped in to say that neither of the other sisters would ever make accountants — because according to her the correct distribution would be £421.43.

An argument started about who was right. When the sisters compared their statements they also found that as well as their income calculations being different the valuation they had obtained for closing stock on 30 June 19X6 also varied in each case.

(a) Showing the calculations to support your answer, provide information of which methods the sisters had used to price out stocks in their various assessments of the partnership's performance. Present your results in tabular form to show the total income for the partnership and the value of the closing stock for each of the methods. *(10 marks)*

(b) Discuss the major conceptual difficulties associated with pricing out stock as far as the measurement of income and value is concerned. Refer to the sisters' calculations where appropriate. *(7 marks)*

(c) Do any of the methods used by the sisters overcome the difficulties that you have discussed and can you make additional suggestions which might prove to be even more helpful to management trying to measure the performance of an organisation? Give reasons for your answer. *(3 marks)*

(Total 20 marks)

ANSWERS
1

(a) (i)

STATEMENT OF PRODUCTION ORDER
(in units)

Orders		Units
Ordered but not despatched		1,000
Orders just received		10,000
		11,000
Stock		
Already on hand	5,000	
Work in progress	2,000	
		7,000
Production order		
For customers		4,000
To bring stock to maximum		15,000
Product order to be placed		19,000

(ii)

STATEMENT FOR MATERIAL ISSUE TO PRODUCE 19,000 DOTTIES
(in kilos)

Material	Kilos required per dottie	Total material requirements
Doh	2	38,000
Ray	3	57,000
Mee	1	19,000
Fah	5	95,000

(iii) ### STATEMENT OF MATERIAL PURCHASE ORDER
(in kilos)

Material	Doh	Ray	Mee	Fah
For production	38,000	57,000	19,000	95,000
Less on hand	3,000	3,000	5,000	20,000
Adjustment for reservation	2,000	nil	nil	1,000
	1,000	3,000	5,000	19,000
	37,000	54,000	14,000	76,000
Plus to make up to maximum	7,000	12,000	7,000	20,000
Purchase order to be placed	44,000	66,000	21,000	96,000

(b) The factors a firm would have to take into consideration when arriving at maximum and minimum levels of stockholdings are:

(i)   The demand for the item. The maximum quantity held should occur at the time new supplies are received, and should be sufficient to meet the expected demand until the next consignment is received. The assumption is that demand is predictable and steady. If the rate of demand varies, a minimum stockholding will be set which will be a safety margin to cover possible excess demands over the norm in any period. The maximum holding will be increased correspondingly.

(ii) The frequency of procurement. This obviously affects the demand that will have to be met between each purchase delivery. The less frequently purchase orders are placed, the higher will be the necessary maximum stockholding (and, of course, the average stockholding).

(iii) Stockholding costs, such as premises charges, insurance and interest on money tied up in stocks. Consideration of these will influence the decision on the frequency, and thus the order quantity, of procurement.

(iv) The lead time between placing a purchase order and receiving the goods. If this is stable, no new factor is introduced; but if it varies a safety stockholding will be needed, affecting the minimum and maximum holdings.

(v) The acceptability of occasional 'stock-out' positions. These can affect production plans and/or customer goodwill. If immediate fulfilment of all material requisitions is necessary, stockholdings must be higher than if delays can be permitted.

(vi) The physical characteristics of the item. Goods that are subject to deterioration or loss during storage should be held in small quantities and reordered frequently. Goods with a long shelf life can be held in larger quantities and produced less frequently.

(vii) The amount of finance available for stockholdings. Referring specifically to Doh and Mee, these will have the same demand pattern and be subject to the same considerations relating to stock-outs. Without information about their respective supply conditions, storage characteristics and price it is not possible to give a complete answer as to why they should have the same maximum and minimum holding levels.

2   The rationale underlying economic order quantity models is that in decision making it is necessary to balance the benefits yielded against the costs involved. In the EOQ model the two contributory variables are:

(a) Stockholding costs, such as premises charges, insurance, interest on the money invested in stocks and the costs of administering those stocks. The stockholding costs for any given total procurement quantity in any period will vary directly with the size of the individual purchase orders placed. If goods are purchased in large batches, the average quantity in stock will be high and stockholding costs will be high, and vice versa.

(b) Ordering costs and purchase prices per unit, which are likely to be lower for large batch quantities.

The EOQ model facilitates the ascertainment of that order quantity, within the range of possible order quantities, at which total costs per annum (and thus average cost per unit) are minimised; in other words, what spending on stockholding costs is justified by the resultant gain through the reduction of procurement costs?

This cost-benefit approach is applicable to most business decisions. In considering the most appropriate level of service to offer customers, for example, its application would depend on the way in which 'service' was defined; but four possible methods can be reviewed:

(i)   Immediate delivery from stock. A policy of ensuring that all customer demands can be met immediately from stock would involve high stockholdings in relation to the annual rate of demand, but would give rise to customer satisfaction and possibly an increase in business. If, alternatively, low stockholdings caused frequent delays in satisfying orders, then although stockholding costs would be low, this could be associated with loss of business from dissatisfied customers and with high costs, not only of placing frequent and possibly urgent orders but also of correspondence with customers apologising for the delay. It is quite possible that occasional out-of-stock positions could occur without the loss of benefits or the increase in costs of paperwork exceeding the saving on stockholding costs; a management decision would take all these variables into account.

(ii) Range of products on offer. By offering a wide range of products, a business may attract new customers, including those who like to obtain all their requirements from a single source. The greater the range, however, the higher the costs of holding and administering inventories. It is also likely that some products will yield less than the normal profit margin, or may have to be regarded as 'loss leaders'. A balance of advantage has to be struck.

(iii) Speed and frequency of distribution service. An improved rate of delivery from warehouse to customer can attract customers but will involve increased capital and vehicle operating costs. The possibility of creating regional depots in order to reduce travel distances and give lighter loads is a typical distribution problem involving complex calculations of costs and benefits.

(iv) Maintenance and repair services after sale. These often constitute a selling point that is attractive to customers. The cost of providing these services has to be measured against both the likely increase in sales of original equipment and the charge that can be made for these services.

3

(a)   The formula for arriving at optimum batch size is:

$$B = \sqrt{\frac{2DS}{H}}$$

where B = optimum batch size
        C = annual demand
        S = set-up costs for each batch
        H = annual holding costs per unit.

In applying this formula to the manufacture of product Exe, we make use of the following figures:
D (annual demand) is given as 4,000 units.
S (set-up costs). These are given as £136, but included in that figure is £66 skilled labour costs. We are told that skilled labour is being given a guaranteed weekly wage. For the company as a whole, therefore, these costs will not vary with the number of set-ups. The only relevant set-up costs are the £70 for machine parts.
H (holding costs). These will comprise the cost of financing stocks and the warehouse rent which varies with the number of units in stock (i.e. the space occupied).
The annual warehouse rent per unit of Exe is simple to calculate. It is 0.40 square metres x £20 = £8.

The annual financing cost, however, is more complex. The value to be financed is the cost of one unit of Exe, incorporating one unit of Dee; but in the decision we are considering we do not have to take account of those fixed costs that the company will have to finance in any event. So we ignore skilled labour and fixed overheads and get the following value:

	Exe	Dee
	£	£
Raw materials	13	8
Labour – unskilled	7	4
Variable overhead	5	3
	25	15

Total unit cost to be financed   40
@ 15% per annum, financing cost is £6 per unit per annum.

The optimum batch size for Exe is thus:

$$\sqrt{\frac{2 \times 4{,}000 \times £70}{£(8 + 6)}} = 200 \text{ units,}$$

so that 20 batches will be made during the year; the average stockholding (half the batch size) will be 100 units. The relevant annual cost of manufacturing in batches of 200 units will be:

	£
Set-up costs 20 batches x £70	1,400
Holding costs 100 units x £(8+6)	1,400
	2,800

Under the existing scheme of making 4 batches of 1,000 units each (average stockholding 500 units) the corresponding cost is:

	£
Set-up costs 4 batches x £70	280
Holding costs 500 units x £(8+6)	7,000
	7,280

The annual savings from pursuing the optimal policy would therefore be £4,480.

(b) For procuct Wye, with annual demand 10,000 units; ordering costs (similar to 'set-up' costs in part (a)) of £100 per order are holding costs per unit of £8 per annum, the economic order quantity would be:

$$\sqrt{\frac{2 \times 10,000 \times £100}{£8}} = 500 \text{ units}$$

This formula however does not take into account the quantity discounts available. To decide on the correct size of a purchase order we need to add together, at each price level, the relevant ordering and holding costs plus the purchase cost of the materials. This is done in the following table:

	Price £20.00 Order Qty 500	Price £19.80 Order Qty 1,000	Price £19.60 Order Qty 2,000
	£	£	£
Cost of materials purchased (10,000 units per annum)	200,000	198,000	196,000
Ordering cost (10,000/order qty x £100)	2,000	1,000	500
Holding costs (order qty/2 x £8)	2,000	4,000	8,000
Total cost	204,000	203,000	204,500

Pink Ltd should therefore purchase Wyes in batches of 1,000.

(c) Some limitations on, or difficulties in the use of, the optimum batch size model as stated in part (a) above are:

(i) The difficulty of obtaining reliable estimates of the cost variables, including the rate of interest to be used.

(ii) The assumption of a constant rate of demand throughout the year. Seasonal variations can be dealt with by confining the use of the model

41

to one season at a time. Random variations are covered by (iv) below.

(iii) The assumption that an ecomomic batch quantity can be set for an individual component without regard to the manufacture of other components entering either into it or into further assemblies of which it forms a part. It is possible for every component to be made in an ecomomic batch quantity yet out of phase with other components, so that completed component stocks have to be held in waiting stores.

(iv) The assumption of certainty of demand, costs and phasing of production. When uncertainty exists more complex models are required.

Any two of the above could have been selected for an answer.

4

(a) Over the six months to June, the value of total sales made by the partnership was 30,000 kilos @ 15p = £4,500.

The figures of total profit estimated were: Alice £1,350; Betty £1,225 (approx); and Claire £1,264.29 (approx).

These differences could arise only from different methods used in costing the goods sold.

As no basis is provided for estimating a standard cost, the most likely methods are FIFO, LIFO and some form of average cost. Which was used can be determined only by trial and error.

	FIFO			LIFO			AVERAGE COST		
	Kilos	*Price*	*Amount*	*Kilos*	*Price*	*Amount*	*Kilos*	*Price*	*Amount*
COST OF SALES			£			£			£
Jan	5,000	10p	500	5,000	10p	500			
Feb	5,000	10p	500	5,000	12p	600			
April	5,000	12p	600	10,000	10p	1,000			
	5,000	10p	500						
May	5,000	10p	500	5,000	11p	550			
June	5,000	11p	550	5,000	12½p	625			
Total	30,000		3,150	30,000		3,275	30,000		3,235.72
Closing stock	5,000	12½p	625	5,000	10p	500	5,000		539.28
Total bought	35,000		3,775	35,000		3,775	35,000		3,775.00

It appears that Alice used FIFO, Betty used LIFO, and Claire used the version of Average Cost which needs explaining.

The question appears to have been slightly unfair on the candidate, since it is likely that he would first have tried out the normal business versions of average cost, i.e. either the average cost of what remained in stock immediately prior to each sale, or the accumulated average cost of all purchases up to the date of each sale. Only after this would he have led to the somewhat unlikely actual solution — that all sales from February to June were valued at the weighted average price of the total purchases for the six months, i.e. £3,775/35,000 = 10.785714p (which has been used in the last column of the above table).

(b)   It will be seen that the FIFO method gives a valuation of closing stocks that is nearly contemporary with the balance sheet date, dependent on when precisely the last purchase was made, and yields a profit figure which reflects the effect of past purchases at a variety of prices. If, for example, prices have been rising, the profit figure will reflect the benefit obtained by buying stocks at the earlier, lower, prices and holding them until they are sold. Some accountants would say that the reported profit includes 'holding gains' (or losses).

The LIFO method matches the latest known price with each sale, on the grounds that stock sold has to be replaced, and it would be incorrect to report a profit unless provision had been made for replacing the stock used (at the latest reported price). Although the method does not completely fulfil this objective, it does give a closer approach to a 'going concern' profit. In doing so, however, it leaves a residual value for closing stocks which can be completely out of line with contemporary prices.

Any form of average cost method will give intermediate answers for both cost of sales and closing stock values; but if a realistic approach is used, the method yields obviously acceptable approximations to 'actual cost' in each case. It therefore avoids the distortion of either cost of sales or inventory values that is implicit in the other methods.

Each method has its advantages. Which is the most 'true and fair' will depend on what are regarded as the correct concepts of (a) profit and (b) the purpose of a balance sheet.

(c)   A concept of the measurement of income and value which appears to provide useful information is that known as 'current cost accounting' one interpretation of which is embodied in Statement of Standard Accounting Practice No. 16. The effects of this system on the periodic statements of account are:

(i)   That assets (including stocks) are shown in the balance sheet at their 'value to the business', which in a continuing business would usually be their replacement cost. Alice's FIFO method comes nearest to valuing stocks at contemporary values, but does not go so far as to use a replacement cost at the balance sheet date. Any adjustment from book value (incurred cost) to replacement cost would be a holding gain to the sisters in this instances; but as it would be an unrealised gain it would be taken to reserves and not through the profit and loss account.

(ii)   That profit should be recognised only after providing for the continuance of the business, possibly by setting aside sums for the replacement of assets (in this case stocks) used. Betty's LIFO method comes nearest to this idea, but again does not go to the extent of charging into cost of sales a replacement price at which no stocks have yet been purchased. Any difference between book value and replacement value of stocks sold would be credited to reserves, in recognition of the fact that it was a holding gain rather than an operating profit.

These comments are based on the assumption that the three sisters are engaged in a continuing business and not merely in a single venture. For a non-continuing business the terminal value of its stocks, and other assets, would be their net realisable value, and a different (probably lower) figure of profit would result.

5 Budgeting and budgetary control

In the measurement and control of performance which is one of the major management responsibilities assisted by management accounting, budgetary control systems are widely used; they feature in every examination syllabus.

For study purposes it is convenient to subdivide the subject under four headings:

Setting budgets, and the admininstration of budgetary control systems — the subject of this chapter.

Budgets must, of course, use the same accounts coding systems and be based on the same accruals concept that you will have studied previously. Budgets must be related to manager responsibilities, and will use, possibly in modified form, the cost centre structure adopted for cost finding. Questions on other aspects of budget administration are mainly concerned with human relationships (dealt with in chapter 12) or, occasionally, with budget instructions and the budget manual as exemplified in Question 1 in this chapter.

With regard to budget setting, questions requiring the preparation of cash budgets occur so frequently that they have been dealt with separately in chapter 6. In other cases, the fact that you are asked to prepare a budget rather than a report based on historical figures is merely incidental to the main purpose of exemplifying some aspect of contribution analysis or other accounting techniques.

Cash budgets, as mentioned above.

Variance analysis. Questions on variance analysis nearly always involve the use of standard costs and will be considered in chapter 8.

Behavioural aspects of planning and control techniques. This is an important examination subject, and equally important in practice. As noted above, it is dealt with in chapter 12.

STUDY REQUIREMENTS

The budgeting concept
The administration of budgetary control; the budget manual; budget centres; the budget period
Fixed and flexible budgets

QUESTIONS

1 As the newly appointed management accountant of Cook's Rubber Products Ltd you have discovered that existing budgeting procedures leave much to be desired. You therefore decide to produce a budget manual to explain to managers and all other affected parties what their duties are.

You are required to set out the information which must be available to enable managers to prepare budgets on a consistent basis so that they can be incorporated into the master budget. *(16 marks)*

2 The balance sheet of Lady Jane Fashions at 31.12.X1 is summarised below:

	£1000	£1000
Fixed assets		700
Current assets		
Stock of finished goods	44.8	
Debtors	200.0	
Cash	157.6	
	402.4	
Current liabilities	2.4	
Net current assets		400
Capital employed		£1,000

Following an advertising compaign around Christmas the firm expects sales to rise in 19X2 but it is not known precisely to what level. It is anticipated that 12,000 items will be sold in the year at an average price of £100, though, with the uncertainty that exists over this figure, you have beeen asked to produce a flexible budget showing the profit if sales are 80%, 90%, 110% and 120% of 12,000. You have also been asked to produce a cash budget showing the balance at the end of each quarter of 19X2 and a budgeted balance sheet at 31.12.X2, both if the 12,000 sales figure is achieved.

You are told that:

— The level of demand is expected to be constant during 19X2 though the actual level achieved will not be confirmed until the end of the first quarter. Production will be of 1,000 garments per month during the first quarter; production in the second quarter will be sufficient to bring the end-of-June stock levels to 2 months; and in the remaining two quarters production will match demand.

— Although it is intended to maintain the average sales price of £100 per item, if sales are to reach the 120% level it is felt that a quantity discount of 10% will need to be given on 20% of sales made.

— All sales are on credit, 50% of debtors pay two months after sale and 50% pay three months after sale. Sales in 19X1 had been constant throughout the year.

— Materials cost is £20 per item. In order to achieve this purchase price stocks have to be bought in bulk on the first day of each quarter and payment made within thirty days. For orders in excess of £50,000 this cost will fall by 5%.

— Labour costs are based on piece-work scales of £3 per item, though the management of Lady Jane Fashions have recently been reminded of a productivity bonus of 60p per item if monthly production from the work-force of 10 reaches 1,000 items. Labour costs are paid one month after they are incurred.

— Overhead costs are partly fixed and partly variable. The variable element amounts to £5 per item payable in the month incurred. The fixed element is expected to be £500,000 of which £100,000 is depreciation of existing fixed assets. Half of the balance is payable monthly, a quarter at the end of June and a quarter at the end of December. If sales reach 120% additional meachinery costing £240,000 will need to be purchased on 1.4.X2 and will be depreciated @ 10% p.a.

— Opening stock represents 1,600 items at unit variable cost. Creditors are for wages.

— Tax and interest charges can be ignored. *(25 marks)*

3 Twelve Bores Ltd owns a 'shooting complex' comprising a grouse moor, a gunshop and accommodation, 'Lockstock Hall', which has 80 double rooms.

The premises are open for 100 days from the 12th August to the 20th November. The management accounts for the year to 20 November 19X1 showed the following results:

	Gun shop		Grouse moor		Lockstock		Total	
	£	%	£	%	£	%	£	%
Sales	64,800	100	97,200	100	259,200	100	421,200	100
Cost of sales	35,640	55	58,320	60	–	–	93,960	22
Consumables	3,240	5	14,580	15	25,920	10	43,740	10
Variable cotsts	38,880	60	72,900	75	25,920	10	137,700	32
Salaries	3,888	6	29,160	30	77,760	30	110,803	26
Insurance and rates	3,240	5	3,888	4	38,880	15	46,008	11
Amortisation/ depreciation	2,592	4	5,832	6	64,800	25	73,224	18
Direct fixed costs	9,720	15	38,880	40	181,440	70	230,040	55
Total costs	48,600	75	111,780	115	207,360	80	367,740	87
Profit/(loss)	16,200	25	(14,580)	(15)	51,840	20	53,460	13

The gun shop is located in the foyer of Lockstock Hall and sales in the gun shop and fees for the grouse moor are perfectly correlated with occupancy of Lockstock Hall.

The average number of rooms let during the season is 60, which is constant throughout the season, and the rate per room £43.20, irrespective of whether the room is let as a single or a double.

Salaries are for the shooting season only, apart from the cost of a gamekeeper-cum-security man who is paid £12,960 p.a. entirely charged to the Hall.

Variable costs of the gun shop and moor vary in proportion to sales. In Lockstock Hall they vary according to occupancy. Insurance, rates, depreciation and amortisation are annual charges. Depreciation and amortisation are charged on a straight line basis.

The dozen directors of the company are worried by the moor's lack of profitability and are considering two possibilities suggested by two of the board members, 'Batty' Mainwaring and 'Toffles' Tollemache.

Batty's suggestion

'Close and sell the moor, bookings will probably go down by six a day for the whole season, but this will be more than made up by the beaters' wages we won't have to pay'.

Toffles' suggestion

'Why don't we open up 100 days earlier, on the May Day Bank Holiday, 4 May, and try and offer the place as a 'summer holiday'? Lettings will probably be only 10 per day, but a travel company, of which I'm a director, will purchase any number of room lettings up to 40 per day at £30 per room per day, provided that the contract is for the same number of rooms per day throughout the whole 200 days of opening. If the contract is signed it will mean that in the summer all the rooms let to the travel company will be in addition to the 10 average room lettings per day achieved by ourselves. During the shoot, however, because the average room lettings per day achieved by the company is 60 out of the 80 rooms available, any lettings to the travel company in excess of 20 will be in substitution for those achieved by the company. The gun shop can be used as a gift shop pre-season, involving conversion costs of £3,500 in May and £3,500 in August.'

It is anticipated that, as in the past, sales in the shop and the moor and variable costs in the Hall will continue to vary in proportion to the number of rooms let, while variable costs in the shop and on the moor will continue to vary in proportion to sales. There is no seasonal variation in levels of prices and salaries.

The directors have also agreed that the enterprise should be capable of returning profits of £120,000.

(a)   Prepare, using Batty's alternative, a budgeted profit and loss account for the gun shop and Hall for the year ending 20 November 19X2, assuming that the moor is closed during the shooting season and that all facilities are closed during the remainder of the year.

(b)   Prepare, using Toffles' suggestion, a budgeted contribution statement for the following year for the shop, moor and Hall on the basis of the travel company taking 40 rooms per day for the 100 days of the shooting and summer seasons and compare the total contribution with the fixed costs and target profit for the year.

(c) Compute, using Toffles' suggestion, the minimum number of rooms per day which will have to be sold to the travel company if the Hall, shop and moor are operated for the two 100-day periods so that the target profit of £120,000 is just about attained.

You may assume that the relationship contained in the 19X0-19X1 accounts continue to be valid.

Ignore taxation and inflation.   *(30 marks)*

4   The trustees of a public hall have produced the following budget for the year commencing 1 July, 19X1:

		£000
Income:		
Lettings at £250 a day		75
Franchise payment: bar/restaurant ..		10
car park		2
		87

	£000	
Expenses:		
Administrative staff	10	
Operating staff	30	
Repairs and renewals ..	30	
Heating and lighting ..	8	
General expenses	2	
Maintenance reserve ..	5	
Financing charges	20	
		105
Loss		18

Letting reservations have been made as under:

	Days
Exhibitions	75
Conferences and meetings ..	105
Theatrical shows	60
Sporting events	60
	300

The 300 days is the maximum letting time available in the year.

Since preparing the budget, the treasurer to the trustees has approached the various organisations with hall reservations and all except the theaterical shows have now agreed to an increase of 10% in the letting fee. Also after negotiations, in addition to their franchise fees, the bar/restaurant operator has agreed to pay 1% of his gross takings and the car park operator a sliding scale fee as under:

Parking on any day			Extra fee per car pence
For the first 500 cars	..	..	Nil
For the next 500 cars	..	..	5
For the next 500 cars	..	..	6
For any additional cars	..	..	7

In the discussions, the theatrical show managers stated that they were near a point of financial balance and could not accept a higher charge. Also they considered there should be a differential charging system as their shows ran for six days at a time and caused less work and expense than other bookings.

An investigation has shown the following facts to be relevant to the problem:

Admininstrative staff 50% full-time and 50% variable with attendances
Operating staff   40% full time and 60% variable with attendances
Repairs and renewals 70% labour cost, of which 60% is variable with attendances; 30% material cost, all of which is fixed.
Heat and light   20% fixed and 80% variable

All other expenses are fixed costs.

	Average attendance per day	Ratio of cars to attendance	Average bar/restaurant purchase per attendance/day £
Exhibitions	4,000	0.4	0.30
Conferences and meetings	900	0.8	8.00
Theatrical shows	1,000	0.4	1.50
Sporting events	1,500	0.5	2.00

There is a clause in the trust deed requiring that lettings to any of the four groups should be within limits of 10% and 45% of the total days available. The contracts for the bar/restaurant and car park franchises are both in the fifth year of seven-year contracts at fixed amounts.

The relative usage of the variable elements of services provided is as follows:

	Per daily usage			
	Admin staff	Operating staff	Repairs & renewals	Heat and light
Exhibitions	5	5	3	7
Conferences and meetings	2	1	1	1
Theatrical shows	1	3	2.5	3
Sporting events	5	4	2	3.5

From the information given:

(a) Calculate a revised budget for the year distinguishing between fixed and variable items.

(b) Prepare a profitability statement for each of the four letting groups.

(c) Calculate a differential daily letting fee for each group based on the revised budget.

(d) Comment briefly on the assertion of the theatrical show managers that their letting fees should be the lowest.

(e) State the percentage of lettings to each group, within the limitations set, which would maximise profit for the year.

(f) Indicate one aspect of the present financial arrangements which you believe requires further investigation, giving reasons for your choice.

Work to nearest £100 in apportionments and to nearest £1 in daily rates.

(30 marks)

ANSWERS

1 The information which a budget manual might contain to enable budgets to be prepared by all managers on a consistent basis and in forms which facilitate consolidation into the master budget includes:

(a) The organisation structure of the business, setting out clearly the responsibilities of each manager and the limits of his authority. Some companies prefer not to publish organisation charts on the grounds that they may give a misleading impression of relative seniorities or levels of manager remuneration; but there should be some definition of functional responsibilities, and each manager should have an individual job specification or terms of reference including details of whom he reports to and who reports to him. In other cases the company's accounts manual may include a code list of cost centres which will provide some indication of the extent of managers' responsibilities. Where none of this information is in existence, or where it is inadequate to indicate budget responsibilities, special budget instructions will be needed.

(b) The classification and coding of the various items of income and expenditure to be covered by the budget. This information again will normally be available in the form of a 'chart of accounts' (or accounts code list) used in coding source documents for bookkeeping purposes. It will be necessary to ensure however that all managers have copies of those parts of the code list which relate to their own responsibilities.

(c) A statement of the period to be covered by the budget and of the shorter accounting periods into which it is to be subdivided (or 'phased') for purposes of control.

(d) Copies of the forms to be used in submitting budgets. Wherever possible the layout of budget forms should be similar to that of the management reports which will be used later to compare budgeted and actual results.

(e) Instructions on what is to be shown on the various forms, and the manner in which particular items are to be calculated. Examples of practical points to be clarified are:

  (i) whether 'sales' are to budgeted initially on the basis of order intake or of invoiced amounts;
  (ii) when costs are expected to increase, whether uniform percentages for particular items are to be used;
  (iii) what rates of salary increase, if any, are to be budgeted by managers;
  (iv) whether average figures are to be used for wage-linked projects such as National Insurance contributions;
  (v) whether advertising costs are to be budgeted departmentally or centrally;
  (vi) whether major items such as Training Levy are to be budgeted on an accrual or a cash basis.

(f) The timetable for the preparation of the budgets.

In order that they may be available for control purposes in the first accounting period of the budget year, budgets will have to be given final approval by the board by a specified date. Working from that date, and bearing in mind that information from one subsidiary budget may be needed for the preparation of another subsidiary budget (e.g. forecast sales volumes will be needed in planning manufacturing capacity), it will be possible to set target dates for the completion of the various subsidiary budgets.

Instructions which are to be binding on all managers must clearly be issued on the authority of the managing director or chief executive; but somebody must be responsible for drafting them, explaining them when necessary and ensuring that they are being complied with as the work of budgeting progresses. The term 'budget officer' may be used to describe this person; but his precise status will vary from company to company.

2

(a) *Flexible budget for 19X2*

Activity	80%	90%	100%	110%	120%
	£000	£000	£000	£000	£000
Gross sales	960	1,080	1,200	1,320	1,440.0
Discount	–	–	–	–	28.8
	960	1,080	1,200	1,320	1,411.2
Variable production costs:					
Materials	189.00	209.00	235.60	262.20	288.80
Labour	30.60	34.80	44.64	49.68	54.72
Overheads	48.00	55.00	62.00	69.00	76.00
	267.60	298.80	342.24	380.88	419.52
Opening stock	44.80	44.80	44.80	44.80	44.80
	312.40	343.60	387.04	425.68	464.32
Closing stock	44.80	48.60	55.20	60.72	66.24
Cost of goods sold	267.60	295.00	331.84	364.96	398.08
Fixed costs	500.00	500.00	500.00	500.00	518.00
Total costs	767.60	795.00	831.84	864.96	916.08
Profit	192.4	285.0	368.16	455.04	495.12

(b) *Cash budget for 19X2 (at 100% activity)*

Quarter	1	2	3	4
	£000	£000	£000	£000
Sales	300	300	300	300
Opening debtors	200	250	250	250
	500	550	550	550
Closing debtors	250	250	250	250
Receipts	250	300	300	300
Payments:				
Materials	57.00	64.60	57.00	57.00
Labour	9.60	11.76	11.28	10.80
Variable overheads	15.00	17.00	15.00	15.00
Fixed overheads	50.00	150.00	50.00	150.00
	131.60	243.36	133.28	232.80
Net cash flow	118.40	56.64	166.72	67.20
Balance B/F	157.60	276.00	332.64	499.36
Balance C/F	276.00	332.64	499.36	566.56

(c) *Budgeted balance sheet at 31. 12. X2*

	£000	£000
Fixed assets		600.00
Current assets		
Stock of finished goods	55.20	
Debtors	250.00	
Cash	566.56	
	871.76	
Current liabilities	3.60	
Net current assets		868.16
Net assets		1,468.16
Capital employed		
Balance at 1. 1. X2		1,100.00
Profit for the year		368.16
Balance at 31.12. X2		1,468.16

Workings

Production (units)

Activity	80%	90%	100%	110%	120%
Quarter 1	3,000	3,000	3,000	3,000	3,000
Opening stock	1,600	1,600	1,600	1,600	1,600
	4,600	4,600	4,600	4,600	4,600
Sales	2,400	2,700	3,000	3,300	3,600
Closing stock	2,200	1,900	1,600	1,300	1,000
Quarter 2					
Sales	2,400	2,700	3,000	3,300	3,600
Closing stock	1,600	1,800	2,000	2,200	2,400
	4,000	4,500	5,000	5,500	6,000
Opening stock	2,200	1,900	1,600	1,300	1,000
Production	1,800	2,600	3,400	4,200	5,000
Quarter 3 & 4					
Production	2,400	2,700	3,000	3,300	3,600
Total	9,600	11,000	12,400	13,800	15,200

Materials cost (£000)

Quarter 1	57	57	57	57	57
2	36	49.4	64.6	79.8	95
3	48	51.3	57	62.7	68.4
4	48	51.3	57	62.7	68.4
Total	189	209.0	235.6	262.2	288.8

Labour costs (£000)

Quarter 1	10.8	10.8	10.8	10.80	10.80
2	5.4	7.8	12.24	15.12	18.00
3	7.2	8.1	10.80	11.88	12.96
4	7.2	8.1	10.80	11.88	12.96
Total	30.6	34.8	44.64	49.68	54.72

Closing stock

	1,600	1,800	2,000	2,200	2,400
Units	£000	£000	£000	£000	£000
Cost					
Materials	32	34.2	38	41.8	45.6
Labour	4.8	5.4	7.2	7.92	8.64
Overhead	8	9	10	11	12
	44.8	48.6	55.2	60.72	66.24

Debtors

These represent 2½ months' sales.

Labour

Payments are $2/3$ of each quarter's cost plus $1/3$ of previous quarter.

3

(a) *Batty's suggestion*

	Gun shop	Lockstock Hall	
	£	£	
Sales	58,320	233,280	
Cost of sales	32,076	–	
Consumable stores	2,916	23,328	
	34,992	23,328	
Salaries	3,888	77,760	
Insurance, rates	3,240	38,880	
Depreciation	2,592	64,800	
	9,720	181,440	
Total costs	44,712	204,768	
Profit	13,608	28,512	£42,120

(b) *Toffles' suggestion*

	Gun shop	Grouse moor	Lockstock	Total
	£	£	£	£
Sales: 4 May, 11 August	54,000	–	163,200	
12 August, 20 November	86,400	129,600	292,800	
	140,400	129,600	456,000	
Variable costs:				
Cost of sales	77,220	77,760		
Consumable stores	7,020	19,440	56,160	
	84,240	97,200	56,160	
Contribution	56,160	32,400	399,840	488,400
Fixed costs:				
Salaries			179,496	
Insurance and rates			46,008	
Depreciation			73,224	
Conversion costs			7,000	305,728
Projected profit				182,672
Required profit				120,000
Surplus				£ 62,672

(c)   *Break-even travel company lettings*

(i)

	With moor	Without moor
19X0/X1	£	£
Revenue	421,200	324,000
Variable costs	137,700	64,800
Contribution	£283,500	£259,200
Contribution/room	£ 4,725	£ 4,320
Travel company contribution/room (reduced by 100 x (£43.20 − £30))	£ 3,405	£ 3,000

(ii)   For reduction lettings by/to 20 rooms)
Reduction in profit/room let:

		£
In shooting season, gain (£4,725 − £3,405)	=	1,320
In pre-season, loss		3,000
Net loss/room		£1,680

A reduction in travel company lettings of 20 rooms would reduce profit by:

20 x £1,680 = £33,600

The surplus of £62,672 is reduced to £29,072.

(iii)   For reductions beyond 20 rooms:

Reductions beyond 20 rooms,
reduction in profit/room let:

	£
In shooting season	3,000
In pre-season	3,405
Total loss/room	£6,405

A further reduction of:

$$\frac{£29,072}{£6,405} = 4.54 \text{ rooms is possible}$$

Therefore the minimum number of rooms to sell to the travel agent are:

40 − 24.54 = 15.46 or 16 rooms

4 This question is typical of budgetary control questions, both in the complexity of its narrative and in the volume of simple arithmetic necessary to arrive at an answer. It has no great conceptual difficulty however, and the requirements are clearly stated. A calm and logical approach will easily yield an acceptable answer. Students are advised to tick off each item of information in the question as it is used.

(a) *Revised budget*   £000

Revised income

	£000
Lettings at £250/day (theatrical shows) 60 days	15
Lettings at £275/day (other) 240 days	66
Franchise payment: Bar/restaurant	10
Car park	2

Additional agreed income:

Bar commission

	Days	Attendance/ day	Total	Average purchase	Total
				£	£
Exhibitions	75	4,000	300,000	0.30	90,000
Conferences, etc.	105	900	94,500	8.00	756,000
Theatrical shows	60	1,000	60,000	1.50	90,000
Sporting events	60	1,500	90.000	2.00	180,000
	300				1,116,000

1% of £1,116,000 =   11.16

Parking

	Days	Cars/ day	Daily surcharge	Total	
Exhibitions	75	1,600	500 @ 5p		
			500 @ 6p		
			100 @ 7p	4,650	
Conferences, etc.	105	720	220 @ 5p	1,155	
Theatrical shows	60	400	—	—	
Sporting events	60	750	250 @ 5p	750	
				6,555	6.555
					110.715

Expenses

	Variable	Fixed	
	£000	£000	
Administrative staff	5	5	
Operating staff	18	12	
Repairs and renewals (variable 70% x 60% x 30)	12.6	17.4	
Heat and light	6.4	1.6	
General expenses	—	2	
Maintenance reserve	—	5	
Financing charges	—	20	
	42	63	105.00
Profit			5.715

Note: Lettings to each group are within the prescribed limits of 10% and 45% of the total 300 days available.

(b) *Analysed profitability statement*

	Exhibitions	Conferences, etc.	Theatrical shows	Sporting events
	£000	£000	£000	£000
Letting	20.625	28.875	15.0	16.5
Bar commission	.9	7.56	.9	1.8
Parking surcharge	4.65	1.155	—	.75
	26.175	37.590	15.9	19.05

Variable cost (see Apportionments below)

Administrative staff	2	1.1	0.3	1.6
Operating staff	7.5	2.1	3.6	4.8
Repairs and renewals	4.7	2.2	3.2	2.5
Heat and light	3.3	.7	1.1	1.3
	17.5	6.1	8.2	10.2
Contribution	8.675	31.49	7.7	8.35
			56.715	

Less:

Fixed	63			
Franchise	12			
Fixed income			51	
Profit			5.715	
Contribution per day	£116	£300	£128	£148

Apportionments

Administrative staff

	Weight	Days	Proportion	£
Exhibitions	5	75	375	2,000
Conferences, etc.	2	105	210	1,100
Theatrical shows	1	60	60	300
Sporting events	5	60	300	1,600
			945	5,000

Operating staff

	Weight	Days	Proportion	£
Exhibitions	5	75	375	7,500
Conferences, etc.	1	105	105	2,100
Theatrical shows	3	60	180	3,600
Sporting events	4	60	240	4,800
			900	18,000

Repairs and renewals

	Weight	Days	Proportion	£
Exhibitions	3	75	225	4,700
Conferences, etc.	1	105	105	2,200
Theatrical shows	2.5	60	150	3,200
Sporting events	2	60	120	2,500
			600	12,600

Heat and light

	Weight	Days	Proportion	£
Exhibitions	7	75	525	3,300
Conferences, etc.	1	105	105	700
Theatrical shows	3	60	180	1,100
Sporting events	3.5	60	210	1,300
			1,020	6,400

(c) At first sight, the wording of this part of the question may be difficult to understand; but the work 'differential' is often used in relation to incremental or 'variable' costs. What is required here is a set of daily rates that will differ only because of the variable costs (less variable items of income) that they have to cover. Each rate will yield an equal daily amount of marginal contribution (profit plus fixed costs).

The total annual contribution calculated in part (b) is £56,715, which, divided by 300 days, gives a required daily amount of £189.05. The required daily letting fees can therefore be built up as follows:

	Exhibitions	Conferences	Theatrical shows	Sporting events	Total
	£	£	£	£	£
Total contribution	14,178.75	19,850.25	11,343.00	11,343.00	56,715.00
Total variable costs	17,500.00	6,100.00	8,200.00	10,200.00	42,000.00
Less variable income	(5,550.00)	(8,715.00)	(900.00)	(2,550.00)	(17,715.00)
Total to be covered by letting fees	26,128.75	17,235.25	18,643.00	18,993.00	81,900.00
DAYS	75	105	60	60	300
DAILY RATES	£348.383	£164.145	£310.717	£316.550	

(d) The actual statement by the theatrical show managers was that there should be a differential charging system; the implication being that the daily cost of theatrical presentations was less than for other bookings. The calculations made in part (c) in fact result in a lower daily rate for theatrical shows than for exhibitions and sporting events. The lowest rate, however, would be that for conferences. Not only is the conferences variable cost (per day and in total) less than that of other forms of entertainment; but conferences also yield higher daily amounts of bar commission and car park surcharge.

(e) This is a simple application of contribution per units of limiting factor, the limiting factor in this instance being the number of days. From part (b), assuming that existing letting rates are to be used, conferences yield the highest amount of contribution per day and would ideally be allocated the maximum 45% of total day. Exhibitions yield the lowest rate of contribution per day, and should be restricted to the minimum 10% of total days.

This leaves 45% of the total days to be allocated between theatrical shows and sporting events. On the basis of contribution per day, theatrical shows should be limited to 10%, leaving 35% for sporting events.

(f) As shown in the calculation of bar commission in part (a), bar and restaurant sales amount to £1,116,000 per year. Under the existing seven-year contract only £10,000 per year is received as a fixed franchise payment from the restaurant operator. Even though this is now supplemented by a 1% commission on sales, the total amount receivable by the trustees is extremely low in relation to the bar and restaurant profits that would normally be earned.

The contract is due for renewal in two years' time; and should be renegotiated on more favourable terms for the trustees.

No information is available on the income obtained by the car park concessionaire; but this contract should also be reviewed.

6   Cash budgets

A company's plans for profit and asset holdings may yield satisfactory trends of growth and return on investment, but will prove impracticable unless funds can be made available to finance them. It is for this reason that the 'cash budget' has great significance in the overall build-up to the master budget for a period.

Cash budgets are also favoured by examiners, probably because they add interest to questions on budget preparation, which might otherwise contain little other than the formal re-presentation of data relating to the profit and loss account and balance sheet.

From this starting point some questions branch out to cover, for example, the differences between a cash flow statement and a source and applications of funds statement, or alternative sources of finance, though not in the detail that would be found in a financial management syllabus.

None of this should offer any great difficulty to the student with a good grounding in accountancy.

Both computational and essay-type questions will be encountered, and two examples of each are given in this chapter.

STUDY REQUIREMENTS

Cash forecasting and budgeting
Source and application of funds statements

1 Textiles Ltd operates a subsidiary, the Sunny Textile Company Ltd, which manufactures ladies swimwear. Following the success of this subsidiary it has been decided to expand it by diversifying into the production of swimwear for all the family. An extension to the Sunny Textile Company Ltd's factory is now being built for this purpose. The contract for this extension is for £100,000. 10% of the contract price had to be paid on signing the contract in December 19X5. Another £50,000 has to be paid on 30 March 19X6 with balance due on the later of 30 May 19X6 or completion.

The financial year of the Sunny Textile Company Ltd runs from 1 April and budgeted figures for the 19X6 calendar year have been produced as follows:

Month	Sales (before discounts allowed)	Purchase of raw materials (before discounts received)	Wages	Fixed over-heads (including depreciation of £1,000 per month)
	£000	£000	£000	£000
Jan	6	10	5	2
Feb	6	10	5	2
Mar	24	10	5	2
Apr	48	10	5	2
May	48	10	5	2
June	48	10	5	7
July	24	10	5	2
Aug	12	–	4	2
Sept	2	10	5	2
Oct	4	10	5	2
Nov	4	10	5	2
Dec	2	10	6	7
Total	£228	£110	£60	£34

In budgeting cash at bank on 1 April 19X6 at £50,000 the company has overlooked the contract payment for the factory extension due on the 30 March 19X6.

Although the Sunny Textile Company Ltd requires payment for its sales in the month following that in which the sale is made, and offers a settlement discount of 5% for accounts settled within this period, experience has taught it to expect only half the payments when due. One quarter of the payments follow during the second month after sale and the balance comes in the third month. Bad debts average 2½% of sales.

It is company's policy to pay for supplies during the month in which they are delivered in order to take advantage of a 10% prompt settlement discount offered by all its suppliers.

The level of stocks at the end of December 19X6 is expected to remain unchanged from that in January. These are valued on a variable cost basis. The architect issued a final certificate for the factory extension on 19 April.

(a) Prepare for the Sunny Textile Company Ltd:

   (i)   a budgeted profit and loss account;
   (ii) a cash budget on a monthly basis;

   both for the six months commencing 1 April 19X6, stating clearly any assumptions that you need to make.   *(15 marks)*

(b) Discuss the value of cash budgets to management, illustrating the points that you make by reference to any implications that you can derive from the cash budget that you have prepared.   *(5 marks)*

(Total 20 marks)

2   In the third week of April the accountant of the S.W. division of Jackson Brothers p.l.c. is reviewing the division's cash budget up to the end of the company's financial year (31 August). Each of the company's divisions has its own bank account but arrangements are made centrally for transfers among them as a need or opportunity arises. Interest is charged (or allowed) on such intra-company transfers at a market-related rate.

The three months of May, June and July are the S.W. division's busiest months, providing two-thirds of its annual profit, but there is always a cash flow problem in this period. In anticipation of a cash shortage, arrangements have been made to borrow (internally) £100,000 over the busy period at an annual interest rate of 15% (chargeable monthly). The agreed borrowing and repayment schedule is as follows:

   1 May borrowing of £30,000
   1 June borrowing of £70,000
   1 July repayment of £20,000
   1 August repayment of £60,000
   1 September repayment of £20,000

The accountant has in front of him the budgeted divisional profit and loss account figures for the four months to 31 August and the profit and loss accounts for March and April — the latter being an estimated statement. These documents can be summarised as follows:

	March	April	May	June	July	August
	£	£	£	£	£	£
Sales revenue	120,000	120,000	230,000	250,000	300,000	160,000
Facotory cost of goods sold	100,000	100,000	182,500	197,500	235,000	130,000
Selling and distribution costs	4,200	4,200	6,400	6,800	7,800	5,000
Administrative costs and interest charges	7,000	7,000	7,375	8,250	8,000	7,250
	111,200	111,200	196,275	212,550	250,800	142,250
Divisional profit	8,800	8,800	33,725	37,450	49,200	17,750
	£120,000	£120,000	£230,000	£250,000	£300,000	£160,000

The accountant is using the following assumptions:

(a) Each factory cost of goods sold figure includes a fixed cost element of £10,000 of which £2,000 is depreciation. The remaining fixed factory cost can reasonably be assumed to be paid as it is charged.

(b) Direct material cost is approximately 75% of the variable factory cost of the firm's products. The suppliers of this direct material are paid in the month following its purchase. Other variable factory costs of production are paid in the month that the production takes place.

(c) Half of the fixed selling and distribution cost is a depreciation charge for motor vehicles. The remaining cost under this heading is paid in the month in which it is charged.

(d) A monthly central administration charge of £1,000 and interest on any borrowings are charged to administrative costs and interest charges and credited to a head office current account. Other administrative costs of approximately £6,000 per month are paid monthly.

(e) The following policies are followed by the division:

(i) The target month end stock level for finished goods is £10,000 plus 25% of the variable cost of next month's budgeted sales — finished goods are valued at variable cost for accounting purposes.

(ii) The target month end stock level for direct materials is £10,000 plus 25% of the material required for next month's budgeted production.

(f) All sales are on credit terms. 20% of the cash from customers is received in the month following that in which the sales were made, the remainder is received in the next month.

(g) The cash at bank and in hand at the end of April is expected to be approximately £10,000.

(a) Prepare the division's cash budget for the months of May and June. Each cash figure should be rounded to the nearest £1,000. *(18 marks)*

(b) The accountant has been experimenting with the use of the following formula for predicting month-end cash holdings:

$$CB = OB + 0.85_{i-2} - 0.12S_{i-1} - 0.37S_i - 0.08S_{i+1} - 15$$

where CB is the predicted closing cash balance in £000 for month i;
    OB is the (estimated) opening cash balance in £000 for month i
and S_i is the sales figure for month i in £000, actual or budgeted as appropriate.
Assuming that this formula is appropriate, comment on the effect on the division's cash holding at the end of May of deviations of ± 10% in the May sales figure from the budgeted figure.
(*Note:* Do not use the formula in part (a) to this question) *(6 marks)*

(c) Consider the possibility of introducing a discount scheme to encourage customers to pay promptly. How would you judge the worthwhileness of such a scheme? *(3 marks)*

(Total 27 marks)

3 (a) Comment on the reasons for planning for the flow of cash within a firm. Specify the benefits to be derived from the production of a detailed cash budget. *(14 marks)*

(b) Outline the major factors to be considered in the preparation of a detailed cash budget. *(6 marks)*

(Total 20 marks)

4 In relation to cash planning in:
    EITHER a commercial company
    OR   a non-profit-orientated organisation

(a) Explain the techniques that can effectively be used for:
    (i) short-term budgeting (say, one year or less);
    (ii) long-term forecasting (say, more than one year).

(b) Discuss briefly the reasons for the differences between the techniques you have given in answer to (a) (i) and (a) (ii) above. *(20 marks)*

ANSWERS

1

(a) *Preparation of budgets*

(i) Budgeted profit and loss account

Carelessness can creep into examination work, and the first thing to note in this question is that the required profit and loss account covers the six months from April to Septemer. Information given for earlier and later months is there for a purpose, but do not waste your time by starting with a sales figure for twelve months!

In calculating the materials cost of sales, we are told that stocks at 31 December will be the same as those at 1 January; but we do not know what fluctuations in stockholding will occur during the year. It seems clear that the 'purchases' in any month are not related to the sales of that month. The best we can do is assume that no price changes have occurred during the year, and therefore that cost of sales has remained consistent at £110,000/228,000 = 48.25% approx of sales value.

Note however that the credit for discounts received will be calculated on the actual purchases for the six months. Wages are apparently not a 'fixed cost', so they must enter into the variable cost of sales and inventories. The wages cost of sales must therefore be assumed at £60,000/228,000 = 26.3% of sales value.

THE SUNNY TEXTILE COMPANY LTD
Budgeted profit and loss account for the six months commencing 1 April 19X6

	£	£	£
Sales		182,000	
Less: Settlement discounts taken (5% of £91,000)	4,500		
Bad debts written off (2½% of £181,000)	4,550		
		9,100	
			172,900
Less: Costs and expenses			
Material cost of sales (48·25% of revenue) say		87,800	
Discounts received (10% of £50,000)		(5,000)	
Wages (26·3% of revenue), say		47,900	
Fixed overheads		11,000	
Depreciation		6,000	
			147,700
Budgeted net profit			£25,200

(ii) Cash budget
In preparing the cash budget, the following assumptions have been made:
— Wages are paid in the months shown.

— In phasing collections from customers, the discount received will be deducted from the 50% collected in the month after sale, and the 2½% bad debts will be deducted from the 25% collected in third month after sale.

Note also that the opening cash balance will be nil (£50,000 less £50,000 paid on 30 March under the contract for the factory extension); and that the final £40,000 under that contract, certified on 19 April, will be payable on 30 May.

THE SUNNY TEXTILE COMPANY LTD

Cash budget for the six months commencing 1 April 19X6 – in £'s

Month	Feb.	March	April	May	June	July	August	September	Total (for 6 mths)
Balance of cash (brought down)			nil	(750)	(25,600)	(5,400)	25,200	54,400	nil
Cash from sales									
January	2,850	1,500	1,350						1,350
February		2,850	1,500	1,350					2,850
March			11,400	6,000	5,400				22,800
April				22,800	12,000	10,800			45,600
May					22,800	12,000	10,800		45,600
June						22,000	12,000	10,800	45,600
July							11,400	6,000	17,400
August								5,700	5,700
Total cash received from debtors during period			14,250	30,150	40,200	45,600	34,200	22,500	186,900
Paid to suppliers			9,000	9,000	9,000	9,000	nil	9,000	45,000
Paid as wages			5,000	5,000	5,000	5,000	4,000	5,000	29,000
Paid as fixed overheads			1,000	1,000	6,000	1,000	1,000	1,000	11,000
Exceptional payments (for buildings)				40,000					40,000
Total cash paid out during period			15,000	55,000	20,000	15,000	5,000	15,000	125,000
Balance of cash (carried forward)			(750)	(25,600)	(5,400)	25,200	54,400	61,900	61,900

(b)   Cash budgets help management with cash planning, indicating those periods in which cash shortages are likely to occur unless action is taken to cover them, and those periods in which there will be surplus funds which might be available for investment. In the case of the Sunny Textile Company Ltd there will be a shortage of cash between April and June. This is mainly attributable to the £40,000 contract payment due in May. If this could be postponed until August, the only remaining problem would be the £750 deficit in April. It is unlikely that the contractor would agree to this; but if he did he would undoubtedly require to be paid interest on the overdue amount.

Other possibilities might be:

(i)   taking credit from suppliers, with the loss of the discount currently obtained;

(ii) attempting to collect debts more quickly; there is no quarantee that this would succeed, even if higher cash discounts were offered.

Bearing in mind that the need for additional finance is of short duration, the most likely source would be a bank overdraft. The presentation of a cash forecast in the form shown would undoubtedly give the bank manager confidence that the company was planning its affairs and was taking account of all possibilities.

The most obvious solution, however, is for the company to approach its parent company, Textiles Ltd. Surplus funds may be available either at group level or in another subsidiary, and the use of these would save the costs of obtaining the money from outside sources.

2

(a) The main mathematical problem in this part of the question is to calculate the variable cost of sales; from this, by adjusting stock changes (valued at variable cost) to derive the variable cost of production; and thence, adjusting material stocks, to arrive at the purchased input.

The procedure is as follows:

	March £	April £	May £	June £	July £	August £
Factory cost of sales, as stated of which:	100,000	100,000	182,500	197,500	235,000	130,000
Variable	90,000	90,000	172,500	187,500	225,000	120,000
Fixed	8,000	8,000	8,000	8,000	8,000	8,000
Depreciation	2,000	2,000	2,000	2,000	2,000	2,000
Month-end stock finished goods £10,000 + 25% of following month's variable cost of sales	32,500	53,125	56,875	66,250	40,000	
Stock at beginning of month		32,500	53,125	56,875	66,250	
Variable cost of production = 1 (a) + 2 − 3 of which:		110,625	176,250	196,875	198,750	
(a) material (75%)		82,969	132,187	147,656	149,062	
(b) other (25%)		27,656	44,063	49,219	49,688	
Closing stock of material, £10,000 + 25% next month's material cost of production	30,742	43,047	46,914	47,265		
Opening stock of material		30,742	43,047	46,914		
Purchases 4 (a) + 5 − 6		95,274	136,054	148,007		
Payments to suppliers			95,274	136,054		

Two other preliminary calculations are necessary before assembling the cash forecast — collections from customers and the subdivision of selling and distribution costs.

	April	May	June
	£	£	£
Collections from customers			
Sales in March	24,000	96,000	
April		24,000	96,000
May			46,000
		120,000	142,000

Selling and distribution costs

It is necessary to distinguish between fixed and variable costs. This can be done only by relating changes in total selling and distribution costs to changes in sales value. Thus between May and June sales income increased by £20,000 and S & D costs by £400. It appears then that variable S & D costs are 2% on sales value. For May and June therefore the analysis is as follows:

	May	June
	£	£
Variable	4,600	5,000
Fixed	1,800	1,800
Of which:		
Depreciation	900	900
Other	900	900

The required cash budgets, rounded to the nearest £1,000, are:

Cash Budgets

	May	June
	£000s	£000s
Cash/bank balance at beginning of month	10	1
Borrowing	30	70
Receipts from customers	120	142
	£160	£213
Payments:	£	£
Suppliers	95	136
Variable factory expense	44	49
Fixed factory expense	8	8
Administrative expense	6	6
Selling and distribution expense:		
Fixed	1	1
Variable	5	5
	159	205
Cash/bank balance at end of month	1	8
	£160	£213

(b) Before calculating the required deviations, most accountants would probably wish to check whether the formula given does in fact correspond with the forecast already made.

The answer appears to be in the affirmative, as shown below:

		£000
OB		10
$9.8S_{i-2}$	$= 80\% \times £120,000$	96
$0.12S_{i-1}$	$= 12\% \times £120,000$	(14.4)
$0.37S_i$	$= 37\% \times £230,000$	(85.1)
$0.8S_{i-1}$	$= 8\% \times £250,000$	(20)
Constant		(15)
		(28.5)
Borrowing (not included in formula)		30
CB		1.5

If the sales figure for May (S_i) had been plus 10%. i.e. £253,000, the closing balance would have been reduced by 37% x £23,000, i.e. £8,510, to a deficit of £7,010. If the sales figure had been minus 10%, the closing balance would have been increased by £8,510 to £10,010.

The reason for these results appears to be that while no collections from customers are received in the month of sale, any predictable change in sales will affect previous months' purchases, for which payment falls to be made in the month following purchase.

A model of this kind can be useful in predicting the effect on cash of deviations from budgeted sales.

(c)   A first consideration would be that discount would have to be given to customers who already pay promptly without the incentive of such a scheme; in other words the company would be paying a nominal rate of discount without any improvement in cash flow.

Secondly a forecast would have to be made of the percentage of customers who would pay more quickly in consequence of the scheme.

A calculation could then be made of the £-days gained and the total discount granted. This would almost certainly reveal an effective discount rate higher than the nominal rate. This real rate would have to be compared with the cost of borrowed or other capital needed to finance the scheme in order to judge whether the project was financially worthwhile.

Once a scheme was introduced it would be difficult to discontinue it. Such a project should not be used to ameliorate difficulties that are only short-term.

3

(a)   The reasons for any type of planning are to predict the outcome of decisions and to provide a basis for comparison with what eventually happens. This comparison, if made before the proposed action has been completed, will enable steps to be taken to correct or modify any deviations from the plan. At worst, the comparison will give guidance for better planning procedures.

The particular reason for planning the flow of cash within a firm is that cash is an essential commodity, without which the firm's plans for profit and asset holdings cannot be achieved.

The benefits to be derived from the preparation of a detailed cash budget, therefore, are:

(i)   to make sure that the company's plans are financially feasible;

(ii)   to identify periods when surplus cash is likely to be available, and should be put to profitable use;

(iii)   to identify when additional funds will be required, and for what period. Action can then be taken in advance to decide the sources from which those funds are to be obtained;

(iv)   to make all managers aware of the cash flow implications of their plans, and to enlist their collaboration in economising in the use of, or improving the inflow of, cash;

(v)   to provide a basis for monitoring actual performance.

(b)   The major factors to be considered in the preparation of a detailed cash budget are:

(i)   The budget period. A cash budget will form part of the master budget of the firm, whether this is a relatively long-term strategic budget or a relatively short-term operating budget. Within these overall planning periods, however, there may be need for very short-term cash budgets (or, more likely, cash forecasts), since cash flows respond to changes in every other aspect of the master budget. The length of the forecast period will determine the amount of detail that can be built into the cash budget.

(ii) The format of budget presentation. A cash budget for presentation to senior managers will probably need to link budgeted cash flow with budgeted profit, i.e. it will take the form of a Source and Application of Funds Statement. A cash budget to be used for day-by-day control will probably be in the form of a receipts and payments corecast.

(iii) The amount of detail needed. In the case of a receipts and payments budgets, the item headings should ideally correspond to those in the books of prime entry (purchase day book, cash receipts and payments books, petty cash imprests, etc) so that comparisons of actual flows against the budget are made using data readily available.

In the case of sales and purchases it will probably be necessary to identify each month's transactions separately in order to forecast their cash flow implications.

(iv) Budget responsibilities. The accountant or financial controller cannot realistically prepare a cash budget on his own. Collaboration will almost certainly be needed from both the sales manager and the purchasing manager in identifying the timing of receipts from customers and payments to suppliers. All managers should be involved in phasing their own expense budgets.

(v)   Degree of accuracy. As with other budgets, some form of sensitivity analysis should be made to indicate a possible range of cash requirements.

4   The answer given below relates to a commercial company. Students who are familiar with a particular non-profit-orientated organisation will be able to identify the different headings under which receipts and payments would be classified.

(a) (i)   Techniques for short-term budgeting

           Sources of information

           For an annual budget, each manager will have forecast the sales, purchases, expenses and asset changes which fall under his particular responsibility, and will have phased them to intermediate control periods. By applying known credit periods, or by asking managers to specify any abnormal credit periods, the cash flow implications of those budgets can be established.

For shorter-term budgets, specific forecasts can be obtained from the various managers.

Form of budget

It is probable that a 'receipts and payments' format will be used, setting out the various items under headings that are readily comparable with information recorded in the various books of account. This will facilitate control.

A specimen format is illustrated below:

	£	£
Bank balance as at (commencement of period)		x
INFLOW:		
Collections from customers	x	
Dividends from investments	x	
		x
		x
OUTFLOW:		
Payments for materials and services	x	
Wages and salaries	x	
Rent, rates, etc	x	
Capital expenditure	x	
Corporation tax	x	
Debenture interest	x	
Dividend payments	x	
		x
Bank balance as at (end of period)		x

Revision of budget

Because of changing circumstances it is inevitable that actual performance will deviate from that budgeted. The financial manager has to ensure that at all times he is able to mobilise the funds necessary for ongoing operations. It is necessary therefore to review actual cash flows against those budgeted at frequent intervals, and to prepare updated forecasts of cash flows. The frequency of these will vary from weekly (or even daily) to six-monthly according to the financial pressures. They should be on a 'rolling' basis, so that the latest cash forecast always covers a period adequate for affective financial planning.

(a)   (ii)   *Techniques for long-term cash forecasting*

Sources of information

A long-term budget is prepared to identify the main strategies appropriate to the achievement of the company's long-term objectives.

It is likely therefore to be largely narrative in style, and will not contain the same amount of detail as a short-term operating budget. Among the main items likely to be identified are:

— development of new products and techniques, showing the expected development costs and the forecast incremental benefits:

— main items of new capital equipment, investment in inventories and changes in staff establishment;

— a broad summary of profits and net asset holdings year by year during the period of the plan;

— a policy statement on the sources from which additional long-term capital is to be obtained.

Form of cash budget

In view of the paucity of detailed information, the cash budget will be in the form of a Source and Application of Funds Statement. An outline of the possible form of such a statement is given below:

	£	£
Expected commencing balance		x
+ Expected profit for the year		x
+ Depreciation for the year *(added back)*		x̲
		x
± Expected changes in working capital (inventory, debtors, etc.)		x̲
		x
− Expected capital expenditure	x	
− Expected tax payments	x	
− Expected dividend payments	x̲	
		x̲
Expected closing balance		x̲

It is likely that the 'expected closing balance' would be an 'expected requirement for new funds'. It would be followed by a suggested sourcing of such funds, as between equity and borrowed capital, and of the additional dividend and interest payments to which that would give rise.

Revision of budget

Long-term budgets are normally revised yearly. The first year of the old plan will be converted into an operating budget, and a further year will be added to the long-term forecast.

Detailed 'control' is not possible against long-range plans, but a statement should be prepared explaining any changes in the long-term funding requirement.

(b)   Reasons for differences between the two techniques

(The following abbreviations are used: 'STB' for short-term budgets and 'LTF' for long-term forecasts.)

Differences

LTFs are broader in scope and less detailed than STBs.

STBs are broken down into monthly (or smaller) control periods but LTFs are yearly totals.

Reasons

Long-term conditions and events are much more difficult to predict and, as the LTFs are not used for day-to-day control, they need not be as precise as STBs.

The STB is a basis for action aimed at maintaining availability of cash to meet commitments as they arise. Liquidity problems may arise following payment of dividends or corporation tax or the purchase of exceptional equipment, but such difficulties can be avoided if anticipated in good time. Remedial action may take the form of tighter control of debt collection, extended credit arranged with creditors, lowering of inventory levels or the negotiation of temporary bank overdraft facilities.

LTFs serve a different purpose, not being concerned with normal cash movement fluctuations or stop-gap action. They are related to long-term planning on a wide scale. Planned growth, introduction of new products, improvements in technology and the like require long 'lead times' and the financial aspects are vitally important. Investment in fixed assets and working capital must be covered by finance provided from profits or from external sources such as the issue of shares or debentures.

7 Applications of standard costing

The majority of questions on standard costing require the calculation of variances from standards, and a selection of such questions is given in chapter 8.

Essay questions occur, however, on the objectives and advantages of standard costing and on methods of setting standards, sometimes having reference to special industries or to special circumstances such as a 'learning' situation. Questions 1–4 in this chapter are representative examples. The introduction of a standard costing system can have alternative objectives, to which different bases for setting standards will be appropriate. It is important that you have these alternatives clearly in mind.

More rarely, a question will require you to calculate standard costs from data provided. Given the right theoretical grounding, such questions should offer no difficulty. Examples are given in Questions 5 and 6 below.

STUDY REQUIREMENTS

Principles and practice of setting performance standards and value standards
Types of standard cost – ideal, basic and current
Learning curves
Behavioural aspects of control accounting

QUESTIONS

1   In discussing the standard setting process for use with budgetary control and/
or standard costing systems, the following has been written: 'The level of standards
appears to play a role in achievement motivation . . .'

(a)   Briefly distinguish between the motivational and managerial reporting objectives of both budgetary control and standard costing. Describe the extent to
which these two objectives place conflicting demands on the standard of performance utilised in such systems.   *(8 marks)*

(b)   Describe three levels of efficiency which may be incorporated in the standards
used in budgetary control and/or standard costing systems. Outline the main
advantages and disadvantages of each of the four levels described.   *(9 marks)*

(c)   Discuss the advantages and disadvantages of involving employees in the
standard-setting process.   *(8 marks)*

(Total 25 marks)

2   Explain the 'learning curve' and discuss its relevance to setting standards.
(5 marks)

3   (a)   Explain the problems concerning control of operations that a manufacturing company can be expected to experience in using a standard
costing system during periods of rapid inflation.

(b)   Explain three methods by which the company could try to overcome
the problems to which you have referred in answer to (a) above, indicating the shortcomings of each method.   *(20 marks)*

4   What advantages and limitations can be identified with standard costing? To
what extent is it practical to use in the same firm both standard costing and a system of costing based on actual incurred historic costs?   *(20 marks)*

5   A company distributing oil products operates two types of motor vehicle,
tank lorries for liquids such as motor fuels and covered vans for packaged goods
such as lubricating oils.

The transport department's budget shows the costs under three divisions, vehicle
operations, vehicle repairs and loading facilities.

From the data given below:

(a)   Prepare the budget for the year 19X7 showing separately for each division the
costs for each vehicle type.

(b)   Calculate standard costs for each vehicle type of:

(i)   operations (cost per operating mile);
(ii) repairs (cost per vehicle operating hour);

(iii)   loading (cost per loading hour).

(c)   Construct a table showing the standard cost, for a covered van only, for journeys of 20 miles, 40 miles and 60 miles.

All calculations in £s to two decimal places.

Data for the year 19X7

	Tank lorries	Covered vans
Number of vehicles	12	5
Journeys per day	3	4
Loading time, hours per journey	1	1½
Miles per day for each vehicle	110	160
Average driving speed, miles per hour	15	20
Number of drivers (always available)	11	5
Repairs and maintenance for each vehicle, hour per week	5	4
	£	£
Driver's basic pay per hour	2.00	1.60
Operating supplies per vehicle-mile	0.25	0.20
Depreciation per vehicle	825	400
Spare parts per vehicle	550	400
Major repairs by outside contractors per vehicle	1,650	800

	Maintenance mechanics	Loading staff
Number of personnel	2	8
Basic pay per hour	£1.80	£1.20

Chargeable to vehicle operations:		Basis of apportionment
Manager's salary and expenses	£8,500	To vehicle-type on number of vehicles operated
Clerical salaries . . .	£3,400	
Rent, rates, heating and lighting	£34,500	To vehicles on a weighting of 3:2 between a tank lorry and a van

The company operates on the basis of a five-day week of 40 hours for 52 weeks each year. All hourly paid personnel work an average 40-hour week for 50 weeks each year and are paid for two weeks' holiday at basic rate. Hours in excess of 40 per week are paid at time and one half.   *(35 marks)*

6   O'Shea Ltd, an engineering company, has a machine shop which machines a single product. At budgeted activity the standard cost of the product per units is

Direct materials	10lb at £1.50 per lb	15.00
Direct labour	2 hours at £4 per hour	8.00
Variable indirect costs	2 hours at £1.20 per hour	2.40
Fixed indirect costs	2 hours at 80p per hour	1.60
		£27.00

Performance reports are prepared monthly. The following report for April 19X4 is in typical format:

	Actual costs	Standard costs applied	Total variance	Variance Price/ rate	Analysis Usage/ efficiency	Volume
	£	£	£	£	£	£
Direct materials	134,200	135,000	800F	5,800F	5,000U	—
Direct labour	77,600	72,000	5,600U	1,600U	4,000U	—
Variable indirect	21,400	21,600	200F	1,400F	1,200U	—
Fixed indirect	15,600	14,400	1,200U	400F	—	1,600U
	248,800	243,000	5,800U	6,000U	10,200U	1,600U

These figures include no credits for scrap. Method studies during the first quarter of 19X4 indicate that the probable standard material loss of scrap through machining is 10% and that the scrap can be sold for 50p per lb, a price suggested as standard. The accounts department state that the actual scrap for April 19X4 weighed 9,600 lb and was invoiced at £4,220.

The method studies further reveal that part of the variance is due to rejected work and to reworking certain items. Rejected work is ascertained only on inspection at completion. The need to rework certain items is invariably ascertained half-way through the labour cycle. Production control report that 500 completed units were rejected during April 19X4 and a further 500 units reworked.

(a) Prepare a revised statement of standard cost per unit, allowing for scrap.
(8 marks)

(b) Prepare a revised version of the machine shop's performance report for April 19X4 accounting for scrap, and showing scrap, reject and rework variances.
(12 marks)

(Total 20 marks)

ANSWERS

1

(a) In both budgetary control and standard costing systems, details of actual performance are compared with predetermined standards and the resulting variances reported. The difference between the two systems is mainly in the detail of the variance analysis that is possible; broadly speaking a standard costing system provides more detailed comparisons than a budgetary control system. Such systems perform various functions including the motivation of staff and providing management with information upon which it can base decisions.

The motivation objective presupposes that with targets to work to, employees will act in a manner that is consistent with the firm's plans. This might be possible only if, allied to the standards set, there is some bonus scheme for achieving or exceeding those standards. The managerial reporting objective requires that a system is set up to provide management with the information it requires to control the operations of the organisation and to make decisions regarding the improvement of performance.

The possible conflict between the two objectives is not pronounced. If it is felt that any conflict presents problems in standard setting, there is always the possibility of setting 'dual standards'. Any standard, to provide motivation, must be fair, what an employee might reasonably be expected to achieve; this too is the sort of standard with which management should expect to compare actual performance.

(b) Various levels of efficiency may be incorporated in standard-setting, resulting in a range of standards:

   (i) 100% efficiency — here standards are set which are unrealistic. 'Ideal standards' (the standards which can be attained under the most favourable conditions possible) result in purely adverse variances and therefore provide neither useful management information nor serve any motivational function.

   (ii) High efficiency — here again the production of a tight standard will eventually act as a poor motivator.

   (iii) Expected efficiency — the use of an 'expected standard' (the standard which it is anticipated can be attained during a future specified budget period) or a 'normal standard' (the average standard which it is anticipated can be attained over a future period of time, preferably long enough to cover one trade cycle); it is what was referred to in (a) above when suggesting that what was required was a fair standard.

   (iv) Poor efficiency — using what might be termed loose standards providing no real management information; it may motivate staff through the operation of a bonus scheme, though this would appear to indicate a poor basic level of remuneration.

Any three of these could been chosen for an answer to the question.

(c)   The main advantage of allowing employees to participate in the standard-setting process stems from the fact that the resulting standards are then not entirely imposed. By involving employees their own aspiration levels can be utilised in the final standards set — either by taking their suggested levels without modification or by using them to modify the management-derived standards. Evidence seems to suggest that a budget which is pitched at the aspiration level of employees is more likely to be accepted by the employees and actually to be effective in motivating them. Hence any evidence which assists in determining the aspiration level is of use for the motivational aspects of budgetary control and standard costing.

If the employee's involvement is apparent rather than of real effect in the determination of standards such pseudo-participation appears to have negative behavioural effects. Hence the message seems to be that no participation is better than false participation.

A further disadvantage is that of variance reporting to management. Unless the variances are based on a comparison of the actual performance with a budget based on expected efficiency those variances reported will provide management with little real information. As employee-derived budget standards may not be based on management's expectations the resulting variances may not be directly useful to management. Similarly the use of standards other than those expected will lead to a difference between the standards used in the planning and those used in the control processes.

2   When new products or processes are introduced, in the early stages the expected time (and cost) per unit are likely to be high; but as employees become familiar with the new requirements this time will diminish progressively until a steady state is reached. Researches, particularly in the aerospace industry, have shown that for any given set of circumstances the rate of familiarisation (or 'learning') is broadly predictable; and that in general terms as cumulative output doubles so the average time per unit will fall by a determinable percentage of the previous average time. This percentage is likely to be between 60% and 85%. The most commonly used model takes the form:

$$y = ax^{-B}$$

where y is the average labour cost at the marginal unit, a is the labour cost of the first unit, x is the cumulative number of units produced, and B is the index of the rate of decrease in labour cost.

The values of x and y can be plotted on graph paper to show the 'learning curve' as in Fig. 7:1.

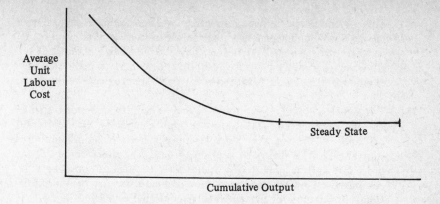

Figure 7:1

Learning curve theory is very relevant to standard setting. If the learning phenomenon is ignored a standard set when the cumulative output is low may be too near α and, since this ignores the cost reductions resulting from learning, favourable variances will tend to appear. Alternatively the standard might be set at the steady state level and this would yield adverse cost variances throughout the 'start up' phase.

3

(a) Rapid inflation introduces difficulties into the interpretation of variances from standard costs, since an adverse cost variance on an operation may be due to unpredicted and unavoidable price changes, and not necessarily because the operation is out of control. Particular instances of this problem are:

 (i) Standard costs may already include forecast assumptions about price changes. There may be difficulty in segregating planned price changes from additional non-controllable effects of inflation.

 (ii) 'Inflation' is often measured by changes in a general index of prices. These may have no relevance to the particular price changes experienced by the business.

 (iii) Rapid price increases could be masked by improvements in productivity. Unless standard costs are modified frequently as prices change, variance analysis into price and efficiency elements will be distorted.

 (iv) Sharp price rises will create doubts in the minds of management as to the validity of standard costs for decision making, e.g. for product pricing.

(b)   Methods of overcoming these problems are:

(i)   To set standards in terms of the price levels prevailing at a given time, say at the commencement of the budget process. A shortcoming may be that managers may feel that they are not being given a proper allowance for inevitable price rises; but this can be overcome to some extent by the certainty with which price variances can be measured.

(ii)   To revise standards frequently having regard to the price changes actually experienced. These might be approximated by the use of internal indices. In fact, for control purposes both technical and price standards should always be kept up to date. The shortcomings of this procedure are the amount of work involved (though not onerous with a computerised system) and also the increased difficulty of interpreting trends of variances when standards are continually changed.

(iii)   To elaborate the scheme of variance analysis so as to reflect causes and responsibilities more precisely. The shortcomings are that this additional analysis might have to be made outside the accounting system and might be practicable only after the event (a 'hindsight' analysis between planning and operational variances).

4   The advantages and limitations of standard costing include:

Advantages

(a)   *Planning.* Provided the technical and cost standards are realistic for the period during which they are to be used, they can assist in planning, in particular by building up budgets with greater certainty than would otherwise be possible.

(b)   *Control.* Variances routinely calculated and reported will provide at least provisional evidence of aspects of the business to which managers need to give special attention. They facilitate 'management by exeption'. It must be borne in mind, however, that accounting variances do not necessarily identify either true causes or true responsibilities. They are the starting point for further investigation.

(c)   *Management reporting.* Management reports should be more easily understood, since they put a consistently based value on deviations from norm of which managers should already be aware, either from physical controls or from records of price changes.

(d)   *Speed of reporting.* Variances are identified and can be reported as they occur – as and when material is purchased or used and work is done. This gives better opportunities for remedial action.

(e)   *Simplified bookkeeping*, particularly for inventories of materials and of work in progress at various stages of completion. This is not a major consideration if the record keeping is computerised.

Limitations

(a) *Validity of standards.* The standards used must have contemporary validity if the variances calculated from them are to be usable for control purposes. This may mean frequent revision of standards, which will destroy the advantages of trend analysis in management reporting and of simplicity in record keeping.

(b) *Availability of input data.* Variance accounting depends on source documents (material requisitions, time sheets, etc) that are accurate, reliably coded and adequately narrated for causes of off-standard items. This imposes a heavy workload on staff who may be unskilled or have little interest in accounting requirements.

(c) *Process to which applied.* The task of setting and maintaining standards is justified only (and may only be possible) where operations are conducted on a repetitive basis. Standard costing is most suited for use in mass production operations, including the manufacture of standardised components which are subsequently incorporated into unique or non-standard products. This comment applies to a 'system' of variance accounting. Under other circumstances it may be possible to set particular standards for use in statistical calculations – e.g. kilometres run per litre of fuel in road vehicle operation. Such 'standards' are commonly referred to as 'performance indicators'.

It can be practical to use in the same firm both standard costing and a system of actual historic costing. The example of standard components being incorporated into non-standard products was referred to above. It will be appreciated, however, that the 'actual' cost of the final product will include a standard cost element unless, using an appropriate scheme of variance coding, variances can be identified with products and this, after being reported, be reintegrated into an actual product cost. It may be worth noting that firms using a standard cost accounting system still have to compute an actual cost of year-end inventories for their annual accounts. This is normally a somewhat arbitrary statistical procedure.

5   This is basically a question on budget prepartion from a complex set of data. There is plenty of scope for arithmetical error, and for cumulative errors if the first-step calculations of required hours are badly done, so careful and logical work is needed; but there should be no conceptual difficulties.

After the budget has been assembled, the examiner requires certain statistical calculations of budgeted unit costs and journey costs. The question is included in this chapter because these performance indicators are referred to as 'standard costs'. There is no implication, however, that they will be used in a standard costing system.

The solution is followed by the supporting calculations.

(a) *Cost budget for 19X7*   (b) *Standard unit costs*

	Lorries	Vans
Mileage	343,200	208,000
Operating hours	22,880	10,400
Loading hours	9,360	7,800
	£	£

Vehicle operations

	Lorries	Vans
Drivers' wages	48,400	17,600
Supplies	85,800	41,600
Depreciation	9,900	2,000
Management	6,000	2,500
Clerical	2,400	1,000
Rent, rates, etc.	27,000	7,500
	179,500	72,200

Per mile

Lorries	Vans
£0.52	£0.35

Vehicle repairs

	Lorries	Vans
Wages	5,940	1,980
Spare parts	6,600	2,000
Major repairs	19,800	4,000
	32,340	7,980

Per operating hour

Lorries	Vans
£1.41	£0.77

Loading facilities

	Lorries	Vans
Wages	12,031	10,025

Per loading hour

Lorries	Vans
£1.29	£1.29

	Lorries	Vans
Total cost	223,871	90,205

(c) *Vans – standard journey costs*

	20 miles		40 miles		60 miles	
	(hours)	£	(hours)	£	(hours)	£
Loading @ £1.29 per hour	(1½)	1.94	(1½)	1.94	(1½)	1.94
Operating @ £0.35 per mile		7.00		14.00		21.00
Repairs @ £0.77 per operating hour	(1)	0.77	(2)	1.54	(3)	2.31
		9.71		17.48		25.25

DRIVERS' TIME AND WAGES – SUPPORTING CALCULATIONS

	Lorries		Vans	
(a) Operating mileage (52 weeks)	12 x 110 x 260	= 343,200	5 x 160 x 260	= 208,000
(b) Operating hours	'a' ÷ 15	= 22,880	'a' ÷ 20	= 10,400
(c) Normal hours (50 wks)	11 x 8 x 250	= 22,000	5 x 8 x 250	= 10,000
(d) Overtime hours	'b' – 'c'	= 880	'b' – 'c'	= 400
(e) Pay for normal hours	'c' x £2	= £44,000	'c' x £1.6	= £16,000
(f) for overtime	'd' x £3	= £ 2,640	'd' x £2.4	= £ 960
(g) for holidays	11 x 80 x £2	= £ 1,760	5 x 80 x £1.6	= £ 640
(h) (Total)	'e + f + g'	= £48,400	'e + f + g'	= £17,600
Supplies	343,200 x £.25	= £85,800	208,000 x £.2	= £41,600
Depreciation	12 x £825	= £ 9,900	5 x £400	= £ 2,000
Management	12 x £500	= £ 6,000	5 x £500	= £ 2,500
Clerical	12 x £200	= £ 2,400	5 x £200	= £ 1,000
Rent, rates, etc (£34,500 ÷ 46 = £750)	36 x £750	= £27,000	10 x £750	= £ 7,500

Mechanics' time
and wages
(a) Required hours (4,160) 12 x 5 x 52 = 3,120   5 x 4 x 52 = 1040 (= ¼)
(b) Normal hours
  2 x 40 x 50 = 4,000
(c) Overtime hours 160
(d) PAY for normal hours
  4,000 x £1.8 = £7,200
(e)   for o/time
  160 x £2.7 = £ 432
(f)   for hols.
  2 x 80 x £1.8 = £ 288
(g)   Total   £7,920
  apportioned (see 'a')   (¾)   £5,940   (¼) £1,980

| Spare parts | 12 x £550 | = £6,600 | 5 x £400 | = £ 2,000 |
| Major repairs | 12 x £1,650 | = £19,800 | 5 x £800 | = £ 4,000 |

Loading time and
  wages
(a) Required hours (17,160) 12 x 3 x 260 = 9,360   5 x 4 x 1½ x 260 = 7,800
(b) Normal hours
  8 x 40 x 50 = 16,000
(c) Overtime hours   1,160
(d) PAY
  for normal hours
  'b' x £1.2 = £19,200
(e) for o/time
  'c' x £1.8 = £ 2,088
(f) for hols.
  8 x 80 x £1.2
        = £   768
(g) Total   £22,056
  apportioned (see 'a')   £12,031   £10,025

6

(a) *Standard cost of product per unit, allowing for scrap*

	£
Direct materials: 10lb at £1.50 per lb	15.00
Less: Scrap recovery 1 lb at £0.50	50
	14.50
Direct labour: 2 hours at £4 per hour	8.00
Variable indirect: 2 hours at £1.20 per hour	2.40
Fixed indirect: 2 hours at £0.80 per hour	1.60
	26.50
Standard cost of 9lb of effective material	14.50
Standard cost of material	1.611 per lb

(b) *Machine shop performance report April 19X4*

	Actual costs	Standard costs applied	Total variance
	£	£	£
Direct materials	134,200	135,000	
Scrap sales	4,220	4,500	
	129,980	130,500	520 (F)
Direct labour	77,600	72,000	5,600 (U)
Variable indirect	21,400	21,600	200 (F)
Fixed indirect	15,600	14,400	1,200 (U)
	244,580	238.500	6,080 (U)

Variance analysis

	Price/ rate £	Usage/ efficiency £	Rejects £	Reworking £	Capacity £	Total variance £
Direct materials	5,800 (F)	2,847 (F)	7,250 (U)			
Scrap	580 (U)	297 (U)	–			
	5,220 (F)	2,550 (F)	7,250 (U)	–	–	520 (F)
Direct labour	1,600 (U)	2,000 (F)	4,000 (U)	2,000 (U)	–	5,600 (U)
Variable indirect	1,400 (F)	600 (F)	1,200 (U)	600 (U)	–	200 (F)
Fixed indirect	400 (F)	400 (F)	800 (U)	400 (U)	800 (U)	1,200 (U)
	5,420 (F)	5,550 (F)	13,250 (U)	3,000 (U)	800 (U)	6,080 (U)

Note: It is assumed that finished units rejected have a nil value, and that no additional material was absorbed when production had to be reworked.

DIRECT MATERIALS
(£1.611 per lb)

	lb	£		lb	£
Cost ledger control					
(C.L.C.)	93,333.3	134,200	Scrap account		
Price variance		5,800	Normal 10% at 50p	9,333.3	4,667
		140,000	abnormal at £1.611	266.7	430
Usage variance	1,766.7	2,847		9,600	5,097
			Rejects	4,500	7,250
			Finished goods	81,000	130,500
	95,100	£142,847		95,100	142,847

SCRAP SALES
(Standard scrap loss 10%, standard scrap recovery 50p per lb)

	lb	£		lb	£
Materials account			Cash	9,600	4,220
normal scrap	9,333.3	4,667	Price variance	—	580
abnormal scrap	266.7	430			4,800
			Yield variance 266.7lb at		
			£1.611 − 0.50		297
	9,600.0	5,097		9,600	5,097

DIRECT LABOUR
(£4 per hour)

	Hours	£		Hours	£
C.L.C.	19,000	77,600	Rejects	1,000	4,000
Rate variance		(1,600)	Reworks	500	2,000
		76,000	W.I.P.	18,000	72,000
Efficiency variance	500	2,000			
	19,500	78,000		19,500	78,000

VARIABLE OVERHEADS
(£1.20 per hour)

	Hours	£		Hours	£
C.L.C.	19,000	21,400	Rejects	1,000	1,200
Expenditure variance		1,400	Reworks	500	600
		22,800	W.I.P.	18,000	21,600
Efficiency variance	500	600			
	19,500	23,400		19,500	23,400

FIXED OVERHEADS
(80p per hour)

	Hours	£		Hours	£
C.L.C.	20,000	15,600	Rejects	1,000	800
Expenditure variance		400	Reworks	500	400
			Capacity variance	1,000	800
		16,000	W.I.P.	18,000	14,400
Efficiency variance	500	400			
	20,500	16,400		20,500	16,400

8 Advanced variance analysis

More questions have been asked on variance analysis than on any other single aspect of the management accounting syllabus; which is fortunate for the student because marks can be gained quite easily by the application of a set of simple rules and a modicum of common sense interpreting the results.

The eight questions in this chapter have been selected as representative of the main permutations of the subject, other than mix and yield variances in process costing which are included in chapter 9.

The main points to which the student should give careful attention are:

— the treatment of idle time, overtime and mix of skills in the calculation of labour variances;

— the detailed formulae for the calculation of overhead variances;

— the limitations of the accounting analysis of variances, and the possible need for additional investigation, e.g. into controllable and non-controllable variances and into planning and operational variances — a subject of some contemporary interest.

Two of the questions include sales variances which, of course, are variances from budget rather than from standard, but which have not been covered by earlier chapters.

STUDY REQUIREMENTS

The calculations and presentation of variance and sub-variances
The investigation and critical analysis of variances

QUESTIONS

1   The AC/DC Company manufactures special electrical equipment in Kowloon. The management has established standard costs for many of its operations and uses a flexible budget. Overhead is applied on a basis of standard labour-hours. The Rectifier Assembly Department operates at the following standard rates:

Materials:
4 sheets soft iron, 9 x 16 in @ £1.12 each	
2 spools copper wire	@ £2.39 each
Direct-labour rate	£2.50 per hour
Combined overhead rate	£2.10 per direct-labour hour

The flexible budget indicates that total overhead would amount to £4,489 and £4,989 at production levels of 500 and 600 units respectively. The production budget for the past month called for 2,340 direct-laoubr hours, £2,925 variable-overhead costs and £1,989 fixed-overhead costs. Only 550 rectifiers were produced, at the costs listed below:

Materials purchased:
3,000 sheets soft iron, £3,300
1,500 spools copper wire, £3,600

Materials used:
2,215 sheets soft iron
1,106 spools copper wire

Direct labour:
2,113 hours, £5,409.28

Overhead:
Variable costs, £2,769
Fixed costs, £2,110

(a)   What is the standard time for assembling a rectifier?

(b)   What is the standard unit cost?

(c)   What was the material price variance during the past month?

(d)   The material usage variance?

(e)   The direct-labour price variance

(f)   The direct-labour efficiency variance?

(g)   Variable-overhead spending variance?

(h)   Variable-overhead efficiency variance?

(i)   Fixed-overhead budget variance?

(j)   Fixed-overhead volume variance?

Work to the nearest penny.

(20 marks)

2   From the data given below, relating to the manufacture of a special lubricant:

(a)   Calculate the operating profit variance for the month of October 19X1.

(10 marks)

(b)   Analyse this difference into its sub-variances covering sales and production changes.   *(11 marks)*

(c)   Explain briefly what you consider to be the main problem indicated by the figures and how this could be overcome.   *(4 marks)*

(Total 25 marks)

Budget operations for one month.
Input, 20 batches of 500 litres each

Direct materials	% of quantity	Price per litre £
X	30	0.60
Y	20	0.30
Z	50	0.45

Direct labour	% of hours	Rate per hour £
Blending	60	2.50
Filtering	30	2.25
Packing	10	2.00
Total labour hours		8,000
Overhead cost: variable		£0.06 per litre
fixed		£5,750
Output		10,000 litres
Selling price		£3.55 per litre

Actual results for the month of October 19X1:

Direct materials used	Litres	Price per litre £
X	2,200	0.80
Y	2,500	9.35
Z	4,800	0.65

Direct labour	Hours	Rate per hour £
Blending	5,000	2.60
Filtering	2,000	2.20
Packing	700	2.00

		£
Overhead cost: variable		655
fixed		5,800

The output of 9,500 litres from 19 batches processed was all sold at an average price of £3.71 per litre.

3

(a) The sales performance of K.K. Promotions Ltd for 19X1 was as follows:

Product	Boots	Clothing	Toiletries	Total
Units	40,000	100,000	180,000	320,000
	£	£	£	£
Revenue	320,000	480,000	500,000	1,300,000
Standard cost	200,000	300,000	140,000	860,000
Profit	120,000	180,000	140,000	440,000

K.K. is in the process of producing the budget for 19X2 and, whilst the above actual figures are useful, the company would like to know what was in the 19X1 budget. Unfortunately this information seems to be lost and only one or two crumbs of information have come to light, i.e.:

(i) Sales margin quantity variance is £33,333$\frac{1}{3}$ (F).

(ii) Average standard margin per unit = £1.66 $\frac{2}{3}$.

(iii) Budgeted sales (in units) of clothing were achieved.

(iv) Boots were sold at the standard selling price.

(v) The standard selling price of boots per unit is as much as a unit of each of the other two product lines put together.

(vi) Sales price variance is £60,000 (A).

Produce the sales budget for 19X1 showing number of units, unit price, cost and profit for each item and in total. Show any supporting calculations. *(16 marks)*

(b) McMenemy Ltd produces a single product which is sold in cans. Batches of 144 such cans are produced by a team of men in two hours at the following cost:

		£
4 craftsmen	@ £4 per hour	16
2 labourers	@ £2 per hour	4
1 trainee	@ £1 per hour	1
7 men at an average of £3 per hour		£21

In period 5 of 19X2, 300 batches were produced at a total cost of £12,450, made up as follows:

	£
Craftsmen, 2,700 hours paid, 2,600 hours worked	8,500
Labourers, 1,600 hours paid, 1,200 hours worked	3,200
Trainees 700 hours paid, 500 hours worked	750
	12,450

Calculate the total labour variance and analyse this into efficiency, idle time, mix and rate variances. *(9 marks)*

(Total 25 marks)

4   A company with two cost centres, 1 and 2, manufactures two products, A and B, whose standard variable costs per article are as follows:

Cost centre	Element	Quantity	Price/rate £	Amount £
Product A				
		Units	*Per unit*	
1	Direct material: X	6	2.50	15.00
2	Y	2	7.50	15.00
		Hours	*Per hour*	
	Direct wages,			
1	grade: I	5	1.70	8.50
1	II ..	3	1.20	3.60
2	III ..	8	0.90	7.20
1	Variable overhead	8	0.30	2.40
2	Variable overhead	8	0.25	2.00
				£53.70
Product B				
		Units	*Per unit*	
1	Direct material: X	8	2.50	20.00
2	Z	3	2.00	6.00
		Hours	*Per hour*	
	Direct wages,			
1	grade: II ..	7	1.20	8.40
2	III ..	6	0.90	5.40
1	Variable overhead	7	0.30	2.10
2	Variable overhead	6	0.25	1.50
				£43.40

Budgeted data for a period of 4 weeks each of 40 hours are:

	Product A	Product B
Standard selling prices per article	£105	£90
Budgeted output of articles on which standard costs are based	165	285
Budgeted sales for period No. 7	160	310

	Cost centre 1	Cost centre 2
Fixed production overhead	£6,630	£4,545

Selling and distribution and administration expenses total £4,500 per period; they are treated as fixed and as a cost of the period.

Actual data for period No. 7 were as follows:

Opening and closing stocks of raw materials and work-in progress were the same.

	Product A articles	Product B articles
Actual output	150	300
Actual sales:		
at standard selling prices	145	250
at £120 each	25	—
at £ 85 each	—	30

Cost centre	Costs:			Price per unit
			Units	£
1	Direct materials: X		3,900	2.30
2	Y		280	7.50
2	Z		1,040	2.10

			Hours	Rate per hour £
1	Direct wages, grade: I		720	1.85
1	II		2,750	1.10
2	III		3,180	0.90

	Cost centre 1	Cost centre 2
	£	£
Overhead: Variable	960	920
Fixed	7,050	4,250

The company absorbs its fixed production overhead into products by means of cost centre direct labour hour rates. All variances are transferred to the profit and loss account.

(a) Calculate for the period No. 7 the following variances for each cost centre:

    (i)   direct material price;
    (ii)   direct material usage;
    (iii) direct wages rate;
    (iv) direct labour efficiency;
    (v)   variable production overhead;
    (vi) fixed production overhead expenditure;
    (vii) capacity;
    (viii) fixed cost productivity.

(b) Present a profit statement of the company for period No. 7.

(c) Comment on the relative performance of the two cost centres.

(30 marks)

5   The Sloflo Valve Company manufactures valves and other instrumentation for the gas industry. Material and labour standards and overhead budgets have been developed for all departments. The budget for the assembly department for 19X6 is shown below, based on planned activity level of 40,000 direct labour hours.

	Fixed costs £	Variable costs Amount £	Variable costs Rate	Total costs £
Standard direct labour cost	–	80,000	–	80,000
Overhead:				
Indirect labour	9,600	12,000	.150	21,600
Maintenance	5,280	6,000	.075	11,280
Labour overhead	4,800	12,000	.150	16,800
Total overhead	19,680	30,000	.375	49,680
Total conversion cost	19,680	110,000		129,680

*Rate per £1 of standard direct labour cost.

Monthly reports are prepared comparing actual departmental costs with budget. The performance report for May 19X6 is shown below:

	Budget £	Actual £	Variance favourable/unfavourable) £
Standard direct labour cost	6,200	7,120	(920)
Overhead:			
Indirect labour	1,730	1,835	(105)
Maintenance	905	948	(43)
Labour overhead	1,330	1,420	(90)
Total overhead	3,965	4,203	(238)
Total conversion cost	10,165	11,323	(1,158)

Notes: There were no labour rate variances. The fixed cost element in the budget was found by taking 1/12 of the annual budget and the variable cost element by multiplying the standard direct labour cost for the month by the appropriate rate per £1 of standard direct labour cost.

The foreman of the assembly shop was incensed by the performance report and its implication that he had overspent. 'Look at labour overhead', he said. 'How can I spend too much? It's a fixed per cent of the wages. And direct labour wages are set by union agreement, so the only way I can spend too much is to work overtime. There were 320 hours of overtime but they cost £320 extra, not £920.'

He went on to maintain that he was charged for costs he couldn't control and instanced two rush orders which Sales insisted should be produced. One was for 500 valves. Normally the department made 1,000 valves at a time and were allowed 1,100 hours for the making including 20 hours' set-up and 20 hours' cleaning time. The set-up and cleaning time is constant however long or short the run. In the event 590 hours were spent making the 500 valves, 50 of the 590 hours being in overtime.

He said that the second order was for 400 meters. Normally his department made 1,000 meters in one batch and were allowed 1,500 hours for the making including 30 hours' set-up and 30 hours' cleaning time. As it happened the 400 batch took 636 hours, 40 of which fell in overtime. 'What's more,' said the foreman, 'in addition to that we wasted 40 hours sitting around waiting for materials and another 100 hours waiting for a machine to be repaired – even though according to the report I've paid £40 extra for maintenance, it didn't prevent the machine breaking down.'

The production manager told the chief accountant about the foreman's complaint and asked for a more meaningful report to be produced for him.

(a) Prepare a revised performance report for May, analysing the spending and efficiency variances and showing the extent to which the efficiency variance can be explained by what the foreman said. Assume that the original performance report and the foreman's figures are correct.

(b) Indicate and comment upon those costs for which the foreman can be held accountable.

(20 marks)

6   The management team of Thorpe Ltd feel that standard costing and variance analysis have little to offer in the reporting of some of the activities of their firm. 'Although we produce a range of fairly standardised products; states the accountant of Thorpe Ltd, 'prices of many of our raw materials are apt to change suddenly and comparison of actual prices with a predetermined, and often unrealistic, standard price is of little use. For some of our products we can utilise the raw material which will, in our opinion, lead to the cheapest total production costs. However, we are frequently caught out by price changes and the material actually used often proves, after the event, to have been more expensive than the alternative which was originally rejected.

'For example, consider the experience over the last accounting period of two of our products, Alpha and Beta. To produce a unit of Alpha we can use either 5 kg of gamma or 5 kg of delta. We planned to use gamma as it appeared it would be the cheaper of the two and our plans were based on a cost of gamma of £3 per kg. Owing to market movements the actual prices changed and if we had purchased efficiently the costs would have been

gamma   £4.50 per kg
delta   £4.00 per kg

'Production of Alpha was 2,000 units and usage of gamma amounted to 10,800 kg at a total cost of £51,840.

'Product Beta uses only one raw material, epsilon, but again the price of this can change rapidly. It was thought that epsilon would cost £30 per tonne but in fact we paid only £25 per tonne and if we had purchased correctly the cost would have been less as it was freely available at only £23 per tonne. It usually takes 1.5 tonnes of epsilon to produce 1 tonne of Beta but our production of 500 tonnes of Beta used only 700 tonnes of epsilon.

'So you can see that with our particular circumstances the traditional approach to variance analysis is of little use and we don't use it for materials although we do use it for reporting on labour and variable overhead costs.'

Analyse the material variances for both Alpha and Beta utilising

(a)   traditional variance analysis;

(b)   an approach which distinguishes between planning and operational variances.
(14 marks)

7   Darms Ltd manufactures only a single type of product which it sells both to independent retailers under its own brand name and also to several national groups of multiple retailers for them to retail under their own brand names. Although the products sold in these two markets are physically identical, except for the brand name, Darms has a two-tiered price structure with a different price for each of the two markets and for invoicing purposes the products are known as Ds (Darms's brand name) and Rs (retailers' own brand name).

The budgeted costs for the first half of the year were based on production and sales levels of 1,000 units. The budgeted figures were:

BUDGETED COSTS

	Per unit	£	Total (£000s)
Production costs			
Direct labour	10 hours at £3 per hour	30	30
Direct materials	20 kg at £2 per kg	40	40
Variable overheads	£1 per labour hour worked	10	10
Fixed overheads	per unit produced	20	20
	Standard production cost	100	100
Delivery costs	per unit delivered	10	10
			110
Other costs			
Fixed sales costs		40	
Fixed administrative costs of the purchasing department		20	60
Total budgeted costs			£170

The figures for the budgeted sales and the sales mix for the first half of the year were:

		£ (000s)
Ds (Darms's own brand name)	500 units at £210	105
Rs (Retailers' brand name)	500 units at £200	100
Total budgeted sales revenues		205

The actual results for the first half of the year were:

DETAILED PROFIT STATEMENT - MONTHS 1 TO 6

	£ (000s)	£ (000s)	£ (000s)
Sales revenues			
Ds 600 units at £230		138	
Rs 400 units at £210		84	222
Cost of goods sold			
Opening stock of finished goods			
200 units at standard cost of £100		20	
Manufacturing costs for 900 units produced			
Direct labour 8,000 hours paid	28		
Direct materials 20,000 kg	35		
Variable overhead	10		
Fixed overhead	23	96	
		116	
Less: Closing stock of finished goods			
100 units at standard cost of £100		10	106
Delivery costs			12
Sales costs			48
Administrative costs of the Purchasing Department			21
Total costs			187
Profit			£35

Douglas Armstrong, the Managing Director, was quite pleased with the results and made the following further points:

Each of the four major operating departments within the firm - selling, purchasing, production and delivery - is largely free to decide how the operations within its own functions are carried out. As the profit achieved equals that planned, each department can feel satisfied with its own performance.

Although production, at 900 units, was less than planned all orders were met, even though to do so required reducing the levels of finished goods held in stock. There were no stocks of raw materials or work in progress at the beginning or the end of the period.

Output was less than planned owing to the temporary closure of production facilities following the failure of the purchasing department to provide an adequate supply of raw materials. Included in the figures of direct labour hours paid are exactly 1,000 hours due to idle time payments resulting from the factory closure caused by the failure in raw materials supply.

(a)   Produce a statement which will be useful to Mr Armstrong in highlighting the reasons for the performance of Darms Ltd for the first half-year. The statement should analyse the performance of each of the four major operating departments and should use variance analysis to the extent it is applicable and useful. *(15 marks)*

(b) (i) Comment on the performance of Darms Ltd and its four major operating departments. *(6 marks)*

(ii) Describe two of the major difficulties inherent in such an analysis of the performance. *(4 marks)*

(Total 25 marks)

8   The Britten Co. Ltd manufactures a variety of products of basically similar composition. Production is carried out by subjecting the various raw materials to a number of standardised operations, each major series of operations being carried out in a different department. All products are subjected to the same initial processing which is carried out in departments A, B and C; the order and extent of further processing then depends upon the type of end product to be produced.

It has been decided that a standard costing system could be usefully employed within Britten and a pilot scheme is to be operated for six months based initially only on department B, the second department in the initial common series of operations. If the pilot scheme produces useful results a management accountant will be employed and the system will be incorporated as appropriate throughout the whole firm.

The standard cost per unit of output of department B is:

	£	£
Direct labour (14 hours at £2 per hour)		28
Direct materials		
output of department A (3 kg at £9 per kg)	27	
acquired by and directly input to department B		
material X (4 kg at £5 per kg)	20	47
Variable overhead (at £1 per direct labour hour worked)		14
Fixed production overheads		
directly incurred by department B (see Note1)		
manufacturing overhead (per unit)	3	
allocated to department B		
general factory overhead (per unit)	8	11
Standard cost per unit		£100

Note 1: Based on normal monthly production of 400 units

In the first month of operation of the pilot study (month 7 of the financial year), department B had no work in progress at the beginning and the end of the month. The actual costs allocated to department B in the first month of operation were:

	£	£
Direct labour (6,500 hours)		14,000
Direct materials		
output of department A (1,400 kg) – (see Note 2)	21,000	
material X (1,900 kg)	11,500	32,500
Variable overhead		8,000
Fixed overhead		
directly incurred manufacturing overhead	1,600	
allocated to department B – (see Note 3)	2,900	4,500
		£59,000

Note 2: Actual cost of output of department A.

Note 3: Based on the actual expenditure on joint manufacturing overheads and allocated to departments in accordance with labour hours worked.

The production manager feels that the actual costs of £59,000 for production of 500 units indicates considerable inefficiency on the part of department B. He says, 'I was right to request that the pilot standard costing system be carried out in department B as I have suspected that they are inefficient and careless - this overspending of £9,000 proves I am right.'

(a) Prepare a brief statement which clearly indicates the reasons for the performance of department B and the extent to which that performance is attributable to department B. The statement should utilise variance analysis to the extent it is applicable and relevant.   *(14 marks)*

(b) Comment on the way the pilot standard costing system is currently being operated and suggest how its operation might be improved during the study period.   *(6 marks)*

(Total 20 marks)

ANSWERS

1

(a) Total overhead:

		£
	600 units	4,989
	500 units	4,489
	100	500

The variable overhead rate is $\dfrac{£500}{100}$ = £5 per unit

Variable overhead hourly rate = $\dfrac{£2,925}{2,340 \text{ hrs.}}$ = £1.25

Standard time = $\dfrac{£5}{£1.25}$ = 4 hours

(b)

			£
Materials	4 sheets x £1.12 = 4.48		
	2 spools x £2.39 = 4.78		
			9.26
Labour	(4 hours x £2.50)		10.00
Variable overhead	(4 hours x £1.25)		5.00
Fixed overhead	(4 hours x (£2.10−1.25))		3.40
		Standard unit cost	£27.66

(c)

			£
Sheets	3,000 x £0.02 (F)	=	60 (F)
Spools	1,500 x £0.01 (U)	=	15 (U)
Materials price variance			£45 (F)

(d)

				£
Sheets	(550 x 4) − 2,215 =	−15 x £1.12	=	16.80 (U)
Spools	(550 x 2) − 1,106 =	−6 x £2.39	=	14.34 (U)
	Materials usage variance			£31.14 (U)

(e) Direct labour price variance

(2,113 hours x £2.50) − £5,409.28   =   £126.78 (U)

(f) Direct labour efficiency variance

(550 units x 4 hours) − 2,113 hours = 87 hours (F) x 2.50
= £217.50 (F)

(g) Variable-overhead spent variance

(2,113 hours x £1.25) − £2.769   =   £127.75 (U)

(h) Variable-overhead efficiency variance

   87 hours (F) x £1.25   =   £108.75 (F)

(i) Fixed-overhead budget variance

   £2,110 − (2,340 hours x £0.85)   =   £121 (U)

(j) Fixed-overhead volume variance

   2,340 hours − (550 x 4 hours)   =   140 hours (U) x £0.85
                                         =   £119 (U)

2

(a) *Operating profit variance*

This would seem to be the difference between the budgeted and actual profit figures, each of which are calculated below.

Budgeted profit
(Budgeted production and sales - 20 batches of 500 l : 10,000 l)

			£	£
Materials	X	3,000 l @ 60p	1,800	
	Y	2,000 l @ 30p	600	
	Z	5,000 l @ 45p	2,250	
		10,000 l		4,650
Labour	B	4,800 hrs @ 2.50	12,000	
	F	2,400 hrs @ 2.25	5,400	
	P	800 hrs @ 2.00	1,600	
		8,000 hrs @ 2.375		19,000
Variable overheads (10,000 l @ £0.06)				600
				24,250
Fixed overheads (57.5p per l)				5,750
Total costs (£3 per l)				30,000
Profit (55p per l)				5,500
Revenue (10,000 l @ £3.55 per l)				£35,500

Actual results
(Actual production and sales - 19 batches of 500 1; 9,500 1)

					£	£
Materials	X	2,200 1	@	80p	1,760	
	Y	2,500 1	@	35p	875	
	Z	4,800 1	@	65p	3,120	
		9,500				5,755
Labour	B	5,000 hrs	@	£2.60	13,000	
	F	2,000 hrs	@	£2.20	4,400	
	P	700 hrs	@	£2.00	1,400	
		7,700				18,800
Variable overheads						655
Fixed overheads						5,800
						31,010
Sales revenue (9,500 1 @ £3.71)						35,245
Total cost						31,010
Actual Profit						4,235
Operating Profit Variance	£5,500 − £4,235	=				1,265 (A)

(b)　*Analysis of variances*

	£	Favourable £	Adverse £
Sales margin:			
Volume (500 @ 55p)			275
Price (9,500 @ 16p)		1,520	
Materials:			
Price X (2,200 @ 20p)	440		
Y (2,500 @ 5p)	125		
Z (4,800 @ 20p)	960		
Total			1,525
Usage X ((2,200 - 2,850) @ 60p)	390		
Y ((2,500 - 1,900) @ 30p)	(180)		
Z ((4,800 - 4,750) @ 45p)	(22.5)		
Total - a mix variance		187.5	
Labour:			
Rate B (5,000 @ 10p)	500		
F (2,000 @ 5p)	(100)		
P -	-		
Total			400
Efficiency B ((5,000 - 4,560) @ £2.50)	1,100		
F ((2,000 - 2,280) @ £2.25)	(630)		
P ((700 - 760) @ £2.00)	(120)		
Total			350
Variable Overhead:			
Rate (9,500 x £0.06 - £655)			85
Fixed overhead:			
Expenditure			50
Volume (500 x £0.575)			287.5
		2,972.5	1,707.5
Operating profit variance			£1,265.0

(c)　*Main problem*

The main problem seems to be the **cost of materials** which is considerably
above budget. This may be due to bad budgeting, in which case there is little
that can be done to improve performance unless a different choice of materials is possible. Alternatively it may be caused by a failure to obtain quantity
discounts or buying from new suppliers offering less favourable terms. The
buying department should be asked to look into the variances and show how

they intend to improve matters.

In addition the large adverse efficiency variance in the Blending Department should give cause for concern, particularly as this labour force also shows an adverse rate variance. This could be accounted for by idle time, particularly with the reduced sales, though it could also be caused by a stretching of hours to enable overtime premiums to be received. Again investigation of the reasons is required and possibly some sort of piece-work system of remuneration should be devised.

3

(a)   Sales budget 19X1

	Boots	Clothing	Toiletries	Total
Units	50,000	100,000	150,000	300,000
	£	£	£	£
Selling price/unit	8	5	3	
Cost/unit	5	3	2	
Profit/unit	3	2	1	
Revenue	400,000	500,000	450,000	1,350,000
Costs	250,000	300,000	300,000	850,000
Profit	150,000	200,000	150,000	500,000

Workings

(i)   Budgeted sales quantity

$$= 320,000 \; - \; \frac{£33,333\tfrac{1}{3}}{£1.66\tfrac{2}{3}} \; = \; 300,000 \text{ units}$$

(ii)   Budgeted profit

$$= 300,000 \text{ units} \; \times \; £1.66\tfrac{2}{3} \; = \; £500,000$$

(iii)   Selling prices

Price of clothing, C, plus toiletries, T, must equal £8
Also from sales price variance:

$$(40,000 \times £8 + 100,000 \times C + 180,000 \times (£8\text{-}C))\text{-}£1,300,000$$

$$= £60,000$$

$$£1,760,000 - 80,000C - £1,300,000 \; = \; £60,000$$

$$C \; = \; \frac{£400,000}{80,000} \; = \; £5$$

$$T \; = \; £3$$

(iv) Sales quantities

No. of boots sold, B, plus toiletries, T, must equal 200,000
Also total profit is £500,000, thus:

$$
\begin{aligned}
B \times £3 + 100,000 \times £2 + T \times £1 &= £500,000 \\
B \times £3 + £200,000 + (200,000 - B) \times £1 &= £500,000 \\
3B + 200,000 + 200,000 - B &= £500,000 \\
2B &= £100,000 \\
B &= £50,000 \\
T &= £150,000
\end{aligned}
$$

(b) Labour variance

	£
Total variance	
Actual labour cost	12,450
Standard cost of 300 batches = 300 x 2 x £21 =	12,600
Total variance	150(F)

Rate variance

C 2,700 x £4 - £8,500	2,300(F)
L 1,600 x £2 - £3,200	-
T 700 x £1 - £750	50(A)
Rate variance	2,250(F)

Idle time variance

C (2,700 - 2,600) x £4	400
L (1,600 - 1,200) x £2	800
T (700 - 500) x £1	200
Idle time variance	£1,400(A)

Mix

	£
Hours worked = 2,600 + 1,200 + 500 = 4,300	
4,300 hours in standard mix @ standard cost =	12,900
Actual mix @ standard cost:	

C 2,600 x £4 =	10,400	
L 1,200 x £2 =	2,400	
T 500 x £1 =	500	
		13,300

Mix variance	£	400(A)

Efficiency

Standard time for 300 batches = 300 x 7 x 2 =	4,200 hours
Actual time =	4,300 hours
Adverse difference =	100 hours
Efficiency variance = 100 x £3 =	£300(A)

113

(a) Cost variances

The calculated variances are shown in the following table. The references in brackets are to the detailed workings reproduced after the table.

		Cost centre 1	Cost centre 2
Direct materials		£	£
(i) Price	(b−a)	780(F)	104(A)
(ii) Usage	(c−b)	1,500(A)	130(A)
Total	(c−a)	720(A)	234(A)
Direct wages			
(iii) Rate	(e−d)	167(F)	nil
(iv) Efficiency	(f−e)	189(A)	162(A)
Total	(f−d)	22(A)	162(A)
(v) *Variable production overhead*	(h−g)	30(F)	170(A)
Fixed production overhead			
(vi) Expenditure	(j−i)	420(A)	295(F)
(vii) Capacity	(k−j)	310(F)	225(F)
(viii) Productivity	(l−k)	340(A)	270(A)
Total	(l−i)	450(A)	250(F)
Total production cost variance		1,162(A)	316(A)

Workings

	Ref.	Cost centre 1	Cost centre 2
Direct material			
Actual usage at actual prices		Units	Units
X		3900 @ £2.3 = 8,970	
Y			280 @ £7.5 = 2,100
Z			1040 @ £2.1 = 2,184
	a	8,970	4,284
Actual usage at standard prices			
X		3900 @ £2.5 = 9,750	
Y			280 @ £7.5 = 2,100
Z			1040 @ £2.0 = 2,080
	b	9,750	4,180

	Ref.	Cost centre 1	Cost centre 2
Standard usage at standard prices			
X (product A)		900	
(product B)		2400	
		3300 @ £2.5 = 8,250	
Y (product A)			300 @ £7.5 = 2,250
Z (product B)			900 @ £2.0 = 1,800
	c	8,250	4,050

Direct wages

	Ref.	Cost centre 1	Cost centre 2
Actual hours at actual rates		Hours	Hours
grade I		720 @ £1.85 = 1,332	
II		2750 @ £1.10 = 3,025	
III			3180 @ £0.9 = 2,862
	d	4,357	2,862
Actual hours at standard rates			
grade I		720 @ £1.7 = 1,224	
II		2750 @ £1.2 = 3,300	
III			3180 @ £0.9 = 2,862
	e	4,524	2,862
Standard hours at standard rates			
grade I (prod. A)		750 @ £1.7 = 1,275	
II (prod. A)		450	1200
III (prod. A)		2100	1800
(prod. B)		2550 @ £1.2 = 3,060	3000 @ £0.9 = 2,700
	f	4,335	2,700
Variable production overhead	g	(as stated) 960	(as stated) 920
Actual		Hours	Hours
Standard product A		1200	1200
B		2100	1800
	h	3300 @ £0.3 = 990	3000 @ £0.25 = 750

	Ref.	Cost centre 1		Cost centre 2	
Fixed production overhead					
Actual expenditure	i	(as stated)	7,050	(as stated)	4,250
Budgeted expenditure	j	(as stated)	6,630	(as stated)	4,545
Actual hours worked at standard absorption rates*	k	3470 @ £2.0 = 6,940		3180 @ £1.5 = 4,770	

		Cost centre 1	Cost centre 2
Standard hours produced at standard absorption rates*		Std. hours	Std. hours
product A		150 x 8 = 1200	150 x 8 = 1200
B		300 x 7 = 2100	300 x 6 = 1800
		3300	3000
	l	3300 @ £2.0 = 6,600	3000 @ £1.5 = 4,500

* Standard fixed overhead absorption rates

	Cost centre 1	Cost centre 2
Budgeted expenditure	£6,630	£4,545
Budgeted production in standard hours	Std. hours	Std. hours
product A	165 x 8 = 1320	165 x 8 = 1320
product B	285 x 7 = 1995	285 x 6 = 1710
	3315	3030
Expenditure per standard hour	£2.0	£1.5

(b) Profit statement

Budgeted operating profit (gross) (see Note 1)		£	£
Product A 160 @ £23.3	=	3,728	
Product B 310 @ £23.6	=	7,316	
			11,044
less Budgeted selling and distribution and administration expenses			4,500
Budgeted operating profit (net)			6,544

Marketing variance (see Note 2):

	Product A	Product B	Total	
(due to)	£	£	£	
selling prices	+375	−150	+225	
sales volume	+233	−708	−475	
	+608	−858		−250

Production cost variance
(as detailed in separate statement)

	£	
Cost Centre 1	−1162	
Cost Centre 2	− 316	
	−1,478	
		−1,728

Actual operating profit (net)	4,816

Note 1: Calculation of standard gross profit margins

	Product A	Product B
	£	£
Variable production costs (as stated)	53.7	43.4
+ Fixed production overhead:	£	£
Cost centre 1 (£2 per hour)	8 hours = 16.0	7 hours = 14.0
Cost centre 2 (£1.5 per hour)	8 hours = 12.0	7 hours = 9.0
	28.0	23.0
	81.7	66.4
Standard gross profit margin	23.3	23.6
Standard selling price	105.0	90.0

Note 2: Calculations of sales (marketing) variances

	Product A	Product B
	£	£
Due to selling prices	25 @ +£15 = +375	30 @ −£5 = −150
Due to sales volume:		
Budgeted sales (articles)	160	310
Actual sales (articles)	170	280
Difference	+10	−30
	+10 @ £23.3 = +233	−30 @ £23.6 = −708

(c) Performance of two cost centres

The total standard cost incurred by the two cost centres can be summarised as follows:

	Cost centre 1	Cost centre 2
	£	£
Materials	8,250	4,050
Labour	4,335	2,700
Variable overheads	990	750
Fixed overheads	6,600	4,500
	20,175	12,000
Percentage of standard cost represented by the total variances reported in (a)	5.76% (A)	2.63% (A)

The major features of the variances in Cost Centre 1 were a heavy saving on direct material price (approx 8%) more than offset by $1,500/8,250 = 18.2\%$ excess usage. This may have been due to the cheaper material being of inferior quality. Poor material might also have been the cause of low productivity, reflected in adverse labour efficiency and fixed overhead productivity variances. These and all other variances however were small relative to the relevant standard costs.

In cost centre 2 there was also an adverse material usage variance, of about 15%, associated in this case with an adverse price variance. Productivity was again below the budgeted level, but only slightly. The final result of cost centre 2 was affected significantly by underspending of £295 on fixed overheads (as compared with overspending of £420 in cost centre 1).

It is open to question whether the budgets for direct material usage were correctly set.

5   (a)

REVISED PERFORMANCE REPORT MAY 19X6

	Budget	Actual	Total variance	Rush orders	Efficiency	Idle time	Expenditure
	£	£	£	£	£	£	£
Standard direct labour cost	6,200	7,120	(920)	(112)	(208)	(280)	(320)
Overhead:							
Indirect labour	1,730	1,835	(105)	(17)	(31)	-	(57)
Maintenance	905	948	(43)	(8)	(16)	-	(19)
Labour overhead	1,330	1,420	(90)	(17)	(31)	-	(42)
Total overhead	3,965	4,203	(238)	(42)	(78)	-	(118)
Total conversion cost	10,165	11,323	(1,158)	(154)	(286)	(280)	(438)

Note: The volume variance due to rush orders, efficiency, and capacity is not shown on the performance report as the comparison is with the actual budget, not a flexed budget.

(b) The foreman can be held accountable for all costs over which he has control. In this case it will depend on the extent of his responsibility, but from the wording of the question they can be taken to be:

(i) *Direct labour costs*

The costs which can be said not to be his responsibility are those due to circumstances outside his control:

£

Idle time caused by waiting for materials and machine repairs. The ordering of materials is probably not his job and hence a delay is not of his making. For machine repairs it would appear that he has maintained the machines satisfactorily and their breakdown is then outside his control (e.g. due to obsolescence).

	£
140 hours at £2 per hour	280
Hours lost due to extra set-up time, etc on rush orders. 56 hours at £2 per hour	112
Overtime caused by rush orders. The premium only is considered not to be his responsibility as no extra cost would be incurred had the orders been completed in normal time.	90
	482
Actual cost	7,120
Foreman's responsibility	£6,638

He would not have been responsible for any wage rate variance as this is outside his control.

(ii) *Overhead costs*

Fixed overheads will probably have been allocated to the department by an accounting department and are not controllable by the foreman. Variable overheads, on the other hand, are presumably controllable by him and he can be held to be accountable for:

	£
Budgeted variable overheads	2,325
Variance not attributable to rush orders	78
	£2,403

Workings

Overtime:

Standard labour rate is $\dfrac{80,000}{40,000}$ =   £2 per hour

Overtime rate is time and a half   £3 per hour
Overtime hours on valves 50 cost £50 extra
Overtime hours on meters 40 cost £40 extra
Specifically caused by
rush orders   90   £90
other overtime   230   £230

Direct labour hours paid for: $\dfrac{7,120 - 320}{2}$ = 3,400 hours
Standard hours for actual
production $\dfrac{6,200}{2}$ = 3,100 hours
Budgeted hours for May $\dfrac{40,000}{12}$ = $3,333\frac{1}{3}$ hours
Idle time   140 hours
Productive hours paid for (3,400 − 140)   = 3,260 hours
Efficiency variance in hours (3,100 − 3,260) =   160 hours

Rush orders:

Valves

Normal set-up and cleaning time apportionable to 500 valves: $\dfrac{40}{2}$ = 20

Actual set-up and cleaning time on the 500 valves   40

Hours lost owing to the rush order   20

Meters

Set-up and cleaning time apportionable to 400 meters: 60 × $\dfrac{400}{1,000}$ = 24

Actual set-up and cleaning time on the 400 meters   60

Hours lost owing to the rush order   36

Total time lost   56 hours
Direct labour cost (@ £2 p.h.)   £112

Note: Time lost owing to inefficient working on the rush orders (20 hours for the valves) is not considered to be a variance attributable to those orders, but as indistinguishable from ordinary under-efficiency.

Overheads:

Budget for May	*Fixed*	*Variable*	*Total*
	£	£	£
Indirect labour	800	930	1,730
Maintenance	440	465	905
Labour overhead	400	930	1,330
	£1,640	£2,325	£3,965

Assuming that the 'no labour rate variances' applies to the variable element of the overheads, there can be no price variance thereon. Expenditure variance arises on the fixed portion only. Actual variable cost is then standard cost of productive hours.

	Indirect labour	Maintenance	Labour overhead
Productive hours paid for	3,260	3,260	3,260
Rate per hour	.3	.15	.3
Actual variable cost	978	489	978
Actual total cost	1,835	948	1,420
Actual fixed cost	857	459	442
Budgeted cost	800	440	400
Expenditure variance	(57)	(19)	(42)
Efficiency variance (hrs)	160	160	160
Variable overhead rate	.3	.15	.3
Variable overhead variance	(48)	(24)	(48)
Applicable to rush orders (56 hrs)	(17)	(8)	(17)
Other	(31)	(16)	(31)

6

TRADITIONAL VARIANCE ANALYSIS

(a) *Alpha*   £

Material price variance
£51,840 − (10,800 × £3)   19,440(U)

Material usage variance
(10,000 − 10,800) × £3   2,400(U)

Total variance   £21,840(U)

Beta

Material price variance
700 × (£30 − £25)   3,500(F)

Material usage variance
(750 − 700) × £30   1,500(F)

Total variance   £5,000(F)

(b) *Planning and operational variances*

Alpha

Total planning variance
10,000 × (£4.50 − £3.00)   £15,000(U)

which could be analysed as follows:

Uncontrollable	10,000 × (£4 − 3)	£10,000(U)
Possibly avoidable	10,000 × (£4.50 − 4)	£ 5,000(U)

Operational variances
                                                                                               £

Material usage
(10,000 − 10,800) × £4.50   3,600(U)

Material price
10,800 × (£4.5 − 4.8)   3,240(U)

                                                                                  £6,840(U)

Total variance   £21,840(U)

Beta

Planning variance

Uncontrollable
750 tonnes × (£30 − 23)   £5,250(F)

Operational variances   £

Material price
700 × (£23 − 25)   1,400(U)

Material usage
(750 − 700) × £23   1,150(F)

                                        £ 250(U)

Total variance   £5,000(F)

Workings

Alpha	*Quantity*	*Unit price*	*Total cost*
	kg	£	£
Original flexed budget (gamma)	10,000	3	30,000
Revised flexed budget (delta)	10,000	4	40,000
Revised flexed budget (gamma)	10,000	4.5	45,000
Actual (gamma)	10,800	(4.8)	51,840
Beta	*Tons*	*£*	*£*
Original flexed budget	750	30	22,500
Revised flexed budget	750	23	17,250
Actual	700	25	17,500

(a) Actual production 900 units

STANDARD COSTS FOR ACTUAL PRODUCTION

		£ (000s)
Direct labour	9,000 hours at £3	27
Direct materials	18,000kg at £2	36
Variable overhead	9,000 at £1	9
Fixed overhead recovery at standard 9,000 at £20		18
Standard cost of delivery 1,000 at £10		10
Labour, hours paid	8,000	
Less: idle time	1,000	
(hours worked)	7,000	

ANALYSIS OF VARIANCES FROM BUDGETED PERFORMANCE – MONTHS 1 TO 6

	£ (000s)
Planned profit	35

Deviations caused by:

	Favourable variances £ (000s)	Adverse variances £ (000s)	
(i) Sales function			
Price variance			
D 600 (£230 – 210)	12		
R 400 (£210 – 200)	4		
Mix variance (see Note 1)	1		
Spending variance £40,000 – £48,000		8	9(F)
(ii) Purchasing function			
Material price variance			
$20,000 \ (£2 - \frac{£35}{20})$	5		
Idle time variance caused by purchasing function, 1,000 × £3		3	
Fixed overhead volume variance (900 × £20) – £20,000 (see Note 2)		2	
Spending variance, £20,000 – £21,000		1	1(A)

	Favourable Variances £ (000s)	Adverse Variances £ (000s)	£ (000s)
(iii) Production function			
Direct labour variances			
Rate 8,000 $(£3 - \frac{£28}{8})$		4	
Efficiency £3 (9,000 − 7,000)	6		
Material usage variance			
£2 (18,000 − 20,000)			
Variable overhead variances			
Spending, 7,000 $(£1 - \frac{£10}{7})$		3	
Efficiency, £1 (9,000 − 7,000)	2		
Fixed overhead spending			
variance, £20,000 − £23,000		3	6(A)
(iv) Delivery function			
Spending variance		2	2(A)
£10,000 − £12,000			
Total variances			Nil
Actual profit			35

Note 1: Mix variance

	£ (000s)
Standard revenue at actual mix	
£210 × 600 + £200 × 400	206
Standard revenue at standard mix	
£210 × 500 + £200 × 500	205
Mix variance	1(F)

Note 2: This variance is allocated to the purchasing function as it was the purchasing function which caused volume to be lower than that planned.

(b) (i) Although in total Darms Ltd achieved its planned profit the net overall variance of zero comprises many significant individual variances. Therefore attention should be paid to the analysis of variances as well as the total, or net, effect.

The major aspects of performance of the four major operating departments are:

Sales function The change in mix contributed little but the change in sales prices was significant and favourable. The sales overhead costs appear to warrant investigation as they are 20% above budget and produce an adverse variance of £8,000.

Purchasing function Material price variance is favourable and significant but may be related to usage variance (see below).

Allocated to the purchasing function is the effect of the inability to provide adequate raw material and this is reflected in both labour idle time variance and the fixed overhead volume variance.

Production function Labour variances within the control of production, i.e. excluding idle time caused by the purchasing function, show a net favourable variance, but this is the result of both favourable and adverse efficiency and rate variances. The adverse material usage variance is quite high but may be partly caused by the favourable price variance, e.g. low quality materials; this variance cannot therefore be considered in isolation, and is possibly a typical example of linkages between variances. Both variable and fixed overhead variances show small adverse variances.

Delivery function An overspending of £2,000 is shown.

(ii) The major difficulties inherent in the analysis include:

— Determining adequate and up-to-date standards.

— Allocating variances to specific departments. Although the idle time variance and fixed overhead volume variances appear to have been clearly caused by the purchasing function and should be allocated to that function, other variances are more difficult to allocate. Examples of this difficulty are the material price and usage variances (mentioned above) which, if related, cannot be considered in isolation as the sole responsibility of any one department.

8

(a) Actual production   500 units
Standards for actual production

			£
Direct labour	7,000 hours at £2	=	14,000
Direct materials			
department A	1,500kg at £9	=	13,500
X	2,000kg at £5	=	10,000
Variable overhead	7,000 at £1	=	7,000

Fixed Overheads

	Normal expenditure (400 units)	Recovered at standard (500 units)	Actual charge
	£	£	£
Directly incurred manufacturing overhead	1,200	1,500	1,600
Allocated	3,200	4,000	2,900

DEPARTMENT B: PERFORMANCE REPORT FOR MONTH 7

	£
Standard cost of 500 units 500 at £100	50,000

Variances, possibly controllable by department B

	Adverse £	Favourable £	Total £
Direct labour			
Wage rate: $6,500 \left(£2.00 - \dfrac{£14,000}{6,500}\right)$	1,000		
Labour efficiency: $£2(7,000 - 6,500)$		1,000	Nil
Direct materials			
From department A			
Usage: $£9 (1,500 - 1,400)$		900	
Material X			
Price: $1,900 \left(£5 - \dfrac{£11,500}{1,900}\right)$ (See Note 1)	2,000		
Usage: $£5 (2,000 - 1,900)$		500	600(A)
Variable overhead			
Spending: $6,500 \left(£1 - \dfrac{£8,000}{6,500}\right)$	1,500		
Efficiency: $£1 (7,000 - 6,500)$		500	1,000(A)
Fixed overhead			
Manufacturing overhead			
Volume: $(£3 \times 500) - £1,200$		300	
Spending: $£1,200 - £1,600$	400		
Allocated overhead			
Volume: $(£8 \times 500) - £3,200$		800	700(F)
Total controllable variances	**4,900**	**4,000**	**900(A)**
Uncontrollable variances			
Material from department A			
Price: $1,400 \left(£9 - \dfrac{£21,000}{1,400}\right)$	8,400		
Allocated fixed overhead			
Spending: $£3,200 - £2,900$		300	8,100(A)
Total uncontrollable variances	**8,400**	**300**	**8,100(A)**

		£
Standard cost		50,000
Controllable variances (See Note 2)	900(A)	
Uncontrollable variances	8,100(A)	9,000
Actual cost		£59,000

128

Note 1: This assumes that department B carried out their own purchasing function. If a central purchasing function was used the price variance is not controllable by department B.

Note 2: Not all these variances may, in the actual circumstances, be within the control of department B.

(b) The standard costing system is not being operated effectively. The reasons include:

(i) The costs attributed to department B include those over which it has some control and can therefore be held responsible for, and some apportioned actual costs which are a function of the efficiency or activity of other parts of the organisation.

(ii) No credit or allowance is given to department B for those uncontrollable costs mentioned above. Hence the deviations from standard which appear to relate to department B are, in fact, partly attributable to that department and partly not.

(iii) The production manager appears to be using the system incorrectly. It should be used to highlight individual variances for further investigation and, if necessary, to indicate where action needs to be taken – the production manager appears to be using the system to support his preconceived, and as yet unproved, ideas.

The system could be improved by attributing to department B only the actual costs over which it has some control. The costs which derive from elsewhere in the organisation should be allocated to B on the basis of standard cost. In this way variances within B are more likely to reflect B's real performance.

9 Applications of process costing

INTRODUCTION

There are four aspects of process costing that occur spasmodically in examination papers, and for which students need to be prepared. They are:

- The identification and accounting treatment of abnormal gains and losses. This is fairly straightforward, so make sure you have no doubts about it.

- The calculation and evaluation of 'equivalent units' when there is partly completed work in process. There is a conceptual difficulty here, and if necessary you should seek out exercises additional to those given in this chapter, so that the method of approach becomes firmly fixed in mind.

- The calculation of mix and yield variances. The formulae for these must be learnt by heart.

- The costing of joint products. For inventory valuation it may be necessary to attribute joint costs to individual products, though none of the available methods is really satisfactory. For decision making there is no problem. Only the incremental costs after the point of separation are relevant.

STUDY REQUIREMENTS

Product costing for process industries
Problems of common costs, joint products and by-products

QUESTIONS

1 Product P63 is made by three sequential processes, I, II and III. In process III a by-product arises and after further processing in process BP, at a cost of £2 per unit, by-product BP9 is produced. Selling and distribution expenses of £1 per unit are incurred in marketing BP9 at a selling price of £9 per unit.

	Process I	Process II	Process III
Standards provide for:			
— normal loss in process of input of	10%	5%	10%
— loss in process having a scrap value per unit of	£1	£3	£5

For the month of April 19X8 the following data are given:

	Process I	Process II	Process III	Process BP
Output in units	8,800	8,400	7,000 of P63	420 of BP9
Costs:	£	£	£	£
Direct materials introduced (10,000 units)	20,000			20,000
Direct materials added	6,000	12,640	23,200	41,840
Direct wages	5,000	6,000	10,000	21,000
Direct expenses	4,000	6,200	4,080	14,280

Budgeted production overhead for the month was £84,000. Absorption is based on a percentage of direct wages.

There were no stocks at the beginning or end of the month.

Using the information given, prepare accounts for:

(a)   each of processes I, II and III;
(b)   process BP;
(c)   (i)   abnormal losses;
      (ii)   abnormal gains;
showing the balances to be transferred to the profit and loss statement.
(20 marks)

2

(a) Explain and discuss the alternative methods of accounting for normal and abnormal spoilage. *(8 marks)*

(b)   Weston Harvey Ltd assembles and finishes trapfoils from bought-in components which are utilised at the beginning of the assembly process. The other assembly costs are incurred evenly throughout that process. When the assembly process is complete the finishing process is undertaken. Overhead is absorbed into assembly, but not finishing, at the rate of 100% of direct assembly cost.

It is considered normal for some trapfoils to be spoiled during assembly and finishing. Quality control inspection is applied at the conclusion of the finishing process to determine whether units are spoiled.

It is accepted that the spoilage is normal if spoiled units are no more than one-eighteenth of the completed good units produced. Normal spoilage is treated as a product cost and incorporated into the cost of good production. Any spoilage in excess of this limit is classed as abnormal and written off as a loss of the period in which it occurs.

Trapfoils are valuable in relation to their weight and size. Despite vigilant security precautions some units are commonly lost, probably by pilferage. The cost of lost units is written off as a loss of the period in which it occurs. This cost is measured as the cost of the bought-in components plus the assembly process, but no finishing cost is charged.

Weston Harvey uses a FIFO system of costing.

The following data summarise the firm's activities during November 19X1:

Opening work-in-process:
Bought-in components	£60,000
Direct assembly cost to 31 October 19X1	£25,000
No. of units (on average one-half assembled)	50,000

Direct costs incurred during November 19X1:
Bought-in components received	£120,000
Direct assembly cost	£40,000
Direct finishing cost	£30,000

Production data for November 19X1	*Trapfoils*
Components received into assembly	112,000
Good units completed	90,000
Spoiled units	10,000
Lost units	2,000

None of the opening work-in-process had at that stage entered the finishing process. Similarly, nor had any of the closing work-in-process at the end of the month. The units in the closing work-in-process were on average one-third complete as to assembly; none had entered the finishing process.

(i)   Calculate the number of units in the closing work-in-process.   *(3 marks)*

(ii) Calculate the number of equivalent units processed in November 19X1, distinguishing between bought-in-components, assembly and finishing.
(6 marks)

(iii) Calculate the total costs to be accounted for in the month of November 19X1, subdivided into the amounts for good units produced, spoilage, lost

units and closing work-in-process. *(8 marks)*
(Total 25 marks)

3 O'Hara produces a chemical compound by a unique chemical process, which he has divided into two departments, A and B, for accounting purposes. The process functions as follows:

The formula for the chemical compound requires one pound of Chemical X and one pound of Chemical Y. In the simplest sense, one pound of Chemical X is processed in Department A and transferred to Department B for further processing, where one pound of Chemical Y is added when the process is 50% complete. When the processing is complete in Department B, the finished chemical compound is transferred to finished goods. The process is continuous, operating 24 hours a day.

No spoilage occurs in Department B.

In Department A conversion costs are incurred uniformly throughout the process and are allocated to good pounds produced.

In Department B conversion costs are allocated equally to each equivalent pound of output.

O'Hara's unit of measurement for work-in process and finished-goods is pounds.

The following data are available for the month of October 19X4:

	Department A	Department B
Work-in-process, 1 October	8,000 pounds	10,000 pounds
Stage of completion of opening stock (one batch per department)	3/4	3/10
Started or transferred in	47,500 pounds	?
Transferred out	46,500 pounds	?
Work-in-process, 31 October	?	?
Stage of completion of closing stock (one batch per department)	1/3	1/5
Total equivalent pounds of material Y added in Department B		44,500 pounds

Prepare schedules computing equivalent pounds of production (materials and conversion costs) for Department A and for Department B for the month of October 19X4 using the first-in, first-out method of stock valuation. *(17 marks)*

4

(a) From three raw materials (Gorgon, Camem and Stil) VLS manufactures a single cosmetic product called Eau de Vie. The standard mix of materials for one batch of output of Eau de Vie is as follows:

Gorgon	100 fl oz at £15.00 per oz	=	1,500
Camem	200 fl oz at £7.15 per oz	=	1,430
Stil	700 fl oz at £0.10 per oz	=	70
	———		———
	1,000		£3,000 = £3 per fl oz

Each batch should produce a standard output of Eau de Vie sufficient to fill 500 bottles.

During June 100 batches of materials were processed, producing enough Eau de Vie to fill 45,000 bottles. The actual consumption and cost of the materials were as follows:

				£
Gorgon	8,000 fl oz at £19.00 per oz	=	152,000
Camem	20,000 fl oz at £6,85 per oz	=	137,000
Stil	80,000 fl oz at £0.10 per oz	=	8,000
	108,000		£297,000 = £2.75 per fl oz

Venuti, Land and South are partners in VLS. Venuti has been working out the standard cost variances for materials in June. He has calculated *inter alia* that the total variance was £27,000 ADV, the mix variance was £29,000 FAV and the yield variance was £30,000 ADV. However, he felt unsure of his methods of calculation, and asked Lang to make check calculations of the variances independently.

Lang agreed with Venuti's figures for the total cost and yield variances, but calculated the mix variance to be £53,000 FAV. South was therefore asked to check both sets of calculations, again working independently.

After a few minutes' work South said that he agreed that the total cost variance was £27,000 ADV, and that he agreed with Lang that the mix variance was £53,000 FAV; however, he calculated the yield variance to be £54,000 ADV.

Calculate the total cost, price, quantity, mix and yield variances (including all workings) as they have probably been worked out by Lang and South.   *(12 marks)*

(b) Comment on the significance of mix and yield variances, using the figures from part (a) to illustrate your answer if you wish.   *(7 marks)*
   (Total 19 marks)

5 A chemical company has a contract to supply annually 3,600 tonnes of product A at £24 a tonne and 4,000 tonnes of product B at £14.50 a tonne. The basic components for these products are obtained from a joint initial distillation process. From this joint distillation a residue is produced which is processed to yield 380 tonnes of by-product Z. By-product Z is sold locally at £5 a tonne and the net income is credited to the joint distillation process.

The budget for the year ending 30 June 19X1 includes the following data:

| | Joint process | Separable costs | | |
		Product A	Product B	By-product Z
Variable cost per tonne of input, in £	5	11	2	1
Fixed costs for year, in £	5,000	4,000	8,000	500
Evaporation loss in process as % of input	6	10	20	5

Since the budget was compiled it has been decided that an extensive five-week overhaul of the joint distillation plant will be necessary during the year. This will cost an additional £17,000 in repair costs and reduce all production in the year by 10%. Supplies of the products can be imported to meet the contract commitment at a cost of £25 a tonne for A and £15 a tonne for B.

Experiments have also shown that the joint distillation plant operations could be changed during the year so that either:

(i) The output of distillate for product A would increase by 200 tonnes with a corresponding reduction in product B distillate. This change would increase the joint distillation variable costs for the whole of that operation by 2%; or

(ii) The residue for by-product Z could be mixed with distillate for products A and B proportionate to the present output of these products. By intensifying the subsequent processing for products A and B acceptable quality could be obtained. The intensified operation would increase product A and B separable fixed costs by 5% and increase the evaporation loss for the whole operation to 11% and 21% respectively.

(a) Calculate on the basis of the original budget the unit costs of products A and B and the total profit for the year.

(b) Calculate the change in the unit costs of products A and B based on the reduced production.

(c) Calculate the profit for the year if the shortfall of production is made up by imported products.

(d) Advise management whether either of the alternative distillation operations would improve the profitability calculated under (c) and whether you recommend the use of either. *(30 marks)*

6   Equinox is the main product of the Solstice Chemical Corporation. The product is manufactured in two processes with all the output from process 1 (chemical C) being transferred to process 2. Additional raw material (chemical D) is added at the start of processing in process 2 and the finished product is packed, in standardised containers, and dispatched to the finished goods store. A standard costing system is used and this is integrated with the company's financial accounting system.

The following standards apply:

	Process 1			**Process 2**	
	Standard specification for 1,000 kilos of C			*Standard specification for 1,000 kilos of Equinox*	
Direct material:			Direct material:		
400 kilos of A at £0.36	£144		1,050 kilos of C at £0.70	£735	
700 kilos of B at £0.08	56		50 kilos of D at £0.50	25	
Direct labour:			Direct labour:		
25 hours at £4.00 per hour	100		5 hours at £4.00 per hour	20	
Variable overhead:			Variable overhead:		
25 direct labour hours at £8.00	200		5 direct labour hours at £9.20	46	
Fixed overhead:			Fixed overhead:		
25 direct labour hours at £8.00	200		5 direct labour hours at £14.00	70	
			Packing material	4	
	£700			£900	

The standards allow for a normal loss in volume of 10% of the good output in each process; this loss occurs evenly throughout the processing.

The following details apply for the operations of a particular week:

Purchases of raw materials	£
8,000 kilos of A at 0.39 per kilo	3,120
16,000 kilos of B at £0.05 per kilo	800
1,500 kilos of D at £0.54 per kilo	810

	Process 1			**Process 2**		
Direct material issued to production	A	8,000 kilos	C	22,000 kilos (transferred from process 1)		
	B	17,000 kilos	D	930 kilos		
Direct labour	530 hrs at £4.10	£2,173	110 hrs at £3.80	£418		
Variable overhead	£4,134		£912			
Fixed overhead	£4,900 (actual)		£1,510 (actual)			
	£5,000 (budgeted)		£1,660 (budgeted)			
Packing material			£95			
Production and work-in-process:	*Kilos*	*Degree of completion*	*Kilos*	*Degree of completion*		
Opening work-in-process	2,100	50%	1,050	50%		
Output (completed production)	22,000	100%	17,000	100%		
Closing work-in-process	2,675	30%	3,225	25%		

Direct material price variances are calculated when the material is purchased. Raw material stocks are, therefore, recorded at standard cost and issued to production at standard cost. All other production expenses are charged at 'actual' from the expense accounts to the process accounts and any variances are transferred from the process accounts to appropriate variance accounts. Such transfers are made weekly. Output transferred from process 1 to process 2 is transferred at standard cost and work-in-process is valued on this basis.

(a) Write up the process accounts for process 1 and process 2.   *(14 marks)*

(b) Comment on the mix of raw materials used in process 1 during the week.
                                                                          (4 marks)

(c) Comment on the profitability of process 2 if chemical C can be sold at £0.90 per kilo and the market price of Equinox is £1.05 per kilo.   *(4 marks)*
                                                                   (Total 22 marks)

ANSWERS

1

(a)

PROCESS I

	Units	Total £		Units	Total £
Direct materials	10,000	20,000	Process II	8,800	52,800
Direct materials			Normal loss	1,000	1,000
added		6,000	Abnormal loss	200	1,200
Direct wages		5,000			
Direct expenses		4,000			
Production overhead		20,000			
	10,000	55,000		10,000	55,000

PROCESS II

	Units	Total £		Units	Total £
Direct materials			Process III	8,400	100,800
Process I	8,800	52,800	Normal loss	440	1,320
Direct materials					
added		12,640			
Direct wages		6,000			
Direct expenses		6,200			
Production overhead		24,000			
Abnormal gain	40	480			
	8,840	102,120		8,840	102,120

PROCESS III

	Units	Total £		Units	Total £
Direct materials			Finished goods	7,000	168,000
Process II	8,400	100,800	Normal loss	840	4,200
Direct materials			Abnormal loss	140	3,360
added		23,200	BP9 net sales		
Direct wages		10,000	value	420	2,520
Direct expenses		4,080			
Production overhead		40,000			
	8,400	178,080		8,400	178,080

(b)

BP9 PROCESS

	Units	Total £		Units	Total £
Process III	420	2,520	Sales proceeds	420	3,780
Process costs		840			
Selling and distribution		420			
expenses					
	420	3,780		420	3,780

(c) (i)

ABNORMAL LOSS A/C

	Units	Total		Units	Total
		£			£
Process I	200	1,200	Scrap value	200	200
Process III	140	3,360	Scrap value	140	700
			Profit & loss		
			a/c		3,660
	340	4,560		340	4,560

(ii)

ABNORMAL GAIN A/C

	Units	Total		Units	Total
		£			£
Scrap value	40	120	Process II	40	480
Profit & loss a/c		360			
	40	480		40	480

Workings

Normal cost per unit

Process I: $\dfrac{£55,000 - £1,000}{9,000}$ = £6

Process II: $\dfrac{£101,640 - £1,320}{(8,800 - 440)}$ = £12

Process III: $\dfrac{£178,080 - £4,200 - £2,520}{(8,400 - 840 - 420)}$ = £24

Production overhead absorption rate

$\dfrac{\text{Budgeted Overhead}}{\text{Direct Wages}}$ = $\dfrac{£84,000}{£21,000}$ = 400%

2

(a) *Methods of accounting for normal and abnormal spoilage*

Broadly, the purpose of accounting for spoilage is twofold: firstly to identify separately the cost of spoilage as opposed to the cost of good production, and secondly to differentiate between normal spoilage, which is an inherent part of production cost, and abnormal spoilage, which should not arise under efficient operating conditions. Basically, normal spoilage is part of planned production cost whereas abnormal spoilage is avoidable and therefore should be controllable by managerial action. The most important difference between the two types of spoilage from an accounting point of view is that normal spoilage is a cost associated with good production and is therefore inventoriable. Abnormal spoilage is clearly an element of inefficiency which should not be built into stock values and should be written off against the profits of the relevant period. A sensible accounting practice is therefore to follow a procedure such as:

(i) Trace and measure all spoilage costs separately.

(ii) Allocate normal spoilage costs to work-in-process or finished goods stock values, dependent on the point at which spoilage is detectable.

(iii) Charge the balance on the spoilage account after allocating normal spoilage to a loss account.

This kind of system would meet the inventory valuation and control information requirements of the business.

An alternative treatment of normal spoilage would be to consolidate it with good production throughout the accounting system so that no separate values are shown. This is a more likely practical solution but is of lower information content.

If a standard costing system is in operation, the normal spoilage would be incorporated into the standard cost. Therefore normal spoilage would not be reported separately. At the end of each reporting period spoilage variances would need analysing into normal and abnormal spoilage.

Another relevant point is the basis for valuing spoilage. It may be preferred to show the cost of abnormal spoilage at marginal cost only. For control purposes the incremental cost would provide more relevant information. Alternatively, if the production of abnormal spoilage was assumed to have consumed scarce fixed manufacturing facilities, a charge might be added to reflect the opportunity cost of capacity.

(b) (i) *Calculation of units in closing work-in-process*

Total number of units to be accounted for 112,000

	Units
Spoiled units	10,000
Lost units	2,000
Units started and finished	40,000
	52,000
Closing work in process (balance)	60,000
	112,000

(*Note:* Units started and finished is derived from 90,000 good units completed − 50,000 units in opening work-in-process.)

(ii)   *Calculation of equivalent units processed*

	Total units	Equivalent units Components	Assembly	Finishing
Units started and finished	40,000	40,000	40,000	40,000
Completion of opening stock	50,000	Nil	25,000	50,000
Spoilage	10,000	10,000	10,000	10,000
Losses	2,000	2,000	2,000	Nil
Closing stock	60,000	60,000	20,000	Nil
	162,000	112,000	97,000	100,000

(iii) *Calculation of total costs to be accounted for in November 19X1*

	£	Total costs £	Equivalent units	Cost per unit (£)
Opening work-in-process				
Bought-in components		60,000		
Direct assembly		25,000		
Overhead		25,000		
		110,000		
Costs for November 19X1				
Bought-in components	120,000		112,000	1.07143
Direct assembly	40,000		97,000	0.82474
Overhead	40,000			
		200,000		
Total cost to be accounted for		£310,000		£1.89617

Closing work-in-process		£
Bought-in components	60,000 × £1.07143	64,285.8
Assembly costs	20,000 × £0.82474	16,494.8
		£80,780.6
Lost units		£
Bought-in components	2,000 × £1.07143	2,142.86
Assembly costs	2,000 × £0.82474	1,649.48
		£3,792.34

Units transferred
£(310,000 − 80,781 − 3,792)   £225,427

This valuation can be verified as follows: £

Opening work-in-process	110,000
Completion of opening work-in-process (25,000 × £0.82474)	20,618
Units started and transferred (50,000 × £1.89617)	94,809
	£225,427

Good units produced and spoilage: finishing

	Total costs £	Equivalent units	Cost per unit (£)
Transferred from assembly	225,427		
Finishing costs	30,000		
	£255,427	100,000	£2.55427

Abnormal spoilage   5,000 units × £2.55427 = £12,771
Good units   (£255,427 − £12,771) = £242,656

3

DEPARTMENT A

Computation of output in equivalent units
for the month ended 31 October 19X4

	Physical flow	Equivalent units Materials	Conversion costs
Quantities			
Work in process, beginning	8,000		
Units started	47,500		
Pounds accounted for	55,500		
Units completed and transferred out during current period	46,500	46,500	46,500
Work-in-process, end:	9,000		
Materials: 9,000 × 1		9,000	
Conversion costs: 9,000 × 1/3			3,000
Pounds accounted for	55,500		
Total work done		55,500	49,500
Less: Old equivalent units for work done on opening stock in previous periods:			
Materials: 8,000 × 1		8,000	
Conversion costs: 8,000 × 3/4			6,000
Remainder, new equivalent units for current period		47,500	43,500

DEPARTMENT B

Computation of output in equivalent units
for the month ended 31 October 19X4

	Physical flow	Equivalent units Transferred in costs	Materials	Conversion costs
Quantities				
Work in process, beginning	10,000(3/10)			
Dept B material added	44,500			
Transferred in	46,500			
Pounds to account for	101,000			
Pounds completed and transferred out during current period	89,000	44,500	44,500	89,000
Work in process, end:	12,000(1/5)			
Transferred-in costs: 12,000 × 1		12,000		
Materials:			—	
Conversion costs: 12,000 × 1/5				2,400
Pounds accounted for	101,000			
Total work done		56,500	44,500	91,400
Less: old equivalent units for work done on opening stock in previous periods:				
Transferred-in costs: 10,000 × 1		10,000		
Materials:			—	
Conversion costs: 10,000 × 3/10				3,000
Remainder, new equivalent units for current period		46,500	44,500	88,400

4

(a) The mix and yield variances calculated by the three partners do not add up to the total material cost variance of £27,000. This must, of course, include a material price variance, so the first step is to calculate that.
From the normal formula:

$$\text{Price variance} = \text{actual quantity} \times (\text{standard price} - \text{actual price})$$

				£
Gorgon	=	8,000 (15 − 19)	=	32,000 (U)
Camem	=	20,000 (7.15 − 6.85)	=	6,000 (F)
Stil	=	80,000 (0.10 − 0.10)	=	Nil
				26,000 (U)

We can now summarise the partners' findings:

Partner	Total cost £	Price £	Variances: Mix £	Yield £	Other £
Venuti	27,000(U)	26,000(U)	29,000(F)	30,000(U)	
Lang	27,000(U)	26,000(U)	53,000(F)	30,000(U)	24,000(U)
South	27,000(U)	26,000(U)	53,000(F)	54,000(U)	

The two partners (Lang and South) whose calculations we are asked to check agree that the mix variance is £53,000(F).
This can be checked as follows:

Mix variance   =   standard price × (actual quantity at standard mix
    − actual quantity used)

If the actual quantity (108,000 fl oz) had been constituted in the standard proportions, they would have been:

Gorgon	100/1,000 × 108,000	=	10,800 fl oz
Camem	200/1,000 × 108,000	=	21,600 fl oz
Stil	700/1,000 × 108,000	=	75,600 fl oz
			108,000 fl oz

The mix variance is therefore:

Gorgon	£15.00 × (10,800 − 8,000)	=	42,000(F)
Camem	£7.15 × (21,600 − 20,000)	=	11,440(F)
Stil	£0.10 × (75,600 − 80,000)	=	440(U)
			53,000(F)

Now for the yield variance.

The basic formula is:

Standard cost per bottle × (actual output − standard output)

From the information given, 1,000 fl oz input with a standard cost of £3,000 should produce 500 bottles of Eau de Vie. The standard cost per bottle is therefore £6.00. The standard output from the actual 108,000 fl oz would be 108 × 500 = 54,000 bottles. In fact, we are told, only 45,000 bottles were filled. The yield variance on this basis would be:

£6 × (45,000 − 54,000)   =   £54,000(U)

− the result arrived at by South.

Why, then do both Venuti and Lang consider the yield to be £30,000(U)?

145

The answer lies in the fact that the input of 108,000 fl oz is said to have been the quantity used for '100 batches'. But the standard input for 100 batches would have been 100 × 1,000 fl oz, i.e. 100,000 fl oz. It appears therefore that before we begin calculating a yield variance we should recognise a 'usage' (or, in the terms of the question, a 'quantity') variance. This would be:

Standard price × (standard quantity for 100 batches − actual quantity *at standard mix* for 100 batches), thus:

Gorgon	£15.00 × (10,000 − 10,800) =	£12,000(U)
Camem	£7.15 × (20,000 − 21,600) =	11,440(U)
Stil	£0.10 × (70,000 − 75,600) =	560(U)
		24,000(U)

This is clearly the unidentified variance in Lang's calculation, shown in the table above.

The revised yield variance, based on batches, then becomes:

Standard cost per bottle × (actual number of bottles − standard number of bottles from actual input quantity)

or £6 × (45,000 − 50,000) = £30,000(U)

Although we are not asked to check Venuti's calculations, it is clear that he has combined the mix and 'usage' variances.

(b) It would appear that the calculation of a 'mix' variance is fairly straightforward (one can ignore what appears to have been a balancing figure in Venuti's workings) but that 'yield' needs careful definition according to what one is attempting to measure. Lang's analysis seems the more informative approach. In general it would be unwise to make decisions on the basis of mix and yield variances without enquiry into the bases used.

5

(a) The procedure for calculating the unit costs of products A and B is:

− From the contract output quantities of A, B and Z, by applying the given evaporation losses, to arrive at the total quantity input to the joint distillation process.

− The total joint process costs will comprise the input quantity at £5 per tonne plus the joint fixed costs of £5,000. From this will be deducted the sales value of by-product Z, less its identifiable costs (output quantity 400 tonnes × £1 per tonne plus fixed costs £500).

− The net joint costs of A and B thus arrived at will have to be apportioned to A and B on some suitable basis. In the absence of other information, the obvious basis is the output quantity of 3,600 + 4,000 tonnes.

– To these apportioned joint costs will be added the 'separable' variable and fixed costs tabulated in the question.

The workings and solution are as follows:

Workings

	A Tonnes	B Tonnes	Z Tonnes
Finished product	3,600	4,000	380
Yield net of evaporation loss	90%	80%	95%
∴ Yield from joint distillation process	4,000	5,000	400
		9,400	

Yield net of evaporation loss in the joint distillation process		94%
∴ Input to joint distillation		10,000 tonnes

Costs of joint distillation:

		£
10,000 tonnes @ £5 var. cost		50,000
Fixed cost		5,000
		55,000

Less: by-product Z			
Sales 380 tonnes @ £5		1,900	
Less: var. cost 400 tonnes @ £1	400		
Fixed cost	500		
		900	
			1,000
			54,000

Assuming a physical units joint cost apportionment, A = 4,000 tonnes, B = 5,000 tonnes, giving a cost at the completion of joint distillation of £6 tonne.

Product	A £	B £
Material ex joint distillation @ £6 tonne	24,000	30,000
Variable cost @ £11 tonne	44,000	–
@ £2 tonne	–	10,000
Fixed cost	4,000	8,000
	72,000	48,000
Yield – tonnes	3,600	4,000
	£	£
Cost per tonne	20	12
Selling price per tonne	24	14.50
Profit per tonne	4	2.50
Total profit	14,400	10,000
	£24,400	

(b) As compared with the calculations in part (a), variable costs will now be calculated on the reduced output figures; fixed costs will remain unchanged; and, in the absence of instructions to the contrary, the additional £17,000 repair costs will be treated as entirely chargeable to the joint process in the year.

Joint cost recalculation:

		£
9,000 tonnes @ £5		45,000
Fixed costs		5,000
Overhaul costs		17,000
		67,000

Less: by-product Z

Sales 342 tonnes @ £5		1,710	
Less: var. cost 360 tonnes @ £1	360		
Fixed cost	500		
		860	
			850
			66,150

Yield of A 3,600 tonnes and B 4,500 tonnes
Cost   £8.166 tonne

Revised costs of products:

	A £	B £
Material ex joint distillation @ £8.166 tonne	29,400	36,750
Variable cost @ £11 tonne	39,600	–
@ £2 tonne	–	9,000
Fixed cost	4,000	8,000
	73,000	53,750
Yield – tonnes	3,240	3,600
	£	£
Cost per tonne	22.53	14.93

(c)

	£	£
Sales proceeds on own manufacture	77,760	52,200
Less: Costs	73,000	53,750
Total profit (loss) on own manufacture	4,760	(1,550)
Loss on sale of imported goods:		
360 tonnes × £1 (£25.00 − £24.00)	(360)	–
400 tonnes × £0.50 (£15.00 − £14.50)	–	(200)
	4,400	(1,750)
		£2650

(d) *Alternative (i)*

			£
Extra variable costs (2% of £45,000)			900

Product	A	B
Distillate change	+200 tonnes	−200 tonnes
Final product change	+180 tonnes	−160 tonnes

	£	£
Variable costs	+2,200	−400
Imports:		
180 tonnes @ £25	−4,500	
160 tonnes @ 15		+2,400
	−2,300	+2,000

$$\underbrace{\qquad\qquad\qquad\qquad}$$

		300	300

	£
Net deterioration in profit if alternative *(i)* is undertaken	600

Alternative (ii)

Available by-product distillate 360 tonnes.
This will be allocated to:

Product A $\frac{4}{9}$ 160 tonnes

Product B $\frac{5}{9}$ 200 tonnes

Total product output will now be:
Product A 3,600 + 160 = 3,760 × 89% = 3,346 tonnes
Product B 4,500 + 200 = 4,700 × 79% = 3,713 tonnes

		£
Lost by-product revenue		1,710
Additional variable costs:		
	£	
A 160 @ £11	1,760	
B 200 @ £2	400	
		2,160
Additional fixed costs:		
A 5% × £4,000	200	
B 5% × £8,000	400	
		600
		4,470

Z variable costs saved 360 tonnes @ £1   360

Import savings:
    A   3,240
         3,346
             106 tonnes @ £25   2,650

    B   3,600
         3,713
             113 tonnes @ £15   1,695
                                      4,705

Net increase in profit if alternative (ii) is undertaken   235

Thus alternative (ii) would improve the profit per (c) by around 9%.

In deciding whether to adopt alternative (ii), however, the following points should be taken into account:

— There may be the risk that the experimental results may not be achieved under production conditions.

— The position of existing customers for product Z needs to be considered. If they are also customers for other products, it may be unwise to alienate them by cutting off their supplies of Z. If the proposed process changes prove unsuccessful, there may be difficulty in regaining the existing outlets for product Z.

— No mention has been made of any staff reorganisation. If a reduction in the number of employees is envisaged, this may cause a deterioration in labour relations and also involve redundancy payments.

— If a reversion is made to the existing production methods, the company may still be committed to some of the additional fixed costs for some period ahead.

6

(a)   This question covers the whole range of variance calculations other than mix and yield, and involves also the calculation of equivalent units, which affect the costing of opening and closing work-in-process and the calculation of variances. Indications have been given of the derivation of the variances, but it has not been considered necessary at this stage of your studies to set out the calculations in detail.

Process 1 Account

	£		£
Opening work-in-process*	900	Unfavourable variances:	
Direct material			
A 8000 × £0.36	2,880	Direct material usage − B	
B 17000 × £0.08	1,360	(17,000 − 15,750) 0.08	100
Direct labour	2,173	Direct labour rate	
Variable overhead	4,134	(4.10 − 4.00) 530	53
Fixed overhead	4,900	Fixed overhead volume	
Favourable variances:		5,000 − (543.75 × 8.00)	650
Direct material usage−A			
(8,000 − 9,000) 0.36	360		
Direct labour efficiency		Completed production:	
(530 − 543.75) 4.00	55	Transferred to Process 2	
Variable overhead efficiency		(22,000 × 0.70)	15,400
(530 − 543.75) 8.00	110		
Variable overhead spending		Closing work-in-process*	875
4,134 − (530 × 8.00)	106		
Fixed overhead spending			
4,900 − 5,000	100		
	£17,078		£17,078

Process 2 Account

	£		£
Opening work-in-process*	828	Unfavourable variances:	
Direct material			
C	15,400	Direct material usage C	
D 930 × £0.50	465	(22,000 − 19,950) 0.70	1,435
Direct labour	418	Direct labour efficiency	
Variable overhead	912	(110 − 86.25) 4.00	95
Fixed overhead	1,510	Variable overhead efficiency	
Packing material	95	(110 − 86.25) 9.20	218.5
Favourable variances:		Fixed overhead volume	
Direct material usage D		1,660 − (86.25 × 14.00)	452.5
(930 − 950) 0.50	10	Packing variance	
Direct labour rate		95 − (17 × 4.00)	27
(3.80 − 4.00) 110	22		
Variable overhead spending		Completed production:	
(912 − 110 × 9.20)	100	Transferred to finished goods	
Fixed overhead spending		store (17,000 × 0.90)	15,300
1,510 − 1,660	150		
		Closing work-in-process	2,382*
	£19,910		£19,910

Working
(Note: Calculations are in terms of output batches of 1,000 kilos)

Process 1	Material input (Equivalent units)	Standard cost	Processing input (Equivalent units)	Standard cost
		£		£
Closing work-in-process	2.5 @ £144 + 56	500	0.75 @ £500	375
Finished production	22.0	4,400	22.00	11,000
	24.5	4,900	22.75	11,375
Opening work-in-process	2.0	400	1.00	500
Standard input and cost for actual production	22.5	£4,500	21.75	£10,875
Process 2		£		£
Closing work-in-process	3.0 @ £735 + 25	2,280	0.75 @ £136	102
Finished production	17.0	12,920	17.00	2,312
	20.0	15,200	17.75	2,414
Opening work-in-process	1.0	760	0.50	68
Standard input and cost for actual production	19.0	£14,440	17.25	£2,346

The equivalent units for work-in-process in the above working are after deduction of accrued normal loss.

(b) The usage of material on process 1 during the week was 8,000 kilos of A and 17,000 kilos of B, i.e. the proportions were 32% A and 68% B. This compares with a standard mix of 36% (approx) : 64%. It is not known whether this was a deliberate decision, but in view of the higher standard price per kilo for material A it would be expected to have a favourable financial effect as is in fact shown by the net favourable usage variances. Bearing in mind that the actual price paid for A (39p per kilo) was above the standard price, whilst the actual price for B was below standard, a further gain in financial terms would have been achieved.

It should be noted, however, that in process 2 there was a heavy adverse material usage variance, accompanied by an adverse labour efficiency variance. It would be worth investigating whether the change in mix resulted in output of poor quality being transferred from process 1.

(c) By carrying out process 2, incremental costs are incurred per 1,000 kilos Equinox as follows:

	£
Material D	25
Direct labour	20
Variable overhead	46
Packing material	4
	95

and against this the sale of 1,000 kilos
Equinox at £1.05 would yield   1,050

giving net incremental revenue of   955

If the 1,050 kilos of material C were sold
without further processing at £0.90 it
would realise   945

So on the facts stated further processing
is more beneficial to the extent of   10

It is assumed that the fixed costs of process 2 are not relevant to the
calculation.

10   Performance evaluation

INTRODUCTION

Performance evaluation means:

(a)   planning what should be achieved by an individual, a department or a company;

(b)   comparing actual performance against what was expected;

(c)   making a judgement on the quality of that performance, having regard to the actual circumstances under which it was achieved; questions on this aspect will be given in chapter 12.

At company, or profit centre, level, assessment of performance is usually based on a series of financial ratios, notably return on capital employed. Details of these should be familiar to students who have completed their readings in financial accounting. Their application to inter-firm comparison is the subject of question 1 below, whilst their use in divisional performance measurement is dealt with in chapter 20.

A widespread method of performance evaluation is by comparison with budgets or standards, using the techniques already covered in earlier chapters. In describing causes of variances from such plans we used the terms 'efficiency' and 'productivity'. Questions 2 and 3 in the present chapter are concerned with particular aspects of the measurement of productivity.

The final two questions in this chapter deal with certain planning techniques which help to ensure that value for money will be obtained. They are value analysis, work study, cost reduction schemes and zero-base budgeting. The general concept of 'cost-benefit analysis' will be illustrated in chapter 19.

Many work-related performance indicators are specific to the types of business in which they are used — 'passenger miles run' in a transport undertaking, 'occupied bed-days' in the provision of accommodation. Such measures can occur in any examination question, and their significance will normally be obvious from the context in which they are used.

STUDY REQUIREMENTS

Performance evaluation techniques
Profitability criteria and ratios

QUESTIONS

1   During 19X0 Alfred Williams retired from the army and with his gratuity purchased a small retail wool shop which he called by his wife's name. Since then he has run the shop with no assistance other than that from his wife Olive. During 19X5 he was asked by the Retail Association of Wool Shops whether he would be prepared to submit his annual accounts anonymously to enable comparisons of trading results to be made with those of other firms.

Mr Williams agreed and sent along his accounts for the year ended 31 March 19X5, which were as follows:

OLIVE'S WOOL SHOP

Profit & loss account for the year ended 31 March 19X5

Sales		£10,145
Less: Cost of goods sold		6,087
Gross profit		4,058
Expenses:		
Wages	£325	
Rates	125	
Heating and light	370	
Insurances	80	
Advertising, print, stationery	510	
Miscellaneous expense	275	
Depreciation	400	
		2,085
Net profit (before taxation)		£1,973

The following additional information had to be supplied:

(i)   Whether the premises were owned or rented, and if the latter, the amount of the rent.

(ii)   Details of the time that the owner and other members of his family spent working in the shop. In their case, Mr. Williams worked for 40 hours each week and his wife for 30.

(iii)   Details of equipment used in the shop (cost, date of purchase, estimated life).

(iv)   The amount shown on the capital account. This was £4,750 at the commencement of the year in question.

Subsequently Mr Williams received the following statement of the 'average' accounts for the wool shops contributing to the scheme, with his own results as 'adjusted' by the Association.

		Olive's Wool Shop	Average wool shop
Sales		£10,145	£12,440
Less: Cost of goods sold		6,087	6,470
Gross profit		4,058	5,970
Expenses:	£		£
Management expenses	2,000		1,850
Wages	865		610
Rates	125		120
Heating and light	370		345
Insurances	80		90
Advertising, printing, etc	510		280
Miscellaneous expenses	275		250
Depreciation	400		400
Interest on capital	475		480
Rent	500		500
		5,600	4,925
Net profit (loss) (before taxation)		(£1,542)	£1,045

Mr Williams and his wife were perplexed at these figures, as from their own accounts they had felt that they were doing very well.

(a) Explain the purpose of the exercise and the reasons for each of the adjustments to the original profit statement. *(10 marks)*

(b) Compare the results of Olive's Wool Shop with those for similar shops which indicate those areas which Mr Williams should investigate. How should Mr Williams view these individual problem areas in order to improve the overall performance of his business? *(10 marks)*
(Total 20 marks)

2   In the context of management accounting:

(a) Define 'added value'.

(b) State briefly how 'added value' differs from 'conversion cost'.

(c) List the advantages a statement of added value has over a normal profit and loss account.

(d) Describe how you would deal with the following items in calculating added value:

(i)   bad debts;
(ii)   Customs and Excise duties;
(iii) employer's pension contributions;
(iv)   fixed assets, self-built by company;
(v)   rents receivable;
(vi)   annual lease payments. *(20 marks)*

3   Within a group of companies are six furniture manufacturers each employing about 2,500 people. Each manufacturer operates as a semi-autonomous unit with its own accounting staff numbering between 90 and 120.

As assistant group management accountant you have been asked to review the accounting manpower utilisation. In the context of such a review:

(a)   Indicate the criteria by which indexes to the productivity of the accounting staff should be selected.

(b)   State what the value of such productivity indexes would be.

(c)   Indicate what productivity indexes you consider could be used for this purpose and how they might be calculated.

(d)   Identify any difficulties you feel might be encountered in the use of these indexes.   *(20 marks)*

4   Describe, and clearly show both the similarities and differences between value analysis and work study, and specify two areas where the techniques can assist, or be utilised by, management accountancy in any or all of its planning, control and performance reporting functions.   *(20 marks)*

5   Explain, and clearly distinguish between, the meaning of the terms
(a)   'cost reduction programme' and
(b)   'zero-based budgeting'.   *(10 marks)*
Describe two applications within any of the functions of management accounting which could be assisted by the utilisation of either of these two techniques. Outline a major difficulty in their application.   *(10 marks)*
                                                                    (Total 20 marks)

ANSWERS

1

(a) The purpose of any scheme of inter-firm comparison is to enable each participating firm to compare its own performance with that of its competitors: not individually, since confidentiality of individual results is normally required by those taking part, but with the average for the industry as a whole. In some schemes three sets of figures are published, the median figures and those for the upper and lower quartiles.

For any meaningful comparison to be made, all sets of accounts must be prepared on a uniform basis, and it is for this purpose that the Association asked for the additional information listed in the question.

The adjustments to Olive's Wool Shop accounts made by the Association were as follows:

(i) Management expenses, £2,000, were included. This is because some firms employ managers to run their businesses. In Olive's Wool Shop Mr Williams managed the business himself. The £2,000 is a reasonable charge for his services to the business as manager.

(ii) Wages were increased from £325 to £865. Mr Williams's wife works in the business. If she did not do so he would have to employ somebody else. The additional £540 is an estimate of the wages attributable to this work.

(iii) Interest on capital, £475, has been introduced. Whatever amount of capital is employed in a business, it has to be rewarded either by dividend distributions (in the case of equity capital) or interest (on borrowed money). Because dividend distributions, if any, are at the discretion of the proprietor, they are not comparable from firm to firm. It is preferable therefore, for inter-firm comparisons, to treat all capital as earning interest at the market rate (in this case apparently 10%) and to charge this interest as a business expense. The resultant 'profit' will be, in effect, an economic profit.

(iv) Some businesses own their premises while others rent them. For comparative purposes it is easiest to make an economic rental charge in all accounts. In doing so care will be needed to eliminate any maintenance or other premises charges that will be included in the rent.

(b) The points for investigation by Olive's Wool Shop, arising out of the comparison with the average wool shop, are as follows:

(i) Gross profit as a percentage of sales value is 40% for Olive's as compared with an average of 48%. It may be that Mr Williams sells a less profitable mix of products than some other firms or that he is paying higher prices for his supplies, possibly because he operates on a small scale and is not obtaining quantity discounts; or that he is applying a lower mark-up than other firms. Dependent on what he believes to be the reason, Mr Williams could decide to modify his existing method of trading.

(ii) Sales at £10,145 are below those of the average firm. This might be, for example, because Mr Williams is operating in a location with few customers; or because, as a retired army man, he is too old to run the shop efficiently; or because, relying on his gratuity, he did not have sufficient capital to carry an adequate range of stocks. Perhaps it would be advisable for him to borrow extra capital and to employ a manager so that the size of the business could be increased.

(iii) Advertising, printing etc. At £510 these expenses are nearly double those of the average firm. They represent about 5% on sales value. It is possible, of course, that Mr Williams is currently engaged in an advertising campaign to boost his business. He should certainly review the effectiveness of this expenditure.

(iv) Heating and light. This is above average. Possible reasons are that Mr Williams is operating in a high cost area, or that he lives above the shop and is charging the business an undue share of bills that are influenced by a high domestic consumption of light and heat.

(v) Net loss. On an economic basis, Mr Williams's business is running at a loss. Unless he regards the business as a hobby, he might do better to sell up and invest his money elsewhere.

2

(a) Added value is the value added by a business to the cost of goods and services purchased from outside; and is achieved by the application of labour and capital. In accounting terms, it is measured as the difference between turnover and the cost of purchased goods and services, after taking account of inventory changes.

(b) Conversion cost is the cost of labour and some overheads added to the cost of direct material in arriving at the total cost of production.

Added value is the cost of labour plus interest and profit added to the value of all purchased materials and services in arriving at sales value.

Conversion cost measures 'cost'. Added value measures economic value created: it can be used as a measure of productivity.

(c) The advantages of an added value statement as compared with a normal profit and loss account are:

(i) It emphasises the joint roles of capital and labour in creating value.

(ii) Such research results as are available indicate that the added value statement is easier to understand than a profit and loss account. The concept of 'profit' calculated on an accruals basis is not easy to understand; nor is 'profit' easy to define.

(iii) In firms where worker participation is encourage, added value (as a measure of productivity) can be used as the basis for incentive schemes.

(iv) Ratios based on added value can provide greater depth of information in inter-firm and inter-divisional comparisons (added value per employee; added value per £ payroll cost; added value per £ capital employed – though this last ratio still requires an acceptable definition of capital employed).

(v) In a profit and loss account, profit appears as a residue available to the shareholders. In an added value statement the final residue, after dividends, is more clearly available for the development of 'the business' in the interests of all participants, including employees.

(d) (i) Bad debts should appear as a loss of added value created, either as a deduction before arriving at 'added value available for distribution' or as a distribution under the general heading of 'financing charges'.

(ii) Customs and Excise duties on purchases are probably best included in the cost of purchases, but if desired could be shown separately under that part of added value 'distributed to the Government', along with corporation tax or income tax on profits.

If VAT is intended to be covered by the heading given in the question, it does not appear in either an added value statement or a profit and loss account – except as a policy matter to display the effect of the firm's role as unpaid tax collector.

(iii) Employer's pension contributions are part of the cost of employee remuneration, and would be shown with wages as part of the distribution of added value.

(iv) In order to show the total of wages paid, the creation of fixed assets for the company's own use could be shown as a separate item after 'sales', and thus enter into the calculation of added value. The alternative, probably less informative, is to exclude all costs of fixed asset creation from the statement.

(v) Rents receivable, except for a property company, do not enter into the added value created by its normal activities, but should be shown as a separate constituent of the added value available for distribution.

(vi) Annual lease payments under an operating lease would be included with other bought-in services in arriving at added value. Payments under a finance lease would enter into the calculation of its capitalised value, which would then be depreciated. There are different opinions on whether depreciation charges should be treated as an expense in arriving at added value (the cost of using assets) or as a distribution of added

161

value, under the heading 'retained for maintenance and expansion of the business'. The treatment adopted in any instance would probably depend on whether the added value statement was prepared under the current cost or the historical cost convention.

3 *General note.* As the various manufacturers in this group are 'semi-autonomous', it is likely that the assistant group management accountant will be reviewing a wide range of accountancy functions such as cost accounting, payroll, at least some aspects of financial accounting and possibly internal cost audit.

(a) It is rather strange that the question asks for criteria in part (a) before defining objectives in part (b). The student might find it helpful to clarify his thoughts about the purposes before deciding what criteria were appropriate. However:

  (i) The indexes selected should be based on information readily available, or obtainable without excessive cost.

  (ii) This information should be available continuously, so that trends can be established. This does not rule out the possibility of measurement against estimates for special non-recurring tasks.

  (iii) Undoubtedly there will be need for comparisons of performance between the various manufacturers, so at least some of the indexes should relate to factors common to the various units.

  (iv) Reliance on observed fact is preferable to reliance on subjective judgement, even though the interpretation of the results will be to some extent subjective.

  (v) The criteria must be accepted as fair by those who are to use them and those whose performance is to be judged. This acceptance will derive mainly from fulfilment of the first four criteria.

(b) The value of these productivity indexes would lie in their use in the planning and control of the use of human resources. The fact that they were to be used might well give rise to action to ensure improved utilisation of manpower in advance of their implementation.

  Their successful development would help to dispel the idea that manpower control is difficult to achieve.

(c) Possible productivity indexes are:

Shop floor payroll clerk cost	Number of direct and indirect operators
Preparation of computer payroll inputs (hours)	1,000 payroll personnel
Number of incoming invoices processed (verified, coded, passed for payment, etc)	Per £ clerical cost.
Attributable wages dept cost	Number of direct and indirect employees.

Internal audit cost	£ added value.
Qualified accounting staff	Total accounting staff

In the case of repetitive clerical operations it may be possible to carry out work study or to use synthetic data to set time standards per unit of output, and to require that clerical time records be accompanied by output records.

Although not direct measures of productivity, such statistics as overtime hours/normal hours worked, absentee hours/normal available hours and number of leavers per period/normal establishment (i.e. labour turnover) all give indirect evidence of the effectiveness of staff control.

(d)   Difficulties likely to be encountered in the use of such indicators will include:

(i)   The difficulty of persuading staff to maintain the necessary detailed records of their utilisation of time. This would be lessened if there were some system of payment by results.

(ii)   The difficulty of apportioning responsibility between inefficient workers and inefficient managers.

(iii) The effects of poor work methods. This could cause differences in performance between different manufacturers.

4   Value analysis and work study are both concerned with efficiency and cost reduction by reducing or eliminating unnecessary expense and activity.

Value analysis, however, is the broader concept. It is consumer oriented.

This technique investigates the product in order to ascertain, for the whole product and each of its constituent parts, what purpose it is intended to serve and whether that purpose is being met effectively and economically. The technique then enables improvements, simplifications and changes to be made to the design of the product and the type, quality and quantity of materials used with a view to reducing costs while still ensuring that the product adequately fulfils its purpose.

Value analysis thus covers design, materials used and manufacturing methods.

Work study, on the other hand, accepts a given product specification and directs itself to ensuring that the conversion of raw material into finished product is carried out by the most effective working methods and at an acceptable level of efficiency.

It is a process whereby the techniques of production are investigated with a view to increasing their efficiency by utilising method study and work measurement. Method study is an analysis of the *way* in which the task should be carried out and work measurement concerns the establishment of a *time* the task should take.

Both techniques will yield results which assist management in shop floor planning and the preparation of budgets.

Both help to identify areas for cost reduction and can be used by management in setting cost reduction programmes.

Both will assist in standard setting and thus improve control through performance reporting.

5

(a) A cost reduction programme is a system, more commonly applied on an *ad hoc* basis than on a routine basis, which forces attention on costs with a view to their reduction. The principal methods by which a cost reduction programme achieves its aim include the use of value analysis, work study and O and M. Costs are critically reviewed in order to determine whether they, and the item which causes the expenditure, are necessary and whether it is possible to improve the manner by which the task is carried out or the product is produced, thereby reducing costs.

(b) Zero-based budgeting is a concept of use in deciding on some departmental budget or spending limits. In many non-manufacturing activities, such as research, advertising and many administrative functions, there is a great deal of discretion as to the level of activity and spending. A similar position arises in those manufacturing departments which are characterised by heavy fixed costs and only a small, relatively unimportant, variable cost element. A common approach is to base the forthcoming budget on the previous period's budgeted or actual expenditure, adding an allowance for inflation, growth, etc. Such an approach tends to give authority to past actions as if they are the correct base from which to proceed. Zero-based budgeting requires that all spending limits, or budget claims, are to be justified on their own merits without reference to previous spending levels. Hence the budget is derived from a 'zero base'.

There are several areas where the techniques can be utilised by management accountancy including:

(i) Budgeting for non-production departments — zero-based budgeting may be useful.

(ii) A cost reduction programme may be of assistance in ascertaining areas of improvement should the need be indicated following the output of a budgetary control system or as part of the feedback process of a budgetary planning exercise.

A major difficulty in the application of a cost reduction programme is the risk that short-term savings may be made in a way that is detrimental to the longer-term prospects of the business. This might be the case where budgets were cut in such areas as research and development, advertising or plant maintenance.

There are several difficulties in the application of zero-base budgeting; in particular:

(i) The identification of alternative levels of achievement and the costs associated with them.

(ii)   The top management decision on the correct 'portfolio' of activities, at selected levels of achievement, which will make the most effective use of the limited resources available to the organisation.

(iii) The time and effort needed to make a thorough examination and analysis of all the activities reviewed, and the possible need to repeat that analysis annually.

11 Service department costs

INTRODUCTION

We are concerned here with the apportionment of service department costs to those other departments which benefit from or make use of the services provided.

This is not a subject that appears specifically in the management accounting syllabuses; indeed the various techniques for exhausting service department costs by apportionment to other departments should have been studied previously in connection with examinations in cost accounting.

Questions do occur, however, from time to time, either on the theoretical value of making such apportionments or requiring a critical analysis of a specific procedure. Both aspects are illustrated in the three questions contained in this chapter.

STUDY REQUIREMENTS

The allocation and apportionment of service department costs to users and products.

QUESTIONS

1   Tootsweets Ltd has prepared the following budget for the year ending 31 December 19X5.

	Notes	Fudge £	Gums £	Rock £	Total £
Sales		200,000	160,000	40,000	400,000
Factory costs:					
Direct materials	(a)	40,000	32,000	8,000	80,000
Fixed overhead	(b)	60,000	48,000	12,000	120,000
Service departments:					
Personnel	(c)	4,000	3,000	1,000	8,000
Maintenance	(d)	6,000	4,000	2,000	12,000
Administration	(e)	40,000	30,000	10,000	80,000
Selling	(f)	30,000	24,000	6,000	60,000
		180,000	141,000	39,000	360,000
Net operating income		£20,000	£19,000	£1,000	£40,000

Notes

(a)   Sugar comprises over 80% of direct materials.

(b)   Fixed overhead includes operating wages.

(c)   Allocated in terms of the number of factory employees engaged in making each product.

(d)   Allocated in terms of factory square footage used for making each product.

(e)   Allocated on the same basis as the costs of the personnel department.

(f)   Allocated in terms of product sales.

The company has 82 employees and occupies 21,000 square feet. Details are as follows:

	Employees	Occupancy (sq ft)
Factory:		
Fudge	20	6,000
Gums	15	4,000
Rock	5	2,000
Offices:		
Personnel	2	500
Maintenance	4	500
Administration	20	5,000
Selling	16	3,000
	82	21,000

For most of 19X5 actual activity and costs have closely approximated to budget. In late autumn, however, the managing director hears a rumour that sugar prices may increase and he suggests to the Board that since rock is the least profitable product its manufacture should be discontinued and the sugar used in its manufacture switched to the other products. The finance director demurs. 'All our products make much the same contribution to overheads and profits,' he says. 'I think that we should review our overheads. The allocation bases are sound, but we should take account, for example, of the fact that Administration does a lot of work for Selling, and Personnel does work for all our departments, not just those engaged in production.'

Without giving calculations:

(a) Give a concise statement of the apparent managerial objective in allocating costs and your views on the validity of such allocations.

(b) Describe two other systematic approaches to overhead allocation and to discuss their relevance to the problem before the Board in the light of your answer to (a). *(20 marks)*

2   The Leviathan Institute of Science and Technology (LIST) is considering whether to charge departments for time used on the central computer, one of its several central services.

LIST has five faculties, incorporating nearly 50 departments. The computer laboratory provides them with a computing service (including both programming and computer operations).

The laboratory has grown rapidly in the last 10 years. The number of staff employed has increased about 10 times, and computing power nearly 1,000 times, in that period. The computer configuration includes a full range of input and output devices, with a large central processing unit. There are 20 terminals located in various user departments.

In common with the other central services (such as personnel, central printing, etc) no system of charging users has so far been operated. Priorities for use have been determined in accordance with guidelines established by the computer committee, on which users are well represented, supplemented occasionally by individual negotiations between the potential user and the laboratory staff. The whole cost of the computing service has been treated as a central overhead, and has not been allocated amongst departments.

The council of the Institute has decided in principle that a system of charging departments for computer usage should be introduced, with a view to controlling and improving the allocation of computer time. The method under consideration is average cost pricing, with fixed prices per unit of service. It has been proposed by R. Hobbes, a consultant engaged by the council.

The proposed system requires that the laboratory prepare a rolling annual budget, in quarterly periods, updated every quarter. Using full absorption costing the budget would spread the total cost over estimated demand in each quarter to produce a charging rate per minute for each of the services available.

When a user wished to use a service he would obtain from the laboratory an estimate of the likely time, and therefore cost, for the job. If the job were undertaken and the actual time were to exceed the agreed estimate, the laboratory would bear the difference as an unfavourable variance; if, on the other hand, the actual time were less than the agreed estimate, half of the difference would be credited to the user department, leaving half for the laboratory.

A user's total expenditure on computing in any financial year would not be allowed to exceed an amount approved as part of the Institute's annual budgeting exercise, and designed to allocate an agreed percentage of computer capacity. However, within this limit users may use outside services if dissatisfied with the proposed internal charge. Similarly, the laboratory would be permitted to sell time to outsiders to the extent that internal demand were insufficient to use the time available.

Outline and discuss the considerations to be taken into account in evaluating the proposed new system of charging for computer usage, assessing its likely motivational and operational effects on the users, the computer laboratory and the Institute. State any further information which you think it necessary to obtain before forming final views. *(25 marks)*

3   An organisation has its own internal printing department. Initially the costs of this department were not charged to users. Three years ago the costs increased significantly when fast photocopying machines were introduced.

In an effort to control the costs, management decided that the service request forms should be priced and the costs charged out to the five operating departments. This entailed the printing room staff recording the time taken to complete the job and details of the materials used. The costs are calculated in the accounting department. The user departments are coded on each slip and this is used to analyse costs by departments. The overall cost of the printing department staff and materials used is also calculated and used as a control check against the total of the individual items.

The work takes about three minutes for each service request form. Three accounting clerks are now used on the pricing and analysis. There are about 8,000 jobs a month averaging about £8 each. Of these 5% are recognised as major items and average about £46 each.

The management accountant believes that his manpower could be reduced by using a statistical cost allocation system. As his assistant, prepare a memorandum for the operating department heads explaining:

(a)   the basic idea of a statistical cost allocation;
(b)   the way the statistical cost allocation would be undertaken;
(c)   the degree of accuracy expected to be achieved, giving an example of a statistical cost allocation;
(d)   the savings in accounting manpower likely to be achieved if the statistical cost allocation were to be adopted. *(20 marks)*

ANSWERS

1

(a) The apparent managerial objective is to allocate all the costs incurred, no matter in what area, over the various products in order to ascertain their individual profitabilities.

Tootsweets Ltd has attempted to meet the objective by finding bases upon which to allocate the various costs of production. Even presuming the bases are valid, the attempt to assess the profitability of each product from the results is not. This is particularly the case when discussing one ingredient as it fails to consider the return per unit of the ingredient. Analysing the results on the basis of the return per £1 of sugar we find that the net operating income per £1 is: fudge 62.5p; gums 74p; rock 15.6p. Although in gross terms the fudge appeared to be the most profitable product, in terms of the income earned per usage of a scarce resource the gums are more profitable. An analysis of this type is also very questionable as there is no reason to suppose that other costs will even be affected by a change to another product mix, e.g. fixed overheads. For an evaluation of the total cost of production and hence a stock valuation, a total absorption cost basis of this type can be valid. However, it is not likely to be so as a basis for managerial decision making.

The finance director is correct in saying that the service department costs should be allocated so as to reflect the work done for other service departments. With this exception one cannot argue with the cost allocations providing the bases themselves are relevant, e.g. that selling costs are dependent upon sales value and not sales volume.

(b) Two other systematic approaches to overhead allocation are as follows:

(i) *Division of costs into fixed and variable elements*
By dividing overheads into those that vary with production and those that do not, one is able to ascertain the return earned by each product before taking into account the fixed costs of the business. Any of these fixed overheads directly traceable to the manufacture of a particular product and not incurred but for that manufacture can be allocated to that product. Other fixed costs are treated as period costs and not attributable to any product. The analysis is then made on the basis of the contribution provided by each product line towards the general fixed overheads and profit of the business. By approaching the problem in this manner the management is provided with suitable information upon which to base decisions, as the results of changing the product mix are immediately apparent.

Tootsweets Ltd has material costs only as direct costs and this approach will reveal the contribution made by each product line towards the overheads and profits. If the return per £1 of sugar is required it is calculable directly in terms of this contribution and it is this result that is the most meaningful. If it is possible to allocate some fixed costs directly this will give an even clearer picture of the relative returns earned by the products.

(ii) *Allocation of costs on a responsibility basis*
Rather than allocate those costs to a product that can be directly attributed thereto, an alternative technique is to allocate costs to the persons responsible for them. Thus administration expenses controllable by the administration manager would be budgeted for under his department. Expenses which are independent of the production of any particular product and which are outside the sphere of influence of the production manager will be budgeted and analysed under the person responsible for them. The production manager will then be held accountable for the costs over which he has control, i.e. materials and some fixed overheads. The allocation of the fixed overheads over the products will still be a problem but an analysis of the direct costs as against revenue per product will be possible.

However, if it is the management's objective to allocate all the overheads to the products in an attempt to ascertain the profitability of each, this system is unsuitable. It is a system primarily used for control purposes and not for management decision making.

2

(a) *Evaluating the proposed new system of charging for computer usage*

The main consideration must be whether the new system is likely to achieve its objective. The objective is to control and improve the allocation of computer time. The existing system allocates time on the basis of guidelines laid down by the computer committee, whereas the proposed system would allocate time on a cost basis through the Institute's annual budgeting exercise. Under both systems each department's time is restricted. It would seem unlikely that allocating time on a cost basis rather than by discussion about the merits of projects would produce a better result, particularly in an academic environment where the benefits of individual projects must be difficult to assess.

(b) *Assessing its likely motivational and operational effects on:*

(i) **Users** These are likely to become more aware of the cost of both programming and computer processing, and will therefore spend more time evaluating proposals before submitting them. They will presumably attempt to undertake cost-benefit analysis on their various proposals. This will prove a difficult exercise and may lead them to give up projects they would have undertaken on other grounds. They will however, be able to budget the cost of their operations more effectively. Moreover, they will not be affected by the inefficiencies of the computer laboratory, as they are being charged with only the agreed estimate for a particular job, and have the freedom to go outside if they consider the internal charges too high.

(ii) **The computer laboratory** The preparation of a quarterly budget should facilitate control over costs and lead to the better utilisation of staff. Computer laboratory staff should be motivated to try to recover their costs through selling computer time both internally and externally. This should lead them to operate more efficiently, so that prices are equal to or less than external prices. Deadlines will be created and there will be pressure to meet schedules; however, there may be a tendency to overestimate time for particular jobs as the laboratory is credited with half of any favourable variance. The morale of the laboratory staff may suffer, as they will view themselves as a service bureau; and the budgeting and negotiation cycle could be time consuming.

(iii) **The Institute** Although the proposals are aimed at controlling and improving the allocation of computer time, it seems that their effect will be to slow the development of systems analysis within the Institute as a whole, as user departments are likely to curtail both current and future consumption of computer services. The new system may lead to the under-utilisation of computer time, owing to the user departments going outside and the computer laboratory finding it difficult to sell outside. Indeed, total costs may even be higher than before, because the user departments have the ability to use outside services.

It is also probable that the Institute will not undertake projects which are desirable on other bases, apart from the cost of computer time. Moreover, the new system is unlikely to encourage the use of the computer laboratory in new research projects, owing to high programming costs.

(c) *Information to be obtained before forming final views*

(i) What do the various departments use the computer for? It is likely that existing programs are too specialised for general commercial use, and therefore the programming staff will have to write such a set of programs before the laboratory is in a position to offer a range of services to outsiders.

(ii) What alternative pricing policies have been considered? With full absorption costing, prices quoted to one department will depend on how much service is being consumed by the other departments. It would seem more sensible to price computer time at market rate, and not to determine individual department budgets by reference to the estimated total cost of the computer department; and it would be more equitable if departments with terminals were charged with the associated fixed cost.

(iii) How will external prices be fixed? They should be at market rate, which may well be below that charged internally. If the laboratory tries to sell outside at average cost, it may not fully utilise capacity.

(iv)   How well does the existing system of time allocation work?

(v)   Was the growth of the computer laboratory planned, and is cost control an important factor? The proposed system could restrict the development of systems analysis, and we therefore need to clarify the council's objectives.

3   Two preliminary points should be borne in mind when tackling this question. First, that you are writing to departmental heads who presumably know nothing about statistical cost allocation, though the idea behind that forbidding title is very simple, i.e. to make charges based on representative samples. You must therefore contrast the proposed system with the method already in use. Second, in part (c) you are required only to 'explain' how an acceptable degree of accuracy is to be achieved, but not to make a calculation of the degree of accuracy in the example you use.

Memorandum: Printing department costs

To: Operating department heads
From: Assistant management accountant

(a)   The cost allocation system currently in use means that you are charged with the actual cost of the materials and print room time which you have requisitioned. Many of these jobs are comparatively minor, and therefore the pricing and analysis procedure is costly. The basic idea of a statistical cost allocation procedure is that a charge basis is determined on a sample which can be deemed to be representative of the whole, and used as a basis of charging the print room costs out, without actually costing each print room order undertaken. The charge basis can be refined as later samples indicate that the pattern of print room usage by operating departments is changing.

A small proportion of print room jobs, about 5%, involve major costs, say of £40 or more. These will probably be excluded from the sampling procedure, and will continue to be specifically costed and allocated. There is no great difficulty in identifying them at the time the work is received by the print room.

(b)   We propose taking the initial sample during the next month; it is important that this shall be large enough to ensure that it is representative both of the operating departments using the print room and of the spread of large and small jobs. Every job in the sample will be individually costed, and from the results we shall develop a formula for spreading future print-room costs over user departments. A very simplified specimen of the type of calculation is given in the next paragraph.

(c)   The degree of accuracy expected is reflected in the confidence limits deriving from the sample. Clearly the larger and better constructed the sample, the greater the degree of confidence that can be attached to the cost allocation. From your point of view as operating department heads, it is important that you feel that charges received from the print room, based upon sample information, do not, in the long run, give an unfair charge to your department in comparison to what would have derived from the current actual cost system. You must appreciate, however, that in the short run a charge may be received for a period in which your department made no use at all of the print room.

Abbreviated illustration (Sample 2,000 orders in one week)

Order cost	Operating department		Value		
	A	B	A £	B £	
£50	40	10	2,000	500	
£40	50	30	2,000	1,200	
£20	50	70	1,000	1,400	
£10	50	200	500	2,000	
£4	900	600	3,600	2,400	
	1,090	910	9,100	7,500	16,600

∴   Until a new sample indicates a change in the work pattern, costs should be split between A and B on a 91/75 basis, or on a 51/58 basis if the first two cost categories are specifically charged.

(d)   At present three accounting clerks are fully occupied in calculating and allocating the actual cost of each order. The future task of costing only major jobs and of taking updated samples from time to time should be handled without difficulty by one person only, leaving him with spare time to assist in other areas of the accounts department.

The proposal should therefore save the cost of at least two people.

12 Behavioural aspects of planning and performance appraisal

INTRODUCTION

The questions exemplified in earlier chapters on budgetary control, standard costing and performance evaluation have been concerned primarily with the mechanics of the systems involved, such as the procedures for setting targets and the calculation of variances.

Every planning and control system, however, has an impact on the behaviour of the people who operate it or are affected by it. The reactions of these people, and the ways in which they may be directed towards the financial benefit of the enterprise as a whole, are the subjects of frequent questions in management accounting examinations.

Five fundamental topics provide the key to answers to such questions. They are:

- the need for 'goal congruence' between the manager and the entity as a whole;
- the need to 'motivate' managers in a way that is consistent with the achievement of the objectives of the entity;
- 'participation' or involvement as a means of achieving goal congruence;
- the importance of good 'communications' between all levels of management;
- the 'sub-optimisation' of the resources of the entity that will occur if the objectives of a sub-system are pursued to the detriment of the overall system goals.

The four questions in this chapter illustrate the relevance of these concepts to particular situations.

STUDY REQUIREMENTS

Management participation in budget preparation — involvement and motivation
Behavioural and organisational aspects of management control

QUESTIONS

1   'Budgeting is too often looked upon from a purely mechanistic viewpoint. The human factors in budgeting are more important than the accounting techniques. The success of a budgetary system depends upon its acceptance by the company members who are affected by the budgets.'

Discuss the validity of the above statement from the viewpoint of both the planning and the control aspects of budgeting. In the course of your discussion present at least one practical illustration to support your conclusions.   *(20 marks)*

2   Many traditional management accounting practices are criticised because they fail to include assumptions about human behaviour.

For TWO of the following areas,
(a)   budgetary control;
(b)   absorption costing;
(c)   installation of a costing and management accounting system,
discuss, with reference to practical situations, how the effects of human behaviour should be recognised in the introduction and operation of the system.
(Total 20 marks)

3   In discussing the standard setting process for use within budgetary control and/or standard costing systems, the following has been written: 'The level of standards appears to play a role in achievement motivation . . .'

(a)   Briefly distinguish between the motivational and managerial reporting objectives of both budgetary control and standard costing. Describe the extent to which these two objectives place conflicting demands on the standard of performance utilised in such systems.   *(6 marks)*

(b)   Describe three levels of efficiency which may be incorporated in the standards used in budgetary control and/or standard costing systems. Outline the main advantages and disadvantages of each of the three levels described.
(6 marks)

(c)   Discuss the advantages and disadvantages of involving employees in the standard setting process.   *(8 marks)*

(Total 20 marks)

4   One characteristic of early standard costing literature was that it rarely considered the effects of people's behaviour on the system. Today behavioural scientists are suggesting that standards need to be established in a way which will enable the legitimacy of these to be recognised.

With reference to any current research or literature in this area or your own experiences, explain the problem and discuss ways in which the management accountant can draw up standards in a way which would make them more likely to be acceptable.   *(20 marks)*

ANSWERS

1   The key section in this quotation is that 'the success of a budgetary system depends on its *acceptance* by the company members . . .'.

Within the context of a company's objectives, budgets are set for two main purposes:

(a)   to allocate resources between managers;
(b)   to measure and evaluate manager performance.

Both aspects are liable to cause critical reaction from the managers concerned.

Managers have their own personal objectives, among which are likely to be the need to demonstrate their 'success' and the need for self-fulfilment. The achievement of these personal objectives in a business environment will be linked with the exercise of responsibility. The delegation of responsibility to managers, however, is accompanied by the risk that they will use the resources entrusted to them to further their own ambitions rather than in the best interests of the organisation as a whole. Examples of this are 'budget padding' (when a manager attempts to obtain a greater share of resources than is necessary for the job he has to do — possibly by 'empire building' to enhance his own importance); and deliberately low budgeting of revenues, so that the manager will be given praise for achieving more than was budgeted.

For a budgetary system to be successful, therefore, managers must be led to see the congruence between their personal goals and those of the organisation for which they work.

A good means of achieving this is by involving managers in budget setting. By participation managers become better aware of company objectives and the need for inter-departmental cooperation; the plans produced are likely to be more realistic, and will be accepted for control purposes by the managers who assisted in their preparation; both morale and management skill will be improved.

Even the most carefully framed budget, however, will not remain valid for control purposes when circumstances change. In judging the results achieved by junior managers, their senior managers must be prepared to give praise for effective adaptation to those circumstances, and not be rigidly constrained by the original plan. Under the latter approach it is possible that the manager under criticism may react in unhelpful ways; either, for example, by spending excessive time in efforts to prove that adverse variances were some other person's responsibility, or by taking action that while improving his own reported results will prejudice the performance of other departments or of the company as a whole. This could happen, for example, when a buyer sought to avoid overspending by purchasing cheap but inferior materials.

To summarise, operating a business is a team activity. If its managers do not share a common approach to the objectives and problems of the business, no accounting techniques can do more than reflect their failure.

2   Answers to all three parts are given.

(a) *Budgetary control*
In its traditional form, budgetary control was largely a collection of
techniques; the assumption being that the people operating the system would
react in a mechanistic way to the imposition of budgets and to an analysis
of variances by cause and responsibility. This, of course, is not true, and it
has to be recognised that people's aspirations and emotions will influence the
way in which budgets are prepared and also the effectiveness of control
against them.

In introducing a system of budgetary control, therefore, it is best to
communicate to managers the objectives to be achieved; to involve them in
budget preparation; and to train them to become better managers and thus to
find personal satisfaction in the success of the organisation. This requires
good leadership, which must also be used in judging a manager's performance
against his budget. To blame a manager for failing to achieve a target under
circumstances not envisaged when the budget was set can lead only to
discontent rather than providing an impetus to new achievements.

(b) *Absorption costing*
Absorption costing is based on the progressive reapportionment of costs
through cost centres until all are identified with production centres, where
they can be absorbed into the cost of saleable products or services. Its
purpose is twofold:

–   to ensure that selling prices are fixed with full knowledge of the total
     costs that have, in some way, to be recovered;

–   during the process, to make cost centre managers aware of the costs
     that have to be incurred elsewhere in the organisation in order to
     support those activities for which they have day-by-day direct
     responsibility.

To avoid behavioural problems in the operation of this system, there are three
desirable features:

(i)   However 'fair' the basis of apportionment, costs apportioned into a
      cost centre should be reported separately from those costs incurred by
      the manager of that cost centre. Only the latter category of costs is
      'controllable' by him in the short term, and it is only in relation to such
      costs that his performance should be judged. If this is not done, a
      disproportionate part of that manager's time may be spent in disputing
      the apportioned costs rather than in running his department.

(ii) The amounts apportioned should, for control purposes, be at budgeted
      amounts. Any excess or saving compared with budget should be
      recognised as the responsibility of the manager of the department
      where the costs were incurred. This could, of course, conflict with the
      price-fixing aim of complete absorption.

(iii) At the time of setting budgets, there should be full discussion of cost apportionment proposals. This may give receiving cost centres an opportunity to challenge the level of service department costs, or at least it will ensure that every manager understands how and why the apportionments are made.

(c) *Installation of costing and management accounting system*

Any such system will process data to produce information. The value of the information will depend on the accuracy of the data introduced; and that data will be provided by people outside the accounting department — the managers at various levels who will be required to fill in forms. The success of the system will depend, therefore, on cooperation by these managers.

Cooperation will be forthcoming only if:

(i) The purpose of the system is explained to the managers, so that they are satisfied that it will help them (or their colleagues) in their work, and also that the information obtained will not be used unfairly in apportioning praise or blame.

(ii) The system is practicable, for example that it does not require excessive written input from staff who will not necessarily be highly literate, and that any coding system used is not over-complex.

(iii) Training is given in the operation of the system, and adequate time allowed for trial running before it is fully implemented.

If these requirements are not satisfied, it is possible that people will not make any particular effort to ensure the smooth running of the system, and may attempt to regress to earlier methods, either in substitution for or in parallel with the new system. Post-implementation checks can, of course, be made to prevent this, but these will never overcome resistance to a system which is not accepted or understood by those who have to operate it.

3

(a) The purposes of setting standards include the following:

(i) to establish targets for achievement by managers and operatives;
(ii) to facilitate the development of business plans;
(iii) to facilitate the reporting of variances, which can be used in appraising performance against standards.

Purpose (i), and to some extent purpose (iii), are motivational objectives. The intention is to motivate employees to improve their performance and in doing so to act in a manner that is in accordance with the firm's plans and interests. Standards set for this motivational purpose must be accepted by the employees as consistent with their own aspiration levels. This commonly means that employees must receive what they regard as adequate remuneration for achieving standards that they do not regard as excessively onerous; in other words, the 'standards' set for motivational purposes are likely to be below what can realistically be achieved.

For planning and control purposes however it is essential to have realistic standards, so that there is conflict between the standards needed for different purposes.

(b)   The three levels of efficiency which may be incorporated in standards are:

(i)   An 'ideal' level of efficiency, i.e. one that might be achieved if operatives were all highly skilled and showed a high level of application to their work at all times — on the British Standard scale their skill and effort rating would be 100. It might be postulated also that there would be no idle time and no loss of work through spoilage. To set standards on this basis would not lead to realistic planning, because such plans could never be fully achieved. It would not assist control, because variances from standard would include both variances from what might have been expected and variances between a realistic expectation and the standards actually set, and these could not be segregated.

It would not result in motivation of employees but the reverse. They would either be discouraged by their inability to meet the standards or would reject the whole control system as unrealistic.

(ii)   An 'expected' level of efficiency. This is the best basis for planning and control. The extent to which it achieves motivation will depend on the way in which remuneration is linked to performance. Employees should recognise such standards as 'fair', particularly if they have been involved in setting the standards; but if the basic time rate of pay is low, the less efficient operatives may find that they are unable to achieve the incentive payments necessary to give them an acceptable standard of living.

(iii)   A low level of efficiency ('loose standards'). The level of efficiency is less than the expected, or likely, performance. This type of standard is unsatisfactory for planning or control purposes, and while it may be highly acceptable to employees it will not provide them with any incentive to improve their performance, or for the more efficient operatives to work to the full extent of their capability.

(c)   The main advantage of allowing employees to participate in the standard-setting process stems from the fact that the resulting standards are then not entirely imposed. By involving employees their own aspiration levels can be utilised in the final standards set — either by taking their suggested levels without modification or by using them to modify the management-derived standards. The evidence of Stedry and others seems to suggest that a budget which is pitched at the aspiration level of employees is more likely to be accepted by the employees and actually to be effective in motivating them.

A second advantage is that management has the benefit of the on-the-job experience of employees, which can sometimes usefully supplement theoretical studies.

The main disadvantages are:

(i)   Employees may well be influenced more strongly by the implications of standard setting for their short-term remuneration than in longer-term improvements in efficiency and the profitability of the business.

(ii) A precedent is set, which can lead to continual disputes about new standards and the revision of existing standards.

(iii) If loose standards result from the participatory process, management control is weakened.

4   This question does not open up any new ground not already covered by the suggested answers to questions 1-3; except for the reference to 'current research or literature'. Students not familiar with the source literature would do best to avoid such a question if they can. As an illustration of the style of approach expected, the model answer published by the professional body which set the question is reproduced below with certain minor modifications:

Standard costing through its communication function and the use of feedback is a control concept. In its traditional approach standards are computed for a product and then, by identifying, collecting and accumulating the costs associated with this product as they become historic, evaluates performance through an examination of the variance between the standard which was set and actual achievement.

The procedure is based upon a number of implicit assumptions. These include: that control flows downwards; that performance can be gauged in terms of accountability; and so on. Standards are set and variances calculated more or less mechanically, and outside certain tolerance limits variances between standards and actual performance are reported to produce a filtering system which enables Management by Exception to take place. Thus we find that standard costing can easily produce a situation in which people have become treated like machines.

Research by people such as Chris Argyris and Edwin Caplan has shown a hostility and mistrust towards such systems by the people whom the systems monitor. They found that such systems may cause conflict and discontent which makes them anti-motivational. This is basically because some standards set are used to provide pressure because of the way in which the standard has been traditionally derived and 'imposed' and then eventually 'policed' from above. Because people at operational levels are rarely provided with reasons why standards have been set at their given levels this causes dissatisfaction.

In recent years, many of the traditional approaches to accounting control have been questioned by the behavioural scientists. One thesis is that because organisational and individual goals differ, the more compatible that they can be made, that is moving the organisation's and the individual's goals into congruence, the better will be the performance of both the organisation and the individual.

This can be assisted by participation in setting standards based on the fact that an individual's past history and future aspirations, together with influences of peers and group norms and the manner and relationship of his supervisor, will all affect operators' attitudes towards their targets. S Becker, an accountant, and D Green, a psychologist, say that the participation of people in the setting of goals that they have to achieve will help the people concerned to identify with their ultimate targets. Becker and Green continue that when there has been group participation in the setting of the group's goals this will lead to the group's identification with the goals and through this improved group morale, coherence, and motivation and a better group performance. In their studies Becker and Green found that the best supervisors were those who related well to the people under them, especially as far as any group planning was concerned.

Andrew Stedry brings in the view that if you can gauge a person's aspiration level then standards should be set at the level of these aspirations. He suggests that aspirations could be manipulated to help the improvement of performance because standards will have been set at a level where they are just attainable.

This is, in fact, something that the traditional view implicitly discusses in terms of tight or loose standards. Stedry continues that as organisations employ a variety of people with a variety of individual needs and goals which will all have an effect on how these people operate in an organisational setting, that because the people concerned are different and have different aspirations and abilities then ideally different standards should be set for different people. This, of course, would have obvious difficulties.

Raymond Miles and Roger Vergin say:

'While behavioural scientists have generally not translated their criticism into detailed prescriptions for the design of control systems, it is possible to abstract from their statement some conditions which they feel must be present in the organisational environment and some requirements which they believe must be met by management control systems:

— Standards must be established in such a way that they are recognised as legitimate. This requires that the method of deriving standards must be understood by those affected, and that standards must reflect the actual capabilities of the organisational process for which they are established.

— The individual organisation member should feel that he has some voice or influence in the establishment of his own performance goals. Participation of those affected in the establishment of performance objectives helps establish legitimacy of standards.

— Standards must be set in such a way that they convey 'freedom to fail'. The individual needs assurance that he will not be unfairly censured for an occasional mistake or for variations in performance which are outside his control.

— Feedback, recognised as essential in traditional control designs, must be expanded. Performance data must not only FLOW UPWARD FOR ANALYSIS BY HIGHER ECHELONS, BUT THEY MUST ALSO BE

SUMMARISED AND FED BACK TO THOSE DIRECTLY INVOLVED in the process.'

Perhaps what Miles and Vergin suggest is too much to hope for as a first step, so to start with, in the consideration of any behavioural implications in standard costing any alienation caused by poor communication should be reduced through the use of clear simple explanations given in laymen's terms to the people at operational level of what is involved. Such a step would help to mitigate some of the behavioural problems in standard costing. As a second step the incorporation of a direct costing system into the standard costing system, remembering that the latter can accommodate the former, will ensure that people are only controlled by the use of costs over which they themselves have some influence.

13　Absorption costing and marginal costing

INTRODUCTION

When we come to consider the use of cost information for decision making, from chapter 14 onwards, we shall find that the costs used are those which will be affected by the decision. Information about such 'relevant costs' will always have to be identified uniquely for each specific decision. Accountants, however, tend to systematise information requirements, and in this context they do so by attempting to identify in general terms those types of cost which are likely to vary with changes in output volume, and those which are more likely to remain 'fixed' over a defined period of time and a defined range of output volumes. Variable costs are then regarded as analagous to the economist's concept of 'marginal costs'.

If this identification is accepted, it is possible that the information value of both historical reports and profit budgets can be improved by presenting them in marginal cost form, rather than by the use of 'total costs' which incorporate the absorption of fixed costs into cost of sales and inventory values. Such presentations can be facilitated by designing the recording system as a 'marginal cost system'.

Although the differentiation between marginal and absorption costing occurs quite early in cost accounting studies, questions on the subject are still set at the management accounting level; they are typified by the four questions in this chapter.

STUDY REQUIREMENTS

Theory of marginal costing and absorption costing
Marginal costing in practice

QUESTIONS

1

(a)   Briefly describe the differences between absorption and direct (marginal or variable) costing. *(6 marks)*

(b)   Discuss the extent to which cost data are useful in the determination of pricing policy. Explain the advantages and disadvantages of presenting cost data for possible utilisation in pricing policy determination using an absorption, rather than a direct, costing basis *(14 marks)*

(Total 20 marks)

2   The following information has been extracted from the books of the My Heir Company by its proprietor concerning a new product that he put into production at the commencement of the period just completed:

Sales   10,000 units sold at £5 each
Production   15,000 units which were produced at the following cost:

	£
Direct materials	15,000
Direct labour	30,000
Variable expenses	6,000
Fixed expenses	12,000

The proprietor of the company has two sons, both of whom are studying accountancy, but at different colleges. He sends each of them a copy of the figures and asks them to produce a statement showing their calculation of the company's profit for the period and the value of its closing stock.

One of the sons, having just been taught full-cost product costing, prepares a statement following that method. The other, who has just learned all about period costing, produces his statement on that basis.

When the father receives the two statements he finds that they provide different profits and stock valuations. Therefore he returns a copy of both statements to each of his sons, asking them to make a check and to find out which one has made a mistake.

(a)   Formulate the TWO statements, presenting these in tabular form, showing the different ways that the sons are likely to have produced their statements.

(8 marks)

(b)   Explain why these two methods give different results. In your discussion, use data from the two statements to illustrate your answer as appropriate and briefly provide the arguments for and against these different approaches.

(12 marks)

(Total 20 marks)

3 Synchrodot Ltd manufactures two standard products, product 1 selling at £15 and product 2 selling at £18. A standard absorption costing system is in operation and summarised details of the unit cost standards are as follows:

STANDARD COST DATA – SUMMARY

	Product 1 £	Product 2 £
Direct material cost	2	3
Direct labour cost	1	2
Overhead (fixed and variable)	7	9
	£10	£14

The budgeted fixed factory overhead for Synchrodot Ltd is £180,000 (per quarter) for product 1 and £480,000 (per quarter) for product 2. This apportionment to product lines is achieved by using a variety of 'appropriate' bases for individual expense categories, e.g. floor space for rates, number of work-staff for supervisory salaries, etc. The fixed overhead is absorbed into production using practical capacity as the basis and any volume variance is written off (or credited) to the profit and loss account in the quarter in which it occurs. Any planned volume variance in the quarterly budgets is dealt with similarly. The practical capacity per quarter is 30,000 units for product 1 and 60,000 units for product 2.

At the March board meeting the draft budgeted income statement for the April/May/June quarter is presented for consideration. This shows the following:

BUDGETED INCOME STATEMENT FOR APRIL, MAY AND JUNE 19X1

	Product 1	Product 2
Budgeted sales quantity	30,000 units	57,000 units
Budgeted production quantity	24,000 units	60,000 units
Budgeted sales revenue	£450,000	£1,026,000
Budgeted production costs		
Direct material	£48,000	£180,000
Direct labour	24,000	120,000
Factory overhead	204,000	540,000
	£276,000	£840,000
Add:		
Budgeted finished goods		
Stock at 1 April 19X1 (8,000 units)	80,000 (3,000 units)	42,000
	£356,000	£882,000
Less:		
Budgeted finished goods		
Stock at 30 June 19X1 (2,000 units)	20,000 (6,000 units)	84,000

	Product 1	Product 2
Budgeted manufacturing cost of budgeted sales	£336,000	£798,000
Budgeted manufacturing profit	£114,000	£228,000
Budgeted administrative and selling costs (fixed)	30,000	48,000
Budgeted profit	£84,000	£180,000

The statement causes consternation at the board meeting because it seems to show that product 2 contributes much more profit than product 1 and yet this has not previously been apparent.

The sales director is perplexed and points out that the budgeted sales programme for the forthcoming quarter is identical with that accepted for the current quarter (January/February/March) and yet the budget for the current quarter shows a budgeted profit of £120,000 for each product line and the actual results seem to be in line with the budget.

The production director emphasises that identical assumptions, as to unit variable costs, selling prices and manufacturing efficiency, underlie both budgets but there has been a change in the budgeted production pattern. He produces the following table:

Budgeted production	Product 1	Product 2
January/February/March	30,000 units	52,500 units
April/May/June	24,000 units	60,000 units

He urges that the company's budgeting procedures be overhauled as he can see no reason why the quarter's profit should be £24,000 up on the previous quarter and why the net profit for product 1 should fall from £4.00 to £2.80 per unit sold, whereas for product 2 it should rise from £2.22 to £3.16.

(a) Reconstruct the company's budget for the January/February/March quarter.
(6 marks)

(b) Restate the budgets (for both quarters) using standard marginal cost as the stock valuation basis. *(8 marks)*

(c) Comment on the queries raised by the sales director and the production director and on the varying profit figures disclosed by the alternative budgets.
(8 marks)
(Total 22 marks)

4 Pattons Ltd produces a single product – the Patt. For the year commencing 1 July 19X5 it budgets to produce 5,000 Patts and sell them at £15.00 each.

The following standard cost card is drawn up for the production of one Patt on 1 July 19X5:

	£
Direct materials	
(10 kilos @ £0.50 per kilo)	5
Direct labour	
(4 hrs @ £1.00 per hour)	4
Variable overhead (See Note 1)	2
Total variable cost	11
Fixed overhead (See Note 2)	1
Total standard cost	£12

Note 1: Variable overheads are recovered on the basis of labour hours.

Note 2: Fixed overheads are recovered on the basis of kilos of material consumed.

Patts are produced using special equipment which can only be leased. The hiring rates for this machinery are 50p per unit produced, with a minimum hire charge of £3,000 per annum. As Pattons Ltd has never produced anywhere near sufficient Patts to cause this minimum hire charge to be exceeded, the minimum rental fee is classified as a fixed cost.

All materials used in the production of Patts are purchased from a single supplier who offers all his customers a discount of 20% in the form of an annual rebate on ALL purchases provided that these exceed 55,000 kilos per annum.

Based on the budget for the year direct labour will be working at full capacity. Once full capacity is exceeded overtime has to be paid to direct labour at time-and-a-half.

For budgeting purposes Pattons Ltd ignores taxation and inflation.

On 1 August 19X5 a large organisation asks Pattons Limited whether it would be prepared to produce 1,000 Patts for them at a price of £10 each. They would require these labelled as Ttaps, their brand name.

The sales manager of Pattons Ltd asks the cost department to produce cost figures to help him decide whether to accept the order. Two sets of figures are produced by the cost department, the first working from the standard cost card and the second using variable production costs. In both cases the figures show that to accept the order would cause the firm a £2,000 loss. However, the marketing director has been wanting an opening into this large organisation for some time and persuades the managing director of Pattons Ltd to let him accept the order as a loss leader, saying that he is prepared to allocate £2,000 from his advertising budget to cover the expected loss.

(a) Draw up the original budget for Pattons Ltd for the year commencing 1 July 19X5. *(3 marks)*

(b) Show how the cost department probably compiled the *two* sets of figures which indicated that acceptance of the order would cause a loss. *(6 marks)*

(c)   In the form of a table showing the company's position *both with and without* the order, exhibit how marginal costs and any contribution associated with the order would be calculated. *(4 marks)*

(d)   If any of the methods used in (b) and (c) above to calculate costs and income differ in content, explain with reference to the figures concerned why the differences occur. What principle should guide the preparation and presentation of information for decision taking? *(7 marks)*

(Total 20 marks)

ANSWERS

1

(a) The differences between direct and absorption costing concern the treatment of fixed manufacturing costs. In absorption costing the fixed manufacturing costs are considered a valid part of the cost of output produced during a period and are therefore attributed to that output. Under absorption costing, therefore, the unit cost (whether the unit is sold or is taken into inventory) contains both directly variable costs and an apportionment of total fixed costs.

Direct costing uses only directly variable costs to derive a unit cost. The fixed manufacturing costs are treated as being a cost of providing production capacity for a period and are considered a period cost rather than a cost of production produced within the period.

(b) Costs and cost structures are important factors to be considered in pricing policy but other factors are of equal or greater importance. Price per unit and quantity sold will frequently be related and knowledge of the relationship, the price elasticity of demand, will be of prime importance in the pricing decision. However, just as price and quantity sold are related so too are quantity produced, itself a function of expected sales, and total cost. Therefore if price is to be set in order to maximise or optimise profit, knowledge of cost structures and cost behaviour will be of great use in determining optimum levels of output and price per unit. Of greatest use will be cost data which allow the decision maker to observe the effect of changes in output on total cost — therefore information concerning cost structures and cost behaviour is of more use than just a figure which purports to be 'cost'.

If cost data are to be presented using absorption costing the figure produced will be a function of the overhead recovery *method* used and the assumed volume of production. At best the figure will be correct only for one level of production and, usually, a different figure of cost will be produced at any other production level. This single cost figure will fail to supply the all important information relating to the behaviour of costs at different output levels. These disadvantages severely reduce the usefulness of absorption costing data to the price setter.

Absorption costing information may have some offsetting advantages over direct costing data for price determination. Absorption costing attempts to include all manufacturing costs in the per unit figure and so no major manufacturing cost can be overlooked, this may overcome the possibility of a substantial part of total activity undertaken being priced to earn a low contribution which is insufficient, in total, to cover all fixed costs. Use of production resources with a finite capacity may have an opportunity cost as alternative use of that capacity is foregone; the use of absorption costing may be considered an imperfect attempt to show that opportunity cost and charge the use of scarce resources to units produced.

On balance, direct costing data together with information concerning fixed costs are likely to be of greater use in price setting than absorption costing data.

2 The term 'period costing' in this question is obviously equivalent to 'marginal costing', under which fixed costs are treated as a period expense rather than being absorbed into product costs.

The alternative presentations may be tabulated as follows:

Fixed overhead treatment	(i)		(ii)	
	Absorbed by product		Expensed in period	
	£	£	£	£
Sales		50,000		50,000
Costs of manufacturing goods produced				
Direct materials	15,000		15,000	
Direct labour	30,000		30,000	
Variable overhead	6,000		6,000	
Fixed overhead (to product)	12,000		—	
	63,000		51,000	
Less: Closing stock (one-third)	21,000		17,000	
Cost of sales		42,000		34,000
			Contribution:	16,000
Fixed overhead (to period)				12,000
Net profit		£8,000		£4,000

(b) The two methods give different results because under method 1 — absorption costing — £4,000 of fixed overheads are carried forward in the closing stock valuation. Under method 2 (marginal costing) all fixed overheads are written off as period costs, giving a lower figure of profit and, of course, a lower value of closing stocks.

Over the whole life of the product, when no stocks will remain unsold, the total net profit reported will be identical under both methods — it is the phasing of that total profit over reporting periods that varies.

The arguments for or against each method can be summarised as follows:

(i) Profit reporting. In favour of absorption costing it can be argued that fixed costs are necessarily incurred in producing the product, so an appropriate apportionment of them should be made to all units (whether sold or remaining unsold). Against this method it can be said that the business could report a profit merely by manufacturing for stock, regardless of the risk that future sales might be at a price lower than their total cost. In practice, of course, this point would be taken into account, and closing inventories would be reduced to net realisable value if this were lower than their cost.

In favour of marginal costing, reported profits will be seen to vary with sales, which is what managers would expect; and the figure of 'contribution' will be more helpful for management decision than a figure of net profit. In addition stock values are kept prudently low. Against the method, profits will reflect sales but not the level of production activity.

(ii) Stock valuation. Inseparable from profit reporting, and covered above.

(iii) Use of product costs for pricing. Under absorption costing, if all products are sold above their full cost the business must make a profit. Full costs provide a pricing 'floor'. The objections to absorption costing are that fixed costs will either have been absorbed on an arbitrary volume base (and may therefore be wrong under current actual circumstances) or that if period actual costs are fully absorbed, total costs will vary from period to period. In addition some products which make a contribution towards fixed costs may be priced out of the market.

Marginal costing avoids these problems, but a strong practical argument against it is that too many sales will be accepted at marginal prices and fixed costs will never be covered.

(iv) Calculation problems. Under absorption costing there is the problem of determining the activity level for the absorption of fixed overhead.

Under marginal costing there is the problem of making a reliable categorisation of costs between fixed and variable.

3   Part (a) of this question is concerned merely with the construction of a budget from data provided, and part (b) is a straightforward re-presentation of the figures on a marginal cost basis. Although the term 'standard marginal cost' is used, it has no concealed implications. No 'actual' costs are available and no variance calculations involved.

(a)   *SYNCHRODOT LTD*

Budgeted income statement for January, February and March 19X1

	Product 1	Product 2
Budgeted sales quantity	30,000 units	57,000 units
Budgeted production quantity	30,000 units	52,500 units
Budgeted sales revenue	£450,000	£1,026,000
Budgeted production costs:		
Direct material	£60,000	£157,500
Direct labour	30,000	105,000
Factory overhead	210,000	532,500
	£300,000	£795,000
Add:		
Budgeted finished goods		
Stock at 1 January 19X1 (8,000 units)	80,000 (7,500 units)	105,000
	£380,000	£900,000

Less:
Budgeted finished goods
Stock at 31 March 19X1 (8,000 units) 80,000 (3,000 units) 42,000

Budgeted manufacturing cost of budgeted sales	£300,000		£858,000
Budgeted manufacturing profit	£150,000		£168,000
Budgeted administrative and selling costs (fixed)	30,000		48,000
Budgeted profit	£120,000		£120,000

(b)   *SYNCHRODOT LTD*

Budgeted income statements for the two quarters to 30 June 19X1

	January/February/March		April/May/June	
	Product 1	Product 2	Product 3	Product 4
Budgeted sales quantity	30,000 units	57,000 units	30,000 units	57,000 units
Budgeted production quantity	30,000 units	52,500 units	24,000 units	60,000 units
Budgeted sales revenue	£450,000	£1,026,000	£450,000	£1,026,000
Budgeted production costs:				
Direct material	£60,000	£157,500	£48,000	£180,000
Direct labour	30,000	105,000	24,000	120,000
Factory overhead	210,000	532,500	204,000	540,000
	£300,000	£795,000	£276,000	£840,000
Add:				
Budgeted opening finished goods stock	32,000	45,000	32,000	18,000
	£332,000	£840,000	£308,000	£858,000
Less:				
Budgeted closing finished goods stock	32,000	18,000	8,000	36,000
Budgeted manufacturing cost of budgeted sales	£300,000	£822,000	£300,000	£822,000
Budgeted manufacturing profit	£150,000	£204,000	£150,000	£204,000
Budgeted administrative and selling costs (fixed)	30,000	48,000	30,000	48,000
Budgeted profit	£120,000	£156,000	£120,000	£156,000

(c)   The sales director, looking at the absorption costing statements, queries why, with equal sales in each quarter, the reported profits should be different. The answer lies in the fact that production volumes were not the same as sales volumes and that fixed overheads were apportioned over production (not sales) units.

The position is as follows:

| | January – March | | April – June | |
	Product 1	Product 2	Product 1	Product 2
Budgeted sales	30,000	57,000	30,000	57,000
Budgeted production	30,000	52,500	24,000	60,000
Units added to (or taken from) stock	–	(4,500)	(6,000)	3,000

For product 1 the fixed overheads appear to be absorbed at the rate of £6 per unit; so whereas the reported profit for January/March is £120,000, that for April/June is lower by 6,000 units @ £6 = £36,000, i.e. £84,000.

For product 2 the fixed overheads are absorbed at the rate of £8 per unit. In January/March 4,500 units are taken from stock, but in April/June 3,000 units are added to stock. The budgeted profit for the second quarter will therefore be 7,500 @ £8 = £60,000 higher than that for the first quarter.

The production director is looking at the net adjustment of £60,000 – 36,000 = £24,000 explained above, and, like the sales director, has assumed that it ought to be related to units sold – not, as is the case, units produced. The changes in profit per unit sold derive from these attributions of fixed overheads to stock changes. The production director's understanding might be helped by an explanation of the difference between marginal contribution and net profit.

4

(a)

PATTONS LTD
Budget for the year commencing 1 July 19X5
(for 5,000 units)

	£	£
Sales (5,000 units @ £15)		75,000
Costs:		
Direct materials (50,000 kilos @ £0.50)	25,000	
Direct labour (20,000 hrs @ £1.00)	20,000	
Variable overheads	10,000	
Total variable costs		55,000
Contribution		20,000
Fixed overheads		5,000
Budgeted net profit		£15,000

(b) The cost clerk probably used the following calculations to indicate that the special order would cause a loss of £2,000:

(i) *Using the standard cost card figures* £

		£
Sales (1,000 @ £10 each)		10,000
Less: Total standard costs (1,000 @ £12 each)	12,000	
Net loss		£(2,000)

(ii) *Using the accountant's variable costs*

	£	£
Sales (1,000 @ £10 each)		10,000
Costs:		
Direct materials (1,000 @ £5.00 *less* 20%)	4,000	
Direct labour (1,000 @ £4.00 per hour +50%)	6,000	
Variable overheads (1,000 @ £2)	2,000	
Total variable costs		12,000
Net loss		£(2,000)

(c) The question here asks for 'marginal costs' in the economist's sense, that is the incremental costs between one position and another.

	Total		
	with order	without order	Marginal difference
	£	£	£
Sales	85,000	75,000	10,000
Costs:			
Direct materials	24,000	25,000	(1,000)
Direct labour	26,000	20,000	6,000
Variable overheads	12,000	10,000	2,000
Contribution	23,000	20,000	3,000
Fixed overheads	5,000	5,000	—
Net profit	18,000	15,000	3,000

(d) Using the approach of the economist, where the incremental revenues and costs are compared it can be seen that the firm will benefit quantitatively by £3,000 if it accepts the order in addition to any qualitative benefits expected by the marketing director.

The approaches of the accountant's variable costs and the economist's marginal costs can be reconciled as follows:

	£
Contribution using the economist's marginal costs	3,000
Less: Rebate on budgeted purchases (20% of £25,000)	5,000
Net loss using the accountant's variable costs	2,000

From the results obtained in the example the variable costs associated with producing the Ttaps are not the same as the marginal costs because of the 'ripple' influences of the increased 'marginal' benefits arising from purchasing larger quantities of materials. Thus the economist examines the effect of changing costs as a whole over the complete production whereas the cost department has considered only the variable costs of the order concerned.

For decision taking the principle to be followed is to compare the additional costs and benefits of a proposed course of action. This renders irrelevant the ways in which an accountant may classify items into fixed and variable, direct and indirect, and so on. It is the ultimate effect of current decisions on future cash flows which should be the overriding consideration.

14   Contribution analysis

INTRODUCTION

It would be most unusual to find an examination paper that did not include a question on the use of cost information for decision making, mainly because this is a major element in the management accountant's role, but also because the subject offers great scope for numerical questions.

These cover a wide range of complexity, and have therefore been classified under five subject headings which are dealt with in chapters 14-18.

The present chapter is concerned with relatively simple questions on contribution and break-even analysis under conditions of certainty.

STUDY REQUIREMENTS

Cost information for decision taking under certainty
Relevant costs
Contribution related to limiting factors
Break-even analysis; profit graphs; margin of safety

QUESTIONS

1   You have recently been appointed financial controller to Burgundy Ltd, a company selling a single product in three sales territories. The profit and loss account for the year ending 31 December 19X2 is as follows:

	Total £	Territory A £	B £	C £
Sales (100,000 units @ £11)	1,100,000	550,000	330,000	220,000
Cost of goods sold, including £100,000 of fixed factory overhead	500,000	250,000	150,000	100,000
Gross margin	600,000	300,000	180,000	120,000
Distribution costs:				
Delivery	68,000	34,000	20,000	13,600
Packing materials	50,000	25,000	15,000	10,000
Packing labour	50,000	25,000	15,000	10,000
	168,000	84,000	50,400	33,600
Selling expenses:				
Salesmen's salaries	50,000	50,000		
Salesmen's commissions	26,400		26,400	
Agents' commissions	11,000			11,000
Sales director's salary	30,000	15,000	9,000	6,000
Advertising, local	80,000	40,000	24,000	16,000
Advertising, national	100,000	50,000	30,000	20,000
	297,400	155,000	89,400	53,000
Total marketing costs	465,400	239,000	139,800	86,600
Administration expenses:				
Variable	50,000	25,000	15,000	10,000
Fixed	100,000	50,000	30,000	20,000
Total administration expenses	150,000	75,000	45,000	30,000
Total expenses	615,400	314,000	184,800	116,600
Operating profit/(loss)	(15,400)	(14,000)	(4,800)	3,400

Territory A contains the company's only factory and central headquarters. This district employs five salaried salesmen.

Territory B is 200 to 400 miles from the factory. The district employs three salesmen on a commission basis and advertises weekly locally.

Territory C is 400 to 600 miles from the factory. The district employs three manufacturers' agents. Local advertising costs are split fifty-fifty between the agents and the company. Cost per unit of advertising space is the same as in Territory A.

The following variable unit costs have been computed:

Delivery per unit	50p, 70p, £1.10 for Territories A, B and C respectively
Packing materials per unit	50p
Packing labour per unit	50p
Administrative expenses	£2 per sales order

Territory A had 17,000 orders, Territory B 6,000 and Territory C 2,000. Local advertising costs were £60,000, £15,000 and £5,000 for Territories A, B and C respectively.

The sales director has heard the 'contribution' approach described at a recent sales convention and is keen to assess the performance of each territory using this method.

(a) Redraft the profit and loss account for 19X2 along contribution lines, showing the profit controllable by each area sales manager. The sales director has agreed that it would not be equitable to allocate fixed manufacturing overhead, national advertising and fixed administration expenses.

(16 marks)

(b) (i) The sales director informs you that a board meeting is to be held next week to discuss the future of Territory A in view of its continuing reported losses. He asks you to prepare a summary of the courses of action most likely to improve profit, which can be used as the basis of discussions. *(6 marks)*

(ii) The salesmen in Territory B have suggested a saturation campaign of local newspaper advertising to cost £30,000. How much must the sales volume in Territory B increase to justify such an additional investment?
(3 marks)

(Total 25 marks)

2   As the first management accountant employed by a manufacturer of power tools you have been asked to supply financial results by product line to help in marketing decision making.

The following account was produced for the year ended 30 September 19X1:

	£000	£000
Sales		1,200
Cost of goods sold:		
Materials	500	
Wages	300	
Production expenses	150	
Marketing costs	100	
		1,050
Net profit		150

A statistical analysis of the figures shows the following variable element in the costs:

	%
Materials	90
Wages	80
Production expenses	60
Marketing costs	70

Below is given, as percentages, the apportionment of the sales and the variable elements of the costs among the five products manufactured.

	Product					Total
	A	B	C	D	E	
Sales	30	15	7	28	20	100
Materials	40	20	10	20	10	100
Wages	15	25	10	25	25	100
Production expenses	30	10	10	30	20	100
Marketing costs	10	30	20	30	10	100

From the information given:

(a) (i) Prepare a statement for the year showing contribution by products.

    (ii) Comment on these contributions.

(b) Calculate the following:

    (i) the break-even sales level;

    (ii) the order of sales preference for additional orders to maximise contribution as a percentage of sales;

    (iii) a revised mix of the £1,200,000 sales to maximise contribution assuming that existing sales by products can only be varied 10% either up or down;

    (iv) a product mix to maximise contribution if manpower availability were reduced by 10% but the product mix could be varied by up to 20%;

(v) the percentage commission which could be offered to an overseas agent on an order of £30,000 worth each of products A, C and E and obtain a 20% contribution on the total sales value.

(30 marks)

3 The Kerkham company manufactures agricultural machinery and is preparing its budget for the year 19X6. An initial review shows that it will not be possible to manufacture all requirements for components A, B, C and D because the normal metal pressing capacity of 20,000 hours would be exceeded.

The company can choose between the alternative courses of action given below to obtain the products in excess of normal production capacity:

(i)   to buy entirely from outside suppliers;
(ii) to buy from outside suppliers and/or use a partial second shift.

The data given below are for the year 19X6:

STANDARD PRODUCTION COST PER UNIT

Component	A £	B £	C £	D £
Variable costs:				
Direct materials	18.50	13.50	12.50	22.00
Direct wages	5.00	4.00	11.00	20.00
Direct expense	5.00	10.00	5.00	30.00
Fixed overhead	2.50	2.00	5.50	10.00
Total production cost	£31.00	£29.50	£34.00	£82.00
Requirements, in units	2,000	3,500	1,500	2,800

Direct expenses relate to the use of the metal presses which cost £5 per machine hour to operate.

Fixed overhead is absorbed as a percentage of direct wages.

Quotations obtained from outside suppliers indicate a willingness to manufacture all or any part of the total requirements at the following prices, each delivered to the factory:

Component	£
A	30.00
B	29.50
C	26.00
D	84.00

Second shift operations would increase direct wages costs by 25% over the normal shift, and fixed overhead by £250 for each 1,000 (or part thereof) second shift hours worked.

Using the information given above and showing your supporting calculations, state:

(a) Which components, and in what quantities, should be manufactured in the 20,000 hours of press time available.

(b) Whether it would be profitable to make any of the balance of components required on a second shift instead of buying them from outside suppliers.

(25 marks)

4   Explain why some figures which are validly incorporated into routine management accounting statements reporting on the efficiency or profitability of a department or product may not be relevant for decision-making purposes concerning those same departments or products.

Outline the relevant costs for decision making purposes.   *(20 marks)*

5   'A break-even chart must be interpreted in the light of the limitations of its underlying assumptions . . .' (From *Cost Accounting: a managerial emphasis* by C. T. Horngren)

(a) Discuss the extent to which the above statement is valid and both describe and briefly appraise the reasons for FIVE of the most important underlying assumptions of break-even analysis.   *(14 marks)*

(b) For any THREE of the underlying assumptions provided in answer to (a) above, give an example of circumstances in which that assumption is violated. Indicate the nature of the violation and the extent to which the break-even chart can be adapted to allow for this violation.   *(6 marks)*

(Total 20 marks)

6   The accountant's approach to cost-volume-profit analysis has been criticised in that, among other matters, it does not deal with the following:

(a) situations where sales volume differs radically from production volume;

(b) situations where the sales revenue and the total cost functions are markedly non-linear;

(c) changes in product mix;

(d) risk and uncertainty.

Explain these objections to the accountant's conventional cost-volume-profit model and suggest how they can be overcome or ameliorated.

(17 marks)

ANSWERS

1

(a)

PROFIT AND LOSS ACCOUNT FOR THE YEAR ENDING 31 DECEMBER 19X2

	Total £000	A £000	B £000	C £000
Sales	1,100	550	330	220
Variable cost of goods sold (£4 per unit)	400	200	120	80
Variable packing costs:				
Materials (50p per unit)	50	25	15	10
Labour (50p per unit)	50	25	15	10
Variable distribution costs (50p, 70p, £1.10)	68	25	21	22
Variable marketing costs:				
Salesmen's commission	26.4	–	26.4	–
Agents commission	11	–	–	11
Variable administration expenses (£2 per order)	50	34	12	4
Total variable costs	655.4	309	209.4	137
Contribution	444.6	241	120.6	83
Fixed controllable costs:				
Salesmen's salaries	50	50	–	–
Advertising, local	80	60	15	5
	130	110	15	5
Profit controllable by area manager	314.6	131	105.6	78
Fixed costs controllable by others:				
Manufacturing	100			
Advertising, national	100			
Sales director's salary	30			
Administration	100			
Operating loss	£(15.4)			

(b) (i) Territory A should not be closed down, as it is making a positive contribution to common fixed costs.

Among the items that should be considered at the board meeting are:

    —   putting Territory A salesmen on commission instead of salary; Territory B produced the same sales per man as the five men in

A, at a far lower cost and with much less local advertising;

— experimenting with the effect of national versus local advertising;

— increasing the number of agents or local advertising in Territory C;

— increasing commission rates;

— a review of common costs to assess if any are avoidable;

— an attempt to reduce variable administrative costs and boost sales per order.

(ii) Assuming the average size of an order is unchanged, the minimum sales increase needed to recoup the outlay is:

$$\frac{\text{Advertising expenditure}}{\text{Contribution per unit}} = \frac{£30,000}{£4.02 \text{ (W)}} = 7,463 \text{ units}$$

If smaller orders resulted, more units would have to be sold.

(W) Contribution per unit sold in Territory B $= \dfrac{£120,600}{30,000} = £4.02$

2

(a) (i)

ANALYSIS OF OVERALL PERFORMANCE

	£000	£000
Sales		1,200
Variable cost of goods sold:		
Materials	450	
Wages	240	
Production expenses	90	
Marketing costs	70	
		850
Contribution		350
Fixed costs		200
Net profit		150

PRODUCT LINE ANALYSIS

	A	B	C	D	E	Total
Sales	360	180	84	336	240	1,200
Material	180	90	45	90	45	450
Wages	36	60	24	60	60	240
Production expenses	27	9	9	27	18	90
Marketing costs	7	21	14	21	7	70
	250	180	92	198	130	850
Contribution	110	—	(8)	138	110	350

(a) (ii) Three of the products (A, D and E) make a contribution towards fixed costs and profit. The other two do not. For those products making a contribution the contribution/sales percentages are:

A	30.56%
D	41.07%
E	45.83%

In making decisions about the future of the various products, at least three factors would have to be considered.

— The stage in the product life. It is possible, for example, that B and C are relatively new products which have not yet achieved full profitability, or that they are reaching the end of their lives, with demand falling.

— Any interrelationship between the products. It is possible that sales of the more profitable products can be made only when a full product range (including products B and C) is offered.

— Whether there are any significant limiting factors on the production or sales that can be achieved. If so the amount of contribution per unit of the limiting factor becomes important.

(b) (i) Assuming a constant mix of sales, average contribution/sales ratio is 350/1,200 − 29.16%.

The break-even sales level is therefore 200/29.16% = £685,714.

(ii) The order of preference, based on contribution/sales ratios, is E, D, A, B, C.

(iii) The mix of sales to maximise contribution, assuming variations from present level of ± 10%, is:

		£000 Sales	£000 Contribution
E	240 + 10%	264	121
D	336 + 10%	369.6	151.8
C	84 − 10%	75.6	(7.2)
B	180 − 10%	162	—
A	Balance = (360 − 8.67%)	328.8	100.5
		1,200	366.1

(iv) Preliminary calculation — contribution per £1 wages (physical manpower not given)

A	110/36	=	306%
B	0/60	=	0
C	(8)/24	=	(33.3%)
D	138/60	=	230%
E	110/60	=	183%

Product mix to maximise contribution under conditions stated:

		£000 Wages	£000 Sales	£000 Contributions
A	360 + 20%	43.2	432	132
C	84 − 20%	19.2	67.2	(6.4)
B	180 − 20%	48.0	144	−
E	240 − 20%	48.0	192	88
D	Balance (336 − 4%)	57.6	322.6	132.5
		216.0	1157.8	346.1

(v)

	A	C	E	
Sales	30	30	30	90
C/sales	30.56%	(9.52%)	45.83%	
	= 9.17	(2.86)	13.75	20.06

20% Contribution   18.00

Available for commission   2.06

% commission $\dfrac{2.06}{90}$ = 2.29%

3

(a)

	A	B	C	D
Machine hours per unit	1	2	1	6
	£	£	£	£
Variable cost per machine hour	28.50	13.75	28.50	12.00
Buying price per machine hour	30.00	14.75	26.00	14.00
Excess of outside price	1.50	1.00	(2.50)	2.00

To minimise costs the company should manufacture those with the greatest excess of buying price over the variable cost, i.e.:

Manufacture	2,800 units of D taking 16,800 machine hours
and	2,000 units of A taking 2,000 machine hours
and	600 units of B taking the remaining 1,200 machine hours

(b) The choice of buying or using a second shift will depend upon the marginal costs involved in the production. It will never be profitable to manufacture C as the outside price is below marginal cost even before the shift premium. For B, however, we must calculate the marginal costs.

Manufacture	1,000	900
	£	£
Variable cost per unit — basic	27.50	27.50
— shift premium	1.00	1.00
	28.50	28.50
Variable costs	28,500	25,650
Extra fixed costs	500	500
	29,000	26,150
Outside price	29,500	26,550

It is therefore beneficial to manufacture all the remaining units of B on second shift, i.e. 2,900 units.

4 Routinely produced management accounting statements are usually based on input data which are to a large extent objectively determined using historic cost, and these data are then manipulated for presentation within the conventions of management accounting. The advantages of relying on this objectively determined input include the fact that it is generally easy to obtain such data and they are consistent with those used in the financial statutory accounts produced under the historic cost accounting conventions, hence the same data bank of information can be used for both financial and maangement accounts, with advantages of consistency and a saving of system operating costs. Actual input costs thus assist in showing what the firm, or a part of the firm, has actually achieved during a period and are therefore quite useful as general purpose information.

For decision-making purposes information is required which is relevant to the particular decision under consideration. In all decisions there must be a 'status quo' (or position the decision-making entity will be in if no decision is taken) and an alternative position (or several positions) which will result as a direct consequence of the decision to be taken. Relevant information is that which relates to the differences between the basic, or status quo, outcome and the others. Therefore the decision should be appraised by making a comparison of the financial effects between the two sets of outcomes. Information concerning events which are common to all outcome possibilities may be ignored, as such events are not decision variables. The decision variables are not to be measured by the historic costs utilised in regular management accounting reports as the historic costs relate to past transactions and are not therefore decision variables for the purpose of any current decision. Past transactions are common to all future or current actions and as such are events common to all outcomes; hence they may be ignored. Relevant information concerns future incremental (or avoidable) costs and revenues (as these can be altered by the current decision) as well as current opportunity values of existing assets.

Relevant costs for decision-making purposes are:

(i) *Opportunity costs of existing assets or past expenditure*

Assets currently held as a result of past expenditure bestow benefits to the owner. It is not the past expenditure which bestows the benefits but the current ownership of the asset, and the benefits can be measured only by considering the uses to which the asset can be put. Hence for decision-making purposes the historic cost is irrelevant as it is the measurement of a past transaction and does not measure the current benefit derivable from the asset. If a current asset is used for one purpose its alternative use will be foregone; for the purposes of deciding whether it is worthwhile to forego this alternative use the benefits which would be derived from that use should be attributed to the asset as its opportunity cost. Opportunity cost is therefore the net revenue which is avoidable as a result of the decision.

(ii) *Incremental, attributable future costs*

Future costs may be relevant but the essential point is that the future costs be avoidable as a result of the decision. If accepting a decision incurs (or saves) a cost and rejecting the decision does not incur (or save) that cost, the cost is a decision variable. For example, apportioned fixed overhead is not relevant but actual changes in total fixed overhead are relevant to the decision which would cause the change.

These are the types of cost relevant for decision making but the actual application of the concepts depends upon the precise decision to be made. There is no such thing as *the* costs for decision purposes which can be applied to an asset or a regular input; there are instead a variety of relevant costs depending upon the nature of the decision to be made.

5

(a) Among the important underlying assumptions of break-even analysis are:

(i) All costs may be classified into fixed and variable elements. This implies that volume is the only cause of cost fluctuation. If it were admitted that factors other than volume were determinants of total costs the total cost curve could not be accurately represented in a two-dimensional form on a break-even chart.

(ii) Fixed costs remain constant over the relevant range of volumes and variable costs per unit are stable over that range. This assumption allows the relationship between total costs and volume to be stated as a simple linear relationship of the form

$$TC = FC + (VC \times volume)$$

where TC = total costs,
        FC = fixed costs,
        VC = variable costs,
        per unit of volume.

Should this assumption be relaxed 'fixed' costs may alter and become 'stepped' — in fact this is easily incorporated into the chart — or the variable cost line may become a curve.

(iii) Selling prices per unit are known and stable over the entire relevant range. As with assumptions (i) and (ii) above for costs this assumption results in total revenues being a linear function of volume. Without this assumption a curvilinear total revenue function could result.

(iv) Either only one product is being considered or the mix of products is known and constant. If one product is being considered sales revenues and costs may be expressed as a function of the volume of that product. If several products are being considered the volume of activity (and hence the total cost) is incapable of a simple description unless the mix of products is known.

(v) A common activity base can be used to describe both sales and production volume. As both sales revenues and total costs are considered simple linear functions of volume it is necessary to express volume for both sales and costs in the same form. For a single product chart that volume may be units or sales revenues; for a multi-product chart the volume will usually be sales revenues.

(vi) There is to be no change in the stock levels. If a change in stock levels is envisaged the costs incurred will relate to a production volume different from sales.

The statement quoted in the question is therefore valid, but says no more than that a break-even chart, like any other financial model, can be only a generalised reflection of reality, and should not be relied on to solve problems which involve some change in the underlying assumptions, or in this instance some extension of the range of volumes over which the data incorporated into the model were observed.

(b) Examples of circumstances in which the underlying assumptions are violated include:

(i) *Variable costs per unit remain stable over the entire relevant range.* This assumption is violated where larger quantities can be obtained at a lower unit cost than smaller quantities — in fact the quantity discounts may cause the cost curve to be discontinuous; if for example orders of less than 2,000 units cost £3 per unit and for orders of 2,000 units and over the unit price *for the whole order* is £2.80 the result will be a cost of £5,700 for 1,900 units but a cost of only £5,600 for 2,000 units. Similarly if there is likely to be a change in productivity, due perhaps to the learning curve, variable costs will alter. These violations result in the simple linear relationship not holding. However, over a restricted range, or several restricted ranges, a linear relationship, or a series of linear relationships, may be a close approximation to reality.

(ii) *Selling price is stable.* The volume of sales may well be a function of selling price and consideration may be given to altering the selling price in order to take advantage of the elasticity of demand. The firm may be offering quantity discounts to encourage high sales. In all these cases total sales revenue is not a linear function of volume, but again a series of linear relationships may be sufficient to approximate the true relationship for the purpose of providing useful information.

(iii) *Sales mix is known.* Most firms have a range of products and the precise mix of sales will not usually be exactly known. A number of factors including fashion, weather and advertising may alter the actual mix of sales from that expected. To include this on a break-even chart will require a range of total cost curves corresponding to the cost functions of each sales mix. This will then give a break-even range rather than a point.

6 This question is very similar to question 5, but relates to the underlying 'cost-volume-profit model' rather than to the break-even chart that is used to illustrate it. Much of the following solution is taken from the model answer published by the examining body concerned, in order to show the style of approach expected.

The conventional form of cost-volume-profit analysis involves the use of a simple linear profit model

$$\pi = (P - V)X - F$$

where π = period profit,
   P = unit selling price,
   V = variable cost per unit sold,
   X = number of units sold,
and F = period fixed cost.

The model is often displayed graphically as a break-even chart.

(a) Since the simple C-V-P model has only one independent variable (X) it can only be used when profit is solely dependent on the entity's sales level (or when it can be adequately approximated in this way). When an entity's sales volume differs radically from its production volume, the cost of goods sold may not be solely a function of sales and it follows that profit in such cases cannot be determined uniquely from a knowledge of the sales volume. When sales volume differs from production volume, the stock valuation method used determines the applicability of the conventional form of C-V-P analysis. If finished goods stock is valued at marginal manufacturing cost (assuming that this is constant), profit continues to be a linear function of sales volume and conventional C-V-P analysis applies. If, however, finished goods stock is valued using one of the versions of full cost, the cost of goods sold (and hence profit) depends not only on the volume sold but also on the volume produced. In such cases profit is no longer a function of a single variable (sales) but of two independent variables (sales and production). This makes it impossible to use the conventional break-even diagram (unless sales volume or production volume is held constant). In this sense conventional C-V-P analysis cannot be used but it is possible to examine the cost-volume-profit relationship in such cases.

(b) The accountant's traditional approach to C-V-P analysis makes use of a linear profit model, but in many cases this will not be adequate, for example under conditions of price-elastic demand, or when the law of diminishing returns affects the total cost function. It is possible to adjust the accounting model to take account of known departures from linear functions, in which case the related break-even chart might take a form similar to the following illustration:

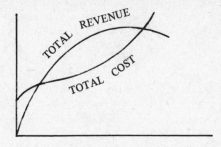

In some cases, however, there may be practical difficulties in constructing the appropriate formulae.

An alternative approach, which is particularly applicable when the firm's selling prices are fixed, involves an emphasis on the 'relevant range'. Although the linear break-even chart appears to describe cost and revenue behaviour for all levels of activity from zero output up to full capacity, it is now generally recognised that any given chart is applicable for a much more restricted range of activity levels. Within this relevant range it is quite possible that a straight line break-even chart is an adequate approximation to a more theoretically correct non-linear model.

(c) Changes in product mix cause difficulties to the graphical form of C-V-P analysis in that (unless all product prices are determined by a uniform mark-up percentage on variable cost) profit will depend not only on sales volume but also on sales mix. This means that (for linear cost and revenue functions) the profit function has the form:

$$\pi = (P_1 - V_1)X_1 + (P_2 - V_2)X_2 + (P_3 - V_3)X_3 + \ldots + (P_n - V_n)X_n - F$$

where the subscripts relate to the individual product lines and there are n such lines. A break-even chart cannot be drawn for such a situation unless a constant product mix is assumed; but it is possible to carry out the underlying analysis using an algebraic model.

(d) The conventional form of analysis does not incorporate considerations of risk and uncertainty.

Sensitivity analysis can be used to calculate the effects of variations in one key variable at a time. If more than one variable is considered to be stochastic, subjective estimates will be required of the probabilities of variation in the elements in the model, and can be combined in a computerised simulation model to show the overall probability of various profit levels.

215

15   Opportunity costs

INTRODUCTION

Many cost-based decisions involve the diversion of facilities from alternative uses, in which cases the potential benefit from opportunities foregone forms part of the cost of the course of action adopted.

This concept of an 'opportunity cost' is easy to appreciate in theory, but is often difficult to apply in practice.

The subject occurs frequently in examination questions, so six examples have been provided in this chapter.

STUDY REQUIREMENTS

Relevant costs for decision making
Opportunity cost

1   Itervero Ltd, a small engineering company, operates a job order costing system. It has been invited to tender for a comparatively large job which is outside the range of its normal activities and, since there is surplus capacity, the management are keen to quote as low a price as possible. It is decided that the opportunity should be treated in isolation without any regard to the possibility of its leading to further work of a similar nature (although such a possibility does exist). A low price will not have any repercussions on Itervero's regular work.

The estimating department has spent 100 hours on work in connection with the quotation and it has incurred travelling expense of £550 on a visit to the prospective customer's factory overseas. The following cost estimate has been prepared on the basis of their study:

INQUIRY 205H/81

Cost estimate

	£
Direct material and components:	
2,000 units of A at £25 per unit	50,000
200 units of B at £10 per unit	2,000
Other material and components to be bought in (specified)	12,500
	64,500
Direct labour:	
700 hours of skilled labour at £3.50 per hour	2,450
1,500 hours of unskilled labour at £2 per hour	3,000
Overhead:	
Department P – 200 hours at £25 per hour	5,000
Department Q – 400 hours at £20 per hour	8,000
Estimating department:	
100 hours at £5 per hour	500
Travelling expenses	550
Planning department:	
300 hours at £5 per hour	1,500
	85,000

The following information has been brought together:

Material A. This is a regular stock item. The stock holding is more than sufficient for this job. The material currently held has an average cost of £25 per unit but the current replacement cost is £20 per unit.

Material B. A stock of 4,000 units of B is currently held in the stores. This material is slow moving and the stock is the residue of a batch bought seven years ago at a cost of £10 per unit. B currently costs £24 per unit but the resale value is only £18 per unit. A foreman has pointed out that B could be used as a substitute for another type of regularly used raw material which costs £20 per unit.

Direct labour. The workforce is paid on a time basis. The company has adopted a 'no redundancy' policy which means that skilled workers are frequently moved to jobs which do not make proper use of their skills. The wages included in the cost estimate are for the mix of labour which the job ideally requires. It seems likely, if the job is obtained, that most of the 2,200 hours of direct labour will be performed by skilled staff receiving £3.50 per hour.

Overhead – Department P. Department P is the one department of Itervero Ltd that is working at full capacity. The department is treated as a profit centre and it uses a transfer price of £25 per hour for charging out its processing time to other departments. This charge is calculated as follows:

	£
Estimated variable cost per machine hour	10
Fixed departmental overhead	8
Departmental profit	7
	£25

Department P's facilities are frequently hired out to other firms and a charge of £30 per hour is made. There is a steady demand from outside customers for the use of these facilities.

Overhead – Department Q. Department Q uses a transfer price of £20 for charging out machine processing time to other departments. This charge is calculated as follows:

	£
Estimated variable cost per machine hour	8
Fixed departmental overhead	9
Departmental profit	3
	£20

Estimating department. The estimating department charges out its time to specific jobs using a rate of £5 per hour. The average wage rate within the department is £2.50 per hour but the higher rate is justified as being necessary to cover departmental overheads and the work done on unsuccessful quotations.

Planning department. This department also uses a charging-out rate which is intended to cover all departmental costs.

(a) Restate the cost estimate by using an opportunity cost approach. Make any assumptions that you deem to be necessary and briefly justify each of the figures that you give. *(10 marks)*

(b) Discuss the relevance of the opportunity cost approach to the situation described in the question and consider the problems which are likely to be encountered if it is used in practice. *(6 marks)*

(c) Briefly discuss the general applicability of opportunity cost in business decision making where a choice exists among alternative courses of action.
(6 marks)
(Total 22 marks)

219

2   L Johnson trades as a chandler at the Savoy Marina. His profit in this business during the year to 30 June 1981 was £12,000; Johnson also undertakes occasional contracts to build pleasure cruisers, and is considering the price at which to bid for the contract to build the Blue Blood for Mr B W Dunn, delivery to be in one year's time. He has no other contract in hand, or under consideration, for at least the next few months.

Johnson expects that if he undertakes the contract he would devote one-quarter of his time to it. To facilitate this he would employ G Harrison, an unqualified practitioner, to undertake his book-keeping and other paperwork at a cost of £2,000.

He would also have to employ on the contract one supervisor at a cost of £11,000 and two craftsmen at a cost of £8,800 each; these costs include Johnson's normal apportionment of the fixed overheads of his business at the rate of 10% of labour cost.

During spells of bad weather one of the craftsmen could be employed for the equivalent of up to three months full-time during the winter in maintenance and painting work in the chandler's business. He would use materials costing £1,000. Johnson already has two inclusive quotations from jobbing builders for his maintenance and painting work, one for £2,500 and the other for £3,500, the work to start immediately.

The equipment which would be used on the Blue Blood contract was bought nine years ago for £21,000. Depreciation has been written off on a straight-line basis, assuming a ten-year life and a scrap value of £1,000. The current replacement cost of similar new equipment is £60,000, and is expected to be £66,000 in one year's time. Johnson has recently been offered £6,000 for the equipment, and considers that in a year's time he would have little difficulty in obtaining £3,000 for it. The plant is useful to Johnson only for contract work.

In order to build the Blue Blood Johnson will need six types of material:

| Material Code | No. of units | | Price per unit (£) | | |
	In stock	Needed for contract	Purchase price of stock items	Current purchase price	Current resale price
A	100	1,000	1.00	3.00	2.00
B	1,100	1,000	2.00	0.90	1.00
C	–	100	–	6.00	–
D	100	200	4.00	3.00	2.00
E	50,000	5,000	0.18	0.20	0.25
F	1,000	3,000	0.90	2.00	1.00

Materials B and E are sold regularly in the chandler's business. Material A could be sold to a local sculptor if not used for the contract. Materials A and E can be used for other purposes such as property maintenance. Johnson has no other use for materials D and F, the stocks of which are obsolete.

The Blue Blood would be built in a yard held on a lease with four years remaining at a fixed annual rental of £5,000. It would occupy half of this yard, which is useful to Johnson only for contract work.

220

Johnson anticipates that the direct expenses of the contract, other than those noted above, would be £6,000.

Johnson has recently been offered a one-year appointment at a fee of £15,000 to manage a boat-building firm on the Isle of Wight. If he accepted the offer he would be unable to take on the contract to build Blue Blood or any other contract. He would have to employ a manager to run the chandler's business at an annual cost (including fidelity insurance) of £10,000, and would incur additional personal living costs of £2,000.

(a) Calculate the price at which Johnson should be willing to take on the contract in order to break even, based exclusively on the information given above.   *(15 marks)*

(b) Set out any further considerations which you think Johnson should take into account in setting the price at which he would tender for the contract.
                                                                (10 marks)
                                                          (Total 25 marks)

Ignore taxation.

3   Bill Davison is 55. He has been in business in Shangri-La as a merchant for over 20 years. His historic cost final accounts for 19X6-19X8 have been as follows (in thousands of roubles):

	19X6		19X7		19X8*	
Income statements						
Sales		135		170		220
Cost of sales		60		70		100
Gross profit		75		100		120
Employees' remuneration	10		15		20	
Establishment costs	20		25		30	
Depreciation of equipment	10		10		10	
		40		50		60
Net profit		35		50		60
Balance sheet on 31 December						
Equipment (net)		60		55		50
Inventory (at cost)		60		70		100
Debtors		30		40		50
		150		165		200
Creditors		30		40		50
Proprietor's capital		120		125		150

*Estimated on 30 November

At Easter 19X8, whilst visiting Copenhagen on a buying trip, Davison had a mild heart attack. He went on a world cruise for three months to convalesce, and now

221

considers himself to be fully recovered.

Last week he telephoned you, as his accountant, to make an urgent appointment. He wanted to discuss two independent offers that he has received.

First, he has been offered R200,000 for his business as from 1 January 19X9, payable in cash on that date.

Second, out of the blue, he has been offered a five-year appointment as full-time director of a welfare foundation for dependants of victims of angina, for which he has done voluntary work for many years. The post carries a fixed annual salary of R25,000. The duties would begin on 1 January 19X9 or as soon thereafter as possible. It is a condition of this appointment that the director may not hold any other executive appointment during the period of his directorship; nor may he hold a controlling stake in any business organisation.

You know that Davison has no other business interest, and that his only other substantial asset is his owner-occupied house, which is not mortgaged. He has no life assurance.

There is no income or capital taxation in Shangri-La. A price index of inventory in Davison's trade (19X2 = 100) was 200 at the end of 19X6, 240 at the end of 19X7 and is expected to be 288 at the end of 19X8.

Davison is calling to see you at 5.30pm this evening.

Set out the issues which you consider that Mr Davison should take into account in deciding how to respond to the two offers which he has received, and state as far as you are able what advice you would give him.   *(15 marks)*

4   Ziro Ltd is considering whether to manufacture a new product – Aggro – for one year. Components for the product will be manufactured in a new factory to be specially leased for the purpose at £10,000 a year. Aggros will be assembled in the existing factory, utilising the same production lines as the firm's other products. The estimated costs per Aggro are shown below:

	Component manufacture	Assembly
	£	£
Material	0.20	
Labour	0.20	0.10
Factory supplies		0.10
Variable overheads	0.30	0.30
Total direct cost	0.70	0.50
Fixed overheads (250% of direct labour)	0.50	0.25
Administrative overheads (50% of total direct cost)	0.35	0.25
Total cost	1.55	£1.00
Add: Total assembly cost	1.00	
Total cost per Aggro	£2.55	

When operating at maximum capacity, the components factory can supply sufficient parts for 24,000 Aggros per year. Surplus capacity after meeting the assembly division's requirements will be used to produce sets of Aggro components for a supermarket which will market them under a different name. The cost of such components will be identical to those produced for the assembly division's use. The supermarket is willing to pay £1 per set of components.

A market research study has suggested that only two prices for the Aggro should be considered, £3.60 and £3.10 per unit. Sales at these prices are estimated to be 15,000 and 22,000 units respectively.

20% of the fixed overheads charged to Aggros relate to the historical cost depreciation of machinery. The machines in the assembly plant do not depreciate in use.

Capacity in the assembly division is already used fully and it is estimated that one unit of an existing product, yielding £1 over and above its variable cost, will have to be sacrificed for each unit of the new product assembled.

The estimated total overhead costs of the component factory are: rent £10,000, other fixed overheads £1,000, administrative costs £5,000.

The machines needed to manufacture the components are available within the firm. They have a value of £10,000 in the firm's books and could be sold for £4,000. If retained on their existing work they will need to be replaced (at a cost of £15,000) in one year's time. If transferred to Aggro production they will have to be scrapped (proceeds nil) at the end of the year.

Advise management whether they should manufacture Aggros, and if so at what volume and price. Add a brief note on your treatment of fixed overheads.

5   The Flaxmin Pedal Car Co. Ltd has recently suffered a strike which lasted for two weeks. During that time no cars were produced. The company issued a press statement to the effect that the cost of the strike was £500,000. This figure was arrived at by the managing director who estimated that production lost was 1,000 cars, each of which could have been sold for £500 giving a total loss of turnover of £500,000.

The company's cost accountant feels that the managing director was overstating the cost of the strike and provides the following statement to support his view:

Expenses avoided:	£
Materials (£100 per car)	100,000
Production labour (£50 per car)	50,000
Depreciation of machinery	175,000
Overheads: 200% on labour	100,000
	425,000
Loss of sales revenue	500,000
Cost of strike	£ 75,000

The following additional information is available:

Depreciation of machinery is based on the conventional straight-line method of calculation. The plant manager estimates that the machinery will fall in value by £20,000 each week regardless of the level of production. In addition he feels that its value will fall by £15,000 for every 100 cars produced.

Overhead expenses are recovered at the rate of 200% on production labour. Most of the overhead expenses are unaffected by the level of production, e.g. rent, rates, maintenance, staff wages, but some, such as power and lighting, vary directly with production. The general manager estimates that the latter type of overhead expense, varying directly with the level of production, amounts to £1,000 for every 100 cars produced.

During the period of the strike the maintenance staff, whose wages are included in the fixed overhead expense, carried out a major overhaul on one of the company's machines using materials costing £1,000. This overhaul would normally have been performed by an outside contractor at a price, including materials, of £10,000.

The sales manager feels that about one half of the production lost could be made up and sold in the next month by the production labour working overtime. Labour is paid at the rate of time and one half for overtime working.

Prepare a statement clearly showing the cost to the company of the strike. State any assumptions which you make and explain any differences between your figures and those of the cost accountant. *(20 marks)*

6 The original budget for the K department of Hilton Ltd for the forthcoming year was as follows:

BUDGET FOR FORTHCOMING YEAR – K DEPARTMENT
Budgeted sales and production – 30,000 units

	Per unit of output	Total for 30,000 units
	£	£000
Sales revenue	10.0	300
Manufacturing costs:		
Material A – one litre per unit	2.0	60
Material B – one kilo per unit	1.5	45
Production labour	2.0	60
Variable overhead	1.0	30
Fixed manufacturing overheads	2.0	60
	8.5	255
Non-manufacturing costs	1.0	30
Total costs	9.5	285
Budgeted net profit for year	0.5	15

As part of Hilton's long-term strategic plan the K department was due to be closed at the end of the forthcoming year. However, rumours of the closure have resulted in the majority of K's labour force leaving the firm, forcing the abandonment of the original budget for the department.

The managing director has suggested that the department could be closed down immediately or, by employing contract labour, could be operated to produce 10,000 or 20,000 units in the year. With the exception of the foreman (see (e) below), the few remaining members of K's production labour force would then be re-deployed within the firm.

The following further information is available:

(a)   Each hour of contract labour will cost £3.00 and will produce one unit of the product. Contract labour would have to be trained at a fixed cost of £20,000.

(b)   There are 30,000 litres of material A in stock. This material has no other use and any of it not used in department K will have to disposed of. Costs of disposal will be £2,000 plus £0.50 per litre disposed of.

(c)   There are 15,000 kilos of material B in stock. If the material is not used in department K up to 10,000 kilos could be used in another department to substitute for an equivalent weight of a material which currently costs £1.8 per kilo. Material B originally cost £1.5 per kilo and its current market price (buying or selling) is £2.0 per kilo. Costs to Hilton of selling any surplus material B will amount to £1.00 per kilo sold.

(d)   Variable overheads will be 30% higher per unit produced than originally budgeted.

(e)   Included in 'Fixed manufacturing overheads' are

(i)   £6,000 salary of the departmental foreman;
(ii)   £7,000 depreciation of the machine used in the department.

If the department is closed immediately the foreman, who will otherwise retire at the end of the year, will be asked to retire early and paid £2,000 compensation.

The only machine used in the department originally cost £70,000 and could currently be sold for £43,000. This sales value will reduce to £40,000 at the end of the year and, if used for any production during the year, will decrease by a further £500 per 1,000 units produced.

(f)   All other costs included in 'Fixed manufacturing overheads' and all 'Non-manufacturing costs' are apportionments of general overheads none of which will be altered by any decision concerning the K department.

(g)   The sales manager suggests that a sales volume of 10,000 units could be achieved if the unit sales price were £9. A sales volume of 20,000 units would be achieved if the sales price per unit were reduced to £8 and an advertising campaign costing £15,000 were undertaken.

(a)   Advise Hilton Ltd of its best course of action regarding department K, presenting any data in tabular form.   *(13 marks)*

(b)   For each of the following separate circumstances show how the advice given in (a) above is altered.

    (i)   Immediate closure of department K would enable its factory space to be rented out for one year at a rental of £8,000   *(2 marks)*

    (ii) The quoted level of efficiency of the contract labour is the *average* for production of the first 5,000 units and any additional production would reflect the effects of the 90% learning curve. Show also the revised contract labour costs.   *(5 marks)*

(Total 20 marks)

Ignore taxation and the time value of money.

ANSWERS

1

(a)

INQUIRY 205H/81

Cost estimate

	£	
Direct material and components:		
2,000 units of A at £20 per unit	40,000	Since the material will be replaced the opportunity cost is the replacement cost.
200 units of B at £20 per unit	4,000	If not used on this job, it seems likely that the material would be substituted for the other material mentioned. The opportunity cost is therefore the current price of the material for which it will be substituted.
Other material and components	12,500	
	56,500	
Direct labour	—	It seems that the labour force are paid, on a time basis, whether or not they are working. If this is true and if no additional labour has to be hired, the opportunity cost is zero.
Overhead:		
Department P 200 hours @ £30	6,000	The department would lose the opportunity of charging out 200 hours at £30 per hour.
Department Q 400 hours @ £8	3,200	£8 is the incremental cost to department Q of one hour of processing time.
Estimating department	—	All the expenses listed in the original estimate are sunk costs and therefore irrelevant.
Planning department	—	It seems likely that there will be no additional costs for the planning department.
	£65,700	

(b) The opportunity cost approach is relevant to the situation described, as the conventional pricing procedures might result in a price which loses a contract which can utilise spare resources and make a positive contribution to Itervero's fixed costs. Some problems, however, can be expected with the use of the opportunity cost approach:

(i)   There may be difficulty in persuading managers of the logic of the method — particularly in view of (iii) below.

(ii) There may be difficulty in defining and evaluating the available alternatives — see section (c) below.

(iii) The conventional cost accounting system used in reporting results will not show the same amount of profit as emerged from the opportunity cost model, even if all revenues and costs are as planned. A practical approach to this problem would be to set a price based on the opportunity cost calculations, but for control purposes to restate the estimate in conventional terms (which in some cases will make it appear that the tender has been made at a 'loss').

(c) Opportunity cost arises as the value displaced by taking one course of action rather than the next best course of action. It can be argued that in order to identify the 'next best course of action' it is necessary to evaluate all possible alternatives. If this were done, and the alternatives were ranked in order of their attractiveness, this ranking would identify the solution, and there would be no need to introduce opportunity cost into the decision-making process. Two comments can be made on this argument:

(i)   In many cases, the majority of possible alternatives will be neither practicable nor desirable on policy grounds, so that there is no practical difficulty in identifying the relevant alternative.

(ii) It will often be found that the real choice is between using one set of resources in one way and another overlapping (but not identical) set of resources in another way rather than the simpler problem of a choice among the alternative uses of a common set of resources. For such problems it is claimed that opportunity cost is appropriate for valuing the resources which are not common to both alternatives. The approach can be used when there are more than two alternatives, and in such cases the non-common resources are valued by reference to their uses outside the set of alternatives which is under consideration.

2

(a) *Calculation of break-even contract price*

The list below sets out the additional costs incurred as a result of accepting the contract; the final break-even contract price is based on these relevant, or opportunity, costs.

	£
G. Harrison	2,000
Supervisor (£11,000 × 1/1.1)	10,000
Craftsmen (2 × £8,000 × 1/1.1)	16,000
Maintenance (£1,000 − £2,500)	(1,500)
Equipment (£6,000 − £3,000)	3,000
Material A (1,000 × £3)	3,000
B (1,000 × £0.90)	900
C (100 × £6)	600
D (100 × £2 + 100 × £3)	500
E (5,000 × £0.20)	1,000
F (1,000 × £1 + 2,000 × £2)	5,000
Other expenses	6,500
Johnson (£15,000 − £10,000 − £2,000)	3,000
Minimum or break-even contract price	50,000

(b) *Other considerations*

(i) *Profit.* Johnson would not be happy simply to break-even on the contract and, when setting the price, add something for profit. The amount added on would be influenced by the factors below.

(ii) *Estimates.* Most of the figures used to establish the price are stated with some certainty. Should any be subject to uncertainty, the price would need to be raised.

(iii) *Tax.* Whereas taxation was ignored in the original calculations it should be taken into account in the final consideration since some of the figures in the original estimate will have different treatments for tax purposes.

(iv) *Interest or cost of capital.* Most of the expenditure is immediate, the benefits are delayed, and there will be some interest cost of the project. The acceptance of the project may also bring forward the purchase of new capital equipment.

(v) *Competitors.* How much would a rival firm quote, what is a reasonable market rate?

(vi) *Personal.* What would Johnson do if he wasn't building Blue Blood? Would he accept the Isle of Wight appointment or would he simply take a holiday? What are the long-term prospects in the Isle of Wight?

(vii) *Customer.* How much is Mr B W Dunn prepared to pay and is he creditworthy?

Advice to Mr Davison

Options open to Davison:

— sell the business for R200,000;

— sell the business and take five year appointment;

— continue in business.

Issues influencing decision, both financial and personal:

(i) What does he want to do with his time? Now being 55, approaching the age of retirement, having suffered a heart attack, he should perhaps take things easy.

(ii) What value does he put on this time? Is the remuneration from the business worth the effort put into it particularly compared with what could be earned from the R200,000 for which it could be sold? Likewise how much effort is involved with the welfare foundation appointment and is that effort worth the fixed salary?

(iii) How serious was the heart attack? Is there the liability of recurrence and is this affected by the possible stress from either job?

(iv) What is the true value of the business? R200,000 appears fair on the basis of the published figures but what are the values of the various assets, what value could be put on goodwill, what are the future prospects of the business? Has anyone else made an offer for the business, has Davison plans to leave it to his children, what is the likelihood of his being able to sell it later when he has firm plans to retire?

(v) What return can he earn on R200,000? How does it compare with the steadily rising profits of the business and the drawings of Davison from it? What are the investment opportunities in Shangri-La?

(vi) How inflation-proof are the various incomes? The income from the welfare post is said to be fixed at R25,000 per annum; with inflation running at 20% that will not be worth much in five years' time. The sales and profits of the business seem to show signs of real growth. To what extent could a lump sum of R200,000 be invested to protect it against inflation?

(vii) Can the business be run by a manager? This again involves decisions about the value Davison puts on his time. Such a manager would need a reasonable remuneration but Davison may feel the money well spent, provided he can find a reliable manager whom he could trust to run the business without continual supervision.

4   The decision on whether or not to manufacture Aggros rests on the following assumptions:

(a)   that machines transferred to component manufacture in the new factory cannot be used for other work if under-utilized there;

(b)   that the machines transferred would not be required to be replaced now on their existing work and that replacement in a year's time will cost £15,000 whether or not transferred, i.e. scrap value in one year is nil;

(c)   that the machines transferred would have remained in service and would not have been sold.

Under these assumptions the opportunity cost of using the machines to produce the new components is nil as no information is given as to contribution lost owing to their transfer. Secondly the manufacturing level for the components must now be maximum capacity as the supermarket price is greater than the variable costs of production.

Budgets for the two selling prices of Aggros are therefore as follows:

		£3.60		£3.10
Sales proceeds	15,000 @ 3.60	54,000	22,000 @ 3.10	68,200
	9,000 @ 1.00	9,000	2,000 @ 1.00	2,000
		63,000		70,200
Variable costs of component manufacture (24,000 × .70p)		16,800		16,800
Variable (opportunity) cost of assembly (£1.50 per unit)		22,500		33,000
		39,300		49,800
Contribution		£23,700		£20,400

The decision is thus to sell at £3.60 if at all. To decide whether or not even to manufacture, the actual fixed costs resulting from the change must be deducted.

Contribution		23,700
Fixed costs:		
Lease	10,000	
Administrative overheads	6,000	
		16,000
Net profit		7,700

Any opportunity cost of the machines should be deducted from this figure to determine whether to switch them from existing work to the production of Aggros. The opportunity cost is the contribution on existing work, or the interest cost of buying a machine a year earlier than you would have done.

Fixed overheads

The fixed overheads in the assembly plant have not been brought into consideration as they will be incurred whether or not Aggros are manufactured. Their absorption is taken into account by using the contribution lost as the measure of the cost of assembling an Aggro.

The component factory fixed overheads are taken into account as they are marginal costs of the new production. They do not depend on the level of production but are a cost to be allocated specifically to the new units.

5   COST OF STRIKE

Notes

		£000	£000
	Contribution lost:		500
	Sales revenue		500
	Variable cost savings:		
	Materials	100	
(a)	Production labour	50	
(b)	Depreciation	150	
(c)	Overheads	10	
		310	
			190
	Less:		
(d)	Saving on overhaul	9	
(e)	Increased contribution next month	82.5	
			91.5
	Cost of strike		98.5

Notes

(a) This is assuming that there is no payment while on strike.

(b) Only the reduction in machine value due to use is saved as the time depreciation is unaffected.

(c) Variable overheads only are saved.

(d) By using internal staff whose wages are a fixed expense to do the overhaul the company is saving the outside contractor's charges but incurring material expense as a result. The net saving is the difference, £9,000.

(e) Increased contribution next month is calculated as follows:

	£000	£000
Increase in sales revenue (500 cars)		250
Variable costs:		
Materials	50	
Production labour (time and a half)	37.5	
Depreciation (use)	75	
Variable overheads	5	
		167.5
Contribution		82.5

There may be other costs of the strike which cannot be enumerated but should be taken into account if possible, such as:

public relations;
loss of definite orders;
interest costs of delaying production;
industrial relations.

6

(a) The alternative courses of action open to Hilton Ltd are:

(i)   to close department K immediately;
(ii)   to operate department K for a further year at 10,000 units;
(iii) to operate department K for a further year at 20,000 units.

The cash flows relating to each of these alternatives (compared in each case with the cash flows which would occur if no action were taken) are:

	Note	*Immediate closure* £000	*Action* *10,000 units* £000	*20,000 units* £000
Cash inflow/savings:				
Sales of production		–	90	160
Sale of machine	1	43	35	30
Material B – savings	2,3	18	9	–
– sales	2	5	–	–
Total inflow/savings		66	134	190
Cash outflows:				
Materials A – disposal arrangements	4	2	2	2
–disposal costs		15	10	5
Material B – purchase		–	–	10
Labour – training		–	20	20
– costs		–	30	60
Variable overhead		–	13	26
Foreman	5	2	6	6
Advertising	–	–	–	15
Total outflows		19	81	144
Net inflow		47	53	46

Note 1	Sales value now £43,000

Note 1   Sales value now £43,000
          Sales value in one year = £40,000 − (£0.50 × production level)
Note 2   Immediate closure releases 15,000 kilos of material B which can be used thus
          (i)   10,000 kilos used as substitute in another department − value £18,000;
          (ii)   5,000 kilos sold − value 5,000 × £1.
Note 3   An activity level of 10,000 leaves 5,000 kilos of B available to be used as the substitute material.
Note 4   Although this cost has been included for the purposes of analysis, it is common to all options open to Hilton and it may be ignored.
Note 5   Immediate closure requires £2,000 paid to the foreman.
          Closure after one year requires only salary to be paid to the foreman.

Hilton Ltd would be advised to operate department K at the level of 10,000 units for the forthcoming year and then to close the department and dispose of its remaining assets.

(b) (i)   If the factory space could be rented for £8,000 this must be treated as a cash inflow relating to immediate closure. The net inflow relating to immediate closure then becomes £55,000. This then becomes the best action.

     (ii) A 90% learning curve means that each time production doubles the *average* time taken to produce each unit falls to 90% of the previous average figure.

           Average per unit for 5,000 units = 1 hour
           Average per unit for 10,000 units = 1 × 0.9 hours = 0.9 hours
           Average per unit for 20,000 units = 0.9 × 0.9 hours = 0.81 hours

           Production labour costs are:
           Production × average time per unit × cost per hour = total cost
           10,000 units ×   0.9 hours   ×   £3   = £27,000 (saving £3,000)
           20,000 units ×   0.81 hours   ×   £3   = £48,600 (saving £11,400)

           Using these figures gives net inflow for each action as follows:

                  Immediate closure   £47,000
                  10,000 units   £56,000
                  20,000 units   £57,400

           Hence Hilton would now be advised to operate department K at 20,000 units for the forthcoming year.

16 Production and capacity decisions

INTRODUCTION

This chapter deals with the problem of computing the level of output at which profit will be maximised when selling price is fixed but either

(i) there are various constraints on the quantity that can be produced, or
(ii) the cost function is non-linear.

Alternative (i) is the more common in examination questions.

Question 1 in this chapter illustrates a simple set of calculations of contribution per unit of limiting factor, while questions 2 and 3 involve the use of linear programming.

Alternative (ii) is exemplified by question 4.

STUDY REQUIREMENTS

Short-run decisions under certainty — contribution analysis and linear programming
Capacity decisions — product mix, alternative methods of manufacture, shutdown problems.

QUESTIONS

1   Following a fire at the factory of Rossi Ltd, the management team met to review the proposed operations for the next quarter. The fire had destroyed all the finished goods stock, some of the raw materials and about half the machines in the forming shop.

At the meeting of the management team the following additional information was provided:

(i)   Only 27,000 machine hours of forming capacity would be available in the forthcoming quarter. Although previously it was thought that sales demand would be the only binding limitation on production it had now become apparent that for the forthcoming quarter the forming capacity would be a limiting factor.

(ii)   It would take about three months to reinstate the forming shop to its previous operational capacity. Hence the restriction on forming capacity was for the next quarter only.

(iv)   Some details of the product range manufactured by Rossi are provided in the following table:

ROSSI'S PRODUCT RANGE

	Product				
	A	B	C	D	E
Sales price	£50	£60	£40	£50	£80
Units of special material required for production					
W or X	2	2	2	1	3
Y	–	–	–	–	6
Z	1	2	1	1	–
Other direct material costs	£6	£12	£6	£5	£13
Other variable production costs	£8	£4	£8	£4	£4
Fixed production costs (based on standard costs)	£6	£3	£6	£3	£3
Forming hours required	5	6	2	10	6

(iv)   The forecasts of demand, in units, for the forthcoming quarter are:

Product	A	B	C	D	E
Units demanded	2,000	2,000	4,000	3,000	4,000

It was originally intended that the number of units produced would equal the units demanded for each product.

(v)   Owing to a purchasing error there is an excess of material W in stock. This has a book value of £6 per unit which is also its current replacement cost. This could be sold to realise £4 per unit after sales and transport costs. Material X could be used instead of material W; material X is not in stock and has a current replacement cost of £5 per unit.

236

(vi) Material Y was in stock at a book value of £2 per unit, which is its normal cost if ordered 3 months in advance, but the stocks of this material were entirely detroyed by the fire. In order to obtain the material quickly a price of £3 per unit would have to be paid for the first 3,000 units obtained in the quarter and any additional units required would cost £6 per unit. These special prices will apply only to this quarter's purchases.

(vii) Some of the stock of material Z was destroyed by the fire. The remaining stocks of 2,000 units have a book value of £7 per unit. The replacement price for Z is currently £8 per unit.

(viii) As a result of the fire it is estimated that the fixed production costs will be £42,000 for the next quarter and the administration and office overheads will amount to £11,500.

(ix) The demand figures shown in (iv) include a regular order from a single customer for

> 3,000 units of C, and
> 3,000 units of E.

This order is usually placed quarterly and the customer always specifies that the order be fulfilled in total or not at all.

(a) Ignoring the information contained in (ix) for this section of the question, determine the optimum production plan for the forthcoming quarter and prepare a statement which indicates to the management of Rossi the estimated financial results of their planned production in terms of total contribution, net current operating profit and financial accounting profit.

(15 marks)

(b) Prepare a statement which clearly shows the management of Rossi Ltd the financial consequence of both the acceptance and the rejection of the order mentioned in (ix). Advise Rossi on the desirability of acceptance of the order in total. Indicate what further information would be useful in arriving at a decision whether to accept or reject the order. *(10 marks)*

(Total 25 marks)

2   A factory owned by your company consists of two departments, machining and finishing. Two products, X and Y, are manufactured. The sales mix of the products has in the past varied considerably with demand but currently there is little difficulty in selling output irrespective of the available mix. However, serious difficulties are now being experienced in the supply of raw materials for product Y and the result is that production of Y will have to be limited to a maximum of 1,800 units per week.

The maximum output from each department per week is as follows:

> Department 1 (machining)   4,000 units of product X, or 2,000 units of product Y, or a proportionate mix of both products

Department 2 (finishing)   2,400 units of product X, or 4,000 units of product Y, or a proportionate mix of both products

Financial data are as follows:

		£
Selling price, per unit:	Product X	18.00
	Product Y	20.00
Variable costs, per unit:	Product X	16.00
	Product Y	17.50
Fixed costs	£1,200 per week.	

(a) Prepare a graph illustrating the various constraints on production.

(b) Prepare a weekly profitability statement to indicate the production mix producing most profit. Workings should be shown.   *(25 marks)*

3   Fleabane Ltd aims to maximise its profits. In one factory it manufactures two liquid products called Erigeron and Stachys. Each is a mix of readily available ingredients which passes through three successive processes of heating, blending and cooling. The finished products are transferred at open market prices to an associated company, which bears all the related storage and transport costs.

Fleabane's management accountant has prepared the following up-to-date cost statement for the two products, expressed in £s per gallon of final product:

		Erigeron		Stachys
Selling price		20		25
Materials and preparation		10		12
		10		13
Variable process costs:				
Heating process	4		1	
Blending process	1		5	
Cooling process	2		3	
		7		9
Contribution margin		3		4

Each process is costed as £1 per hour of process time per gallon. The processing facilities have no alternative use.

On Fleabane's receipt of an enquiry for the delivery of an extra 1,000 gallons of each product during the coming month:

(a) Draft a statement showing how Fleabane should respond to this enquiry, assuming that the remaining unused capacity available in the coming month is 4,000 hours for the cooling processs and 6,000 hours for each of the other two processes.   *(6 marks)*

(b) Draft a statement showing how Fleabane should respond to this enquiry on the assumption instead that each process has only 3,000 hours of unused capacity available in the coming month, showing the following:

(i)   Fleabane's optimal production plan;   *(13 marks)*

(ii)   the range of contribution margins per product within which the optimal production plan will not alter.   *(6 marks)*

(Total 25 marks)

Note: Parts (a) and (b) of this requirement are entirely independent of each other.

4   A company has two presses both capable of producing 20,000 specialised components a year selling for £6 each. Production on each press is flexible with the sole limitation that the economic batch quantity is 5,000 units.

Management anticipates that the components will be required only for a further five years and that the full 40,000 units will not be required every year.

	Total cost per annum	
Production level		
Thousand units	Press A £000	Press B £000
0	25	35
5	60	50
10	63	55
15	70	60
20	82	98

The total cost at zero level includes for each press £5,000 for depreciation and £5,000 for apportioned production overhead. The balance is for direct labour and services which could be used elsewhere if one press were to be sold.

From the data given above:

(a)   Prepare a table to show for each 5,000 step up to 40,000 units the press or presses to use to minimise total costs.

(b)   Indicate the level of production which maximises total profit.

(c)   Calculate whether it would be of financial benefit to sell one press for £90,000 on the assumptions that it would have a scrap value of only £10,000 in five years' time and that the average annual sales during this period would be 75% of capacity. (Ignore inflation and taxation and use 12% per annum as the cost of capital.)

(25 marks)

ANSWERS

1   Optimum production plan determination

This requires a calculation of contribution per key factor incorporating opportunity costs.

Product	A £	B £	C £	D £	E £	E[1] £
Sales price	50	60	40	50	80	80
Materials						
W (or X)	8	8	8	4	12	12
Y	–	–	–	–	18	36
Z	8	16	8	8	–	–
Other material costs	6	12	6	5	13	13
Other variable costs	8	4	8	4	4	4
	30	40	30	21	47	65
Contribution/unit	20	20	10	29	33	15
Forming hours/unit	5	6	2	10	6	6
Contribution/key factor	4	3 1/3	5	2.9	5½	2½
Demand	2,000	2,000	4,000	3,000	4,000	
Total forming hours	10,000	12,000	8,000	30,000	24,000	

The column for product E^1 shows the contribution from E after using the initial 3,000 units of Y, i.e. after producing the first 500 units of E. The relevant cost of W (or X) is the net realisable value of W; X would not be used.

The optimal production plan, obtained by picking the products with the largest contribution per key factor, i.e.:

Product	Units	Forming hours
E	500	3,000
C	4,000	8,000
A	2,000	10,000
B	1,000	6,000
		27,000

(ii)   Profit statement

Note: The distinction between net current operating profit and financial accounting profit is not clear in this instance and is assumed to be a reference to first the use of the opportunity costs as in (i) above and then a use of book values.

	A	B	C	E	Total
Sales (in units)	2,000	1,000	4,000	500	
Contribution/unit	£20	£20	£10	£33	
	£000	£000	£000	£000	£000
Total contribution	40	20	40	16.5	116.5
Fixed costs:					
Production				42	
Administration				11.5	
					53.5
Net current operating profit					63
Opportunity cost adjustment					29
Financial accounting profit					34

Note: The opportunity cost adjustment is required to convert profit based on opportunity costs to one based on book values. This represents the requirement of material W (15,500 units) at book value £6 less opportunity cost £4, i.e. £31,000, and the first 2,000 units of Z used at £7 less £8, i.e. £2,000. The net of these two, £29,000, is shown in the statement.

(b) *Consideration of regular order of C and E*

(i) **Financial consequences**

Product	Contribution /unit	Order accepted Units	Order accepted Contribution	Order rejected Units	Order rejected Contribution
	£		£000		£000
A	20	200*	4	2,000	40
B	20	–	–	2,000*	40
C	10	4,000	40	1,000	10
D	29	–	–	–	–
E	33	500	16.5	500	16.5
E^1	15	2,500	37.5	–	–
			98		106.5

The loss of contribution if the order is accepted is £8,500.

*The figures with asterisks are the remaining production possibilities given the limited 27,000 hours' capacity. If the order is rejected, remaining demand of C is only 1,000 units.

(ii) **Other considerations**

– whether losing the order this quarter will affect future orders from this customer;

– whether not supplying other customers might affect future demand;

– potential growth in demand from either the regular order or other customers as influenced by the previous factors;

- whether selling or not selling one product will affect sales of another product;

- the figures quoted apply only to this quarter since thereafter Y will be obtained more cheaply and X might be used instead of W.

2

(a) *Production constraints*

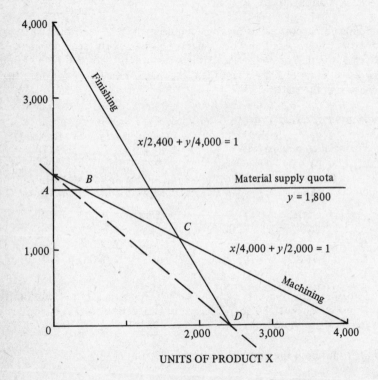

UNITS OF PRODUCT X

Area ABCD0 contains all feasible solutions.

(b) *Production mix producing optimal profit.*

The dotted line on the graph produces a contribution of £5,000. A higher profit will be obtained by plotting another line, parallel to the first but further away from the origin. For the solution to be feasible the line must pass through ABCD0. By inspection it can be seen that a line passing through the point C produces the highest profit.

C is at the intersection of

Machinery	$x/4{,}000 + y/2{,}000$	=	1	(1)

and

Finishing	$x/2{,}400 + y/4{,}000$	=	1	(2)

Multiply (2) by 2 and subtract (1)

$$x/1{,}200 - x/4{,}000 = 1$$
$$2.33x = 4{,}000$$
$$x = 1{,}714.29$$
$$y = 1{,}142.86$$

Weekly profit = (1,714.29 × 2)
+ (1,142.86 × 2.50)
– 1,200
= £5,085.71

If an integer solution is required a trial and error approach must be adopted.

x	y	*Machinery*	*Finishing*	*Profit*
1,715	1,142	0.99975	1.00008	Not feasible
1,715	1,141	0.99925	0.99983	5,082.50
1,716	1,141	0.99950	1.00025	Not feasible
1,714	1,142	0.99950	0.99966	5,083.00
1,714	1,143	1.00000	0.99991	5,085.50
1,713	1,144	1.00025	0.99975	Not feasible
1,712	1,144	1.00000	0.99516	5,084.00

Maximum integer solution $x = 1{,}714$
$y = 1{,}143$

3

(a) The optimal production plan will be that which maximises the contribution. If E is the number of gallons of Erigeron produced and S that of Stachys then the total contribution is given by:

$$C = 3E + 4S$$

This expression is to be maximised subject to the number of hours available for each process:

Heating	$4E + S$	$\leqslant$	6,000
Blending	$E + 5S$	$\leqslant$	6,000
Cooling	$2E + 3S$	$\leqslant$	4,000

and to the minimum and maximum requirements:

$$0 \leqslant E, S \leqslant 1{,}000$$

Only one of the time constraints is limiting, that for the cooling process.

The maximum contribution will therefore be obtained when the highest contribution per cooling process hour is chosen:

Erigeron	£1.50 per process hour
Stachys	£1.33$^1/3$ per process hour

Optimal production plan:

1,000 gallons of Erigeron plus as many as possible of Stachys to utilise fully the cooling process time, i.e. 666$^2/3$ gallons.

(b) (i) The constraints on time now become:

Heating	4E + S	⩽	3,000
Blending	E + 5S	⩽	3,000
Cooling	2E + 3S	⩽	3,000

These are represented on the graph below from which the optimal production plan can be seen to be 631.6 gallons of Erigeron and 473.7 gallons of Stachys.

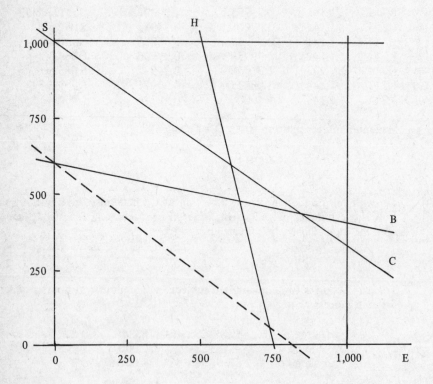

(ii) The optimal production plan will change only when the objective function becomes parallel to the limiting constraints, i.e.:

If e is contribution per unit Erigeron then:

Objective function $= eE + sS$

Gradient $= -e/s$

Gradients of constraints	$H : -4$
	$B : -\frac{1}{5}$
Limiting conditions	e/s	$= 4 ; \frac{1}{5}$
Keeping e at 3	s	$= \frac{3}{4} ; 15$
Keeping s at 4	e	$= 16 ; \frac{4}{5}$

Thus the contribution margins of each can range from $\frac{4}{5}$ to 16 per unit for Erigeron and from $\frac{3}{4}$ to 15 per unit for Stachys before the optimal production decision will change, assuming that the contribution margins per unit of each remain fixed as given when considering the change in the other.

4

(a)

Cumulative output (units)	Use press:	Press A Units	Cost £000	Press B Units	Cost £000	Total cost £000	Revenue £000	Profit £000
0		0	25	0	35	60	0	(60)
5,000	B	0	25	5,000	50	75	30	(45)
10,000	B	0	25	10,000	55	80	60	(20)
15,000	B	0	25	15,000	60	85	90	5
20,000	A and B	10,000	63	10,000	55	118	120	2
25,000	B	10,000	63	15,000	60	123	150	27
30,000	A	15,000	70	15,000	60	130	180	50
35,000	A	20,000	82	15,000	60	142	210	68
40,000	B	20,000	82	20,000	98	180	240	60

The above table is constructed from consideration of the marginal cost of each press for each step, i.e.:

Step		Press A £000		Press B £000
At nil usage		25		35
Moving from:				
0 – 5,000	(60 – 25)	35	(50 – 35)	15
5,000 – 10,000		3		5
10,000 – 15,000		7		5
15,000 – 20,000		12		38

(b)   The level of production which maximises total profit is therefore 35,000 units (profit £68,000 from the above table).

(c)   If neither press was sold, annual sales would be 75% × 40,000 = 30,000 units giving a profit, from the table in part (a), of £50,000. As we are now comparing alternatives, the £5,000 apportioned overhead is irrelevant, being a common cost; the £5,000 depreciation is also irrelevant because we are concerned with cash flows. The relevant cash benefit from using two presses would therefore be £50,000 add back £20,000 = £70,000 per annum.

Alternative 1.   Keep both machines.

$$NPV = 70{,}000 \times \text{cumulative discount factor for 5 years at 12\%}$$
$$= 70{,}000 \times 3.61 = £252{,}700$$

Alternative 2.   Sell one machine.

If press B is sold the company would operate at 20,000 units and obtain an annual cash flow of 120,000 − (82,000 − 10,000) = £48,000

If press A is sold the company would operate at 15,000 units and obtain an annual cash flow of 100,000 − (60,000 − 10,000) = £50,000
∴ Sell press A

$$NPV = (50{,}000 \times 3.61) + 90{,}000 - (10{,}000 \times 0.57) = £264{,}800$$

∴ Sell press A.

17 Sales pricing policy and decisions

INTRODUCTION

An occasional essay-type question will be encountered, dealing with the theory of sales pricing, and question 1 in this chapter covers the main points.

The more usual type of question, however, involves the sales level at which profit will be maximised, and will be concerned with a monopolistic situation in which a demand curve can be established, the object being to identify the volume at which marginal cost is equal to marginal revenue. Most of these can be answered by a suitable tabulation of the data provided, though the amount of work involved can be reduced by applying differential calculus. All the questions in this chapter assume conditions of certainty.

STUDY REQUIREMENTS

Pricing policy and contribution theory — influence of customer demand patterns, elasticity of demand, marketing strategy
Pricing in practice
Elements of calculus

QUESTIONS

1   Cost affects supply and demand affects revenue.

Discuss the factors that would affect price setting in both (a) a competitive market and (b) an oligopolistic situation. *(20 marks)*

2   Alvis Taylor has budgeted that output and sales of his single product, Flonal, will be 100,000 units in 19X2. At this level of activity his unit variable costs are budgeted to be £50 and his unit fixed costs £25. His sales manager estimates that the demand for Flonal would increase by 1,000 units for every decrease of £1 in unit selling price (and vice versa), and that at a unit selling price of £200 demand would be nil.

Information about two price increases has just been received from suppliers. One is for materials (which are included in Alvis Taylor's variable costs), and one is for fuel (which is included in his fixed costs). Their effect will be to increase both the variable costs and the fixed costs by 20% over the budgeted figures.

Alvis Taylor aims to maximise profits from his business.

(a)   Calculate, before the cost increases:

   (i)   the budgeted contribution and profit at the budgeted level of sales of 100,000 units;

   (ii)   the level of sales at which profits would be maximised, and the amount of those maximum profits. *(7 marks)*

(b)   Show whether and by how much Alvis Taylor should adjust his selling price in respect of the increases in:

   (i)   fuel costs;

   (ii)   materials costs. *(6 marks)*

(c)   Show whether and by how much it is worthwhile for Alvis Taylor, following the increases in costs, to spend £1,000,000 on a TV advertising campaign if this were confidently expected to have the effect during 19X2 (but not beyond then) that demand would still fall by 1,000 units for every increase of £1 in unit selling price (and vice versa), but that it would not fall to nil until the unit selling price was £210. *(5 marks)*

(d)   Comment on the results which you have obtained in (a) - (c) above and on the assumptions underlying them. *(7 marks)*

(Total 25 marks)

3

(a) The Los Salemos Drug Company is the manufacturer and distributor of a new wonder drug designed to relieve tension and reduce inhibitions. The company's market consists principally of people connected with the entertainment industry on the west coast of the United States. The company prices the drug at full cost plus 100%. The current variable costs of production are as follows:

> Ingredient 'X': 8 milligrams @ $10 per milligram
> Labour: 5 minutes @ $80 per hour
> Ampoules: 1 @ $1.50 per ampoule

The company's fixed costs (which include the cost of distribution) are currently $320,000 per annum and are absorbed on the basis of budgeted production for the year.

The company is currently setting the price of the drug for the coming year and wishes to take into account expected price increases attached to the various elements of cost. These are as follows:

Element of cost	Expected price increase
Ingredient "X"	10%
Labour rate	50%
Ampoules	$33^{1}/_{3}\%$
Fixed costs	$12\frac{1}{2}\%$

The company's budgeted production and sales for the coming year is 9,000 ampoules.

Calculate:

(i) the selling price of the drug for the coming year on the company's usual basis;
(ii) the company's profit at the budgeted level of activity;
(iii) the break-even point in units and sales value;
(iv) the profit/volume ratio;
(v) the maximum amount that the company should be prepared to spend on advertising to increase sales to 10,000 ampoules. *(10 marks)*

(b) Having received the projected profit figure for the coming year, the chairman of the company, Don Cordoba, has asked the Market Protection Organisation to help in producing a more sophisticated approach to pricing. They have investigated the market and believe that, with some influence being exercised with clients, the following demand pattern will emerge.

Selling price $	Demand Units
200	17,000
220	16,000
240	15,000
260	11,000
280	9,000
300	7,000

It has been suggested to you that the chairman would appreciate the following information:

(i)   the optimal selling price and production level (with supporting calculations) assuming that the demand pattern shown above is accurate;
(ii) the additional profit (if any) compared to the selling price calculated in (a)(i) above;
(iii) the cost per milligram of ingredient 'X' at which the company would be indifferent between charging the price calculated in (a)(i) and (b)(i).

(15 marks)

(Total 25 marks)

4   French Ltd is about to commence operations utilising a simple production process to produce two products, X and Y. It is the policy of French to operate the new factory at its maximum output in the first year of operations. Cost and production details estimated for the first year are:

Product	Production resources per unit			Variable cost per unit		Fixed production overheads directly attributable to product	Maximum production – units
	Labour hours	Machine hours	Direct labour £	Direct materials £		£000	000s
X	1	4	5	6		120	40
Y	8	2	28	16		280	10

There are also general fixed production overheads concerned in the manufacture of both products but which cannot be directly attributed to either. These general fixed production overheads are estimated at £720,000 for the first year of operations. It is thought that the cost structures of the first year will also be operative in the second.

Both products are new and French is one of the first firms to produce them. Hence in the first year of operations the sales price can be set by French. In the second and subsequent years it is felt that the market for X and Y will have become more settled and French will largely conform to the competitive market prices that will become established. The sales manager has researched the first year's market potential and has estimated sales volumes for various ranges of selling price. The details are:

Product X			Product Y		
Range of per unit sales prices		Sales volume	Range of per unit sales prices		Sales volume
£	£	000s	£	£	000s
up to	24.00	36	Up to	96.00	11
24.01 to	30.00	32	96.01 to	108.00	10
30.01 to	36.00	18	108.01 to	120.00	9
36.01 to	42.00*	8	120.01 to	132.00	8
			132.01 to	144.00	7
			144.01 to	156.00*	5

*Maximum price

The managing director of French wishes to ascertain the total production cost of X and Y as, he says: 'Until we know the per unit cost of production we cannot properly determine the first year's sales price. Price must always ensure that total cost is covered and there is an element of profit – therefore I feel that the price should be total cost plus 20%. The determination of cost is fairly simple as most costs are clearly attributable to either X or Y. The general factory overhead will probably be allocated to the products in accordance with some measure of usage of factory resources such as labour or machine hours. The choice between labour and machine hours is the only problem in determining the cost of each product – but the problem is minor and so therefore is the problem of pricing.'

(a) Produce statements showing the effect the cost allocation and pricing methods mentioned by the managing director will have on

(i)   unit costs;
(ii) closing stock values;
(iii) disclosed profit for the first year of operations.   *(8 marks)*

(b) Briefly comment on the results in (a) above and advise the managing director on the validity of using the per unit cost figures produced for pricing decisions.   *(4 marks)*

(c) Provide appropriate statements to the management of French Ltd which will be of direct relevance in assisting the determination of the optimum prices of X and Y for the first year of operations. The statements should be designed to provide assistance in each of the following cases:

(i)   Year II demand will be below productive capacity.
(ii) Year II demand will be substantially in excess of productive capacity.

In both cases the competitive market sales prices per unit for year II are expected to be

X – £30 per unit
Y – £130 per unit

Clearly specify, and explain, your advice to French for each of the cases described.   *(8 marks)*
          (Total 20 marks)

Ignore taxation and the time value of money.

ANSWERS

1

(a) *Price setting in a competitive market*

Under conditions of perfect competition, each firm is faced with a fixed average selling price determined by the output of the whole industry, i.e. the selling price (or demand) curve is horizontal, and the marginal revenue curve is also horizontal.

Each competitor will act logically by producing up to the point where his own marginal cost curve meets that demand curve and marginal cost is equal to marginal revenue.

The total output of the industry as a whole will tend to be increased to the point where the industry's marginal cost curve intersects the demand curve. Under competitive conditions therefore the industry as a whole does not maximise the profits that could be earned.

Individual businesses will differ in cost efficiency; in addition some competitors will be seeking to expand their market share, whilst customers will be 'shopping around' for low-priced bargains. Under such circumstances the prices of particular products will tend to be bid down to a point where the least efficient firm will be selling at a price which barely covers, or does not cover, its variable cost.

The requirements for a perfect market are a homogeneous product; lack of collusion between buyers or sellers; and perfect information. To the extent that these conditions are not met in practice the market may approach a condition of oligopoly.

(b) *Price setting in an oligopolistic situation*

In an oligopolistic situation firms in the industry recognise their inter-dependence. Although the situation is characterised by there being a few sellers, similar supply and demand situations face the oligopolist firms in the market as do a monopolist. Therefore supply prices tend to increase, and greater demand will only be forthcoming if products are sold at continually decreasing prices, as consumers face diminishing marginal utility from the products that they purchase. If the oligopolists are of similar size they are likely to be greatly influenced by each other's actions. Although the same rules concerning price floors will apply to competitive and oligopolistic situations, if there is spare capacity the oligopolist may be reluctant to sell at marginal cost if this is likely to smack of dumping as far as the other firms in the industry are concerned. In some cases spare capacity may even be bought up by the industry and disposed of. As far as price ceilings are concerned all the oligopolists will tend to price about the same level – even if there is no overt collusion. However, this level will be influenced by the demand for the industry's products, the supply and the structure of the oligopoly and expected government reaction. There will be a tendency for the oligopolists to participate in the various forms of non-price competition, such as advertising, services or the use of hidden price cutting in the form of providing longer periods of credit, hidden discounts and so on, rather than for them to go in for overt price cutting. Price leadership may occur in such market structures, where the price leader provides a bench mark of the industry's prices.

2

(a) (i) *Budgeted figures*

The demand curve shows that a selling price of £200 would result in no sales, £199 would result in sales of 1,000 and £100 would produce sales of 100,000. Thus if budgeted sales are to be achieved a selling price of £100 must be adopted.

Budgeted contribution =	100,000 × (£100 − £50)	= £5,000,000
Fixed costs =	100,000 × £25	= £2,500,000
Budgeted profit =	£5m − £2.5m	= £2,500,000

(ii) *Optimum sales level*

This could be found in several ways, using a tabulation approach, equating expressions for marginal cost and marginal revenue or differentiating an expression for contribution. The last two methods are shown:

The demand curve is $Q = (200 - P) = 1,000$

where $Q =$ demand and P unit selling price

Revenue, $R = Q \times P = (200P - P^2) \times 1,000$

$$\text{Marginal revenue} = \frac{dR}{dQ} = \frac{dR}{dP} \times \frac{dP}{dQ} = \frac{dR/dP}{dQ/dP}$$

$$= \frac{(200 - 2P) \times 1,000}{-1,000}$$

$$= 2P - 200$$

$$\text{Marginal cost} = 50$$

Profit is maximum when $2P - 200 = 50$
$$P = 125$$

∴ To achieve maximum profits a sales price of £125 must be adopted.

This would produce sales of $Q = (200 - 125) \times 1,000 = 75,000$ Flonals

Contribution would be 75,000 × (£125 − £50) =	£5,625,000
Fixed costs are	= £2,500,000
Maximum profit	= £3,125,000

Note: The same result could be found from differentiating the expression for contribution:

$$
\begin{aligned}
C &= Q \times (P - 50) \\
&= (200 - P) \times 1,000 \times (P - 50) \\
&= 1,000 \times (250P - P^2 - 10,000)
\end{aligned}
$$

The gradient of this line is given by:

$$
\frac{dC}{dP} = 1,000 \times (250 - 2P)
$$

The expression for C is maximised (or minimised) when $dC/dP = 0$, i.e. when:

$$
\begin{aligned}
1,000 \times (250 - 2P) &= 0 \\
\text{or} \qquad\qquad P &= 125
\end{aligned}
$$

This optimum selling price of £125 is as found in the initial solution above with sales of 75,000 produced and maximum profit of £3,125,000 achieved.

(b) (i) *Fuel cost increases*

This is an increase in fixed costs and therefore the expressions above for marginal cost, marginal revenue and contribution are unaffected, and no change is needed to selling price (profit down £500,000).

(ii) *Material cost increases*

This is an increase in unit variable cost of £10 and so the expressions for marginal cost and contribution will change and with them the optimum selling price.

Now, marginal revenue $= 2P - 200$ and marginal cost £60.

Profit is maximum where:

$$
\begin{aligned}
2P - 200 &= 60 \\
P &= 130
\end{aligned}
$$

Therefore selling price should be increased by £5 (to £130) (demand now 70,000; contribution £4.9m).

(c) *Advertising decision*

(i) Without the advertising campaign:

Contribution	= 70,000 × (£130 − £60)	= £4,900,000
Fixed cost	= £2.5m × 1.2	= £3,000,000
Profit		= £1,900,000

(ii)   With the advertising campaign

Contribution = Demand X contribution per unit
$$C = (210 - P) \times 1{,}000 \times (P - 60)$$
$$= 1{,}000 \times (270P - P^2 - 12{,}600)$$

Contribution is maximum where $dC/dP = 0$

$$dC/dP = 1{,}000 \quad \times \quad (270 - 2P)$$

Contribution is maximum when:

$$1{,}000 \times (270 - 2P) = 0$$
$$P = 135$$

Contribution = $(210 - 135) \times 1{,}000 \times (135 - 60)$
= $75{,}000 \times £75$
= £5,625,000
Fixed costs = £3m + £1m = £4,000,000
Profit = £1,625,000

Thus the effect of the advertising campaign is to reduce profit by £275,000. The campaign is not worthwhile.

(d)   *Comments on results and assumptions*

(i)   **Comments**

In part (a) it can be seen that with information about the manner in which price affects demand a more profitable method of determining suitable selling prices and establishing output and sales levels is available. This also applies to part (b) where it is noticed that any increase in fixed costs should not affect selling price (and therefore demand), though in practice many firms would tend to pass these cost increases on to the customer. This policy, which may go against an initial interpretation of the theoretical argument, may not necessarily be that unwise, since it is likely that any competitors of Alvis Taylor would push their prices up and customers' wage income might also be rising.

It is intuitively obvious that any change in unit variable cost would affect the pricing and output decision as illustrated in (b)(ii). The calculations in part (c) ignore any long term benefit that such a campaign might bring, with the result that the demand curve could stay altered for more than one year and therefore the £1m advertising costs be effectively spread.

(ii)   **Assumptions**

Throughout the problem we have assumed that unit variable cost and total fixed costs do not change at different activity levels. The estimates for these costs are assumed reliable when making decisions based on them. When considering the price increases we have ignored the possibility of using alternative materials or possibly even an alternative type of fuel. However, the crucial underlying assumption is that our sales manager has correctly assessed the way in which selling price influences demand.

3

(a) (i) *Calculation of selling price*

		$
Ingredient 'X':	8 milligrams @ $11 per milligram	88.00
Labour:	5 minutes @ $120 per hour	10.00
Ampoules:	1 @ $ per ampoule	2.00
Fixed costs:	320,000 (1.125) ÷ 9,000 units	40.00
Total cost		140.00
Profit margin:	100%	140.00
Selling price		$280.00

(ii) *Profit at budgeted level of activity*

9,000 units @ $140 per unit $1,260,000

(iii) *Break-even point*

In units

$$\frac{\text{Fixed costs}}{\text{Contribution per unit}} = \frac{\$320,000(1.125)}{\$(280-100)} = \$2,000$$

In sales value

Break-even point in units × selling price = 2,000 × $280 = $560,000

(iv) *Profit volume ratio*

$$\text{P/V ratio} = \frac{\text{Contribution}}{\text{Selling price}} = \frac{\$180}{\$280} = 64.3\%$$

(v) *Maximum expenditure on advertising to increase sales to 10,000 ampoules*

The maximum amount the company should be prepared to spend is equal to the additional contribution that they would earn.

1,000 units @ $180 = $180,000

(b) (i) *Optimal selling price and production level*

Selling price	Variable cost	Contribution per unit	Demand	Total contribution
$	$	$	Units	$
200	100	100	17,000	1,700,000
220	100	120	16,000	1,920,000
240	100	140	15,000	2,100,000*
260	100	160	11,000	1,760,000
280	100	180	9,000	1,620,000
300	100	200	7,000	1,400,000

*The optimal selling price is $240 and the optimal production level is 15,000 units.

(ii) *Additional profit compared to selling price of $280*

$2,100,000 − $1,620,000 = $480,000

(iii) *Cost per milligram of ingredient 'X' at which company would be indifferent between selling prices of $280 and $240*

For company to be indifferent, the total contribution earned at the different selling prices must be the same.

Let x = cost per milligram of Ingredient 'X'

Contribution at selling price of $280

$(280 − 12 − 8x) \times 9,000$ $= 2,412,000 − 72,000x$

Contribution at selling price of $240

$(240 − 12 − 8x) \times 15,000 = 3,420,000 − 120,000x$

∴ $2,412,000 − 72,000x$ $= 3,420,000 − 120,000x$
∴ $120,000x − 72,000x$ $= 3,420,000 − 2,412,000$
∴ $48,000x$ $= 1,008,000$
∴ $x = \$21$;

4

(a) Calculation of overhead recovery rate for general fixed production overhead of £720,000.

Product	Labour hours	Machine hours
	000s	000s
X	40	160
Y	80	20
	120	180
Recovery rate per hour	£6	£4

CALCULATION OF COST PER UNIT

	Labour hours recovery method		Machine hours recovery method	
	X	Y	X	Y
	£000	£000	£000	£000
Direct labour	200	280	200	280
Direct materials	240	160	240	160
Directly attributable overhead	120	280	120	280
General factory overhead	240	480	640	80
Total cost	800	1,200	1,200	800
Units produced (000s)	40	10	40	10
Cost per unit	£20	£120	£30	£80
Price at cost + 20%	£24	£144	£36	£96

(ii) & (iii)   CALCULATION OF CLOSING STOCK VALUES
AND DISCLOSED PROFIT

	Labour hour recovery method			Machine hour recovery method		
	X	Y	Total	X	Y	Total
Cost per unit	£20	£120		£30	£80	
Price per unit	£24	£144		£36	£96	
Sales quantity (000s)	36	7		18	10	
						(See Note 1)
	£000	£000	£000	£000	£000	£000
Sales revenues	864	1,008	1,872	648	960	1,608
Opening stock	0	0	0	0	0	0
Manufacturing costs	800	1,200	2,000	1,200	800	2,000
	800	1,200	2,000	1,200	800	2,000
Less: Closing stocks	80	360	440	660	0	660
Cost of goods sold	720	840	1,560	540	800	1,340
Disclosed profit	144	168	312	108	160	268

Note 1: Sales limited to maximum production

(b) Demand in this instance is price-elastic, so the quantity that can be sold will be determined by the selling price, which in the above calculations is based on 'cost' figures that are heavily dependent on the accounting convention used. There is no guarantee that this procedure will give rise to an optimal result.

In the circumstances of French Ltd it would be better if prices were derived *after considering* cost structures and sales reaction to price levels, and not merely *as a consequence* of accounting costs containing apportionments of fixed costs which are not useful for pricing decisions.

(c) In order to provide information useful for this pricing decision, the correct 'value' per unit of closing stocks must be derived. This value of closing stock is the opportunity value of closing stock and can be derived, for each of the two distinct cases specified in the question, thus:

(i) *Year II demand lower than productive capacity*

Here the only benefit which stock in hand at the end of year I actually bestows on French Ltd is that such stocks save the need to produce those stocks in the following year. Therefore their variable costs of £11 and £44 are relevant as they are the per unit costs saved in year II.

(ii) *Year II demand substantially in excess of productive capacity*

As demand exceeds productive capacity any units of stock in hand at the end of year I will facilitate extra sales in year II; these sales would be lost if the stock in hand were not present. Hence the relevant opportunity values are the sales price of £30 and £130 per unit.

French should now seek to maximise the following:
sales revenue – year I; *plus*
opportunity value of closing stock (based on revenues or cost savings to be realised in year II); *less*
total costs incurred.

However, as total costs incurred in year I are constant at £2,000,000 they may be ignored for the purposes of this decision. Hence the management of French should seek to maximise the other two items.

CALCULATION OF OPTIMUM PRICES FOR YEAR I

Product X

Price per unit	Sales quantity	Sales revenue	Closing stock quantity	Case I – 'Value' =£11		Case II – 'Value'=£30	
				Worth of closing stock	Total 'worth'	Worth of closing stock	Total 'worth'
£	000s	£000	000s	£000	£000	£000	£000
24	36	864	4	44	908	120	984
30	32	960	8	88	1,048*	240	1,200
36	18	648	22	242	890	660	1,308*
42	8	336	32	352	688	960	1,296

Product Y

Price per unit	Sales quantity	Sales revenue	Closing stock quantity	Case I – 'Value'=£44		Case II – 'Value'=£130	
				Worth of closing stock	Total 'worth'	Worth of closing stock	Total 'worth'
£	000s	£000	000s	£000	£000	£000	£000
96	10	960	0	0	960	0	960
108	10	1,080	0	0	1,080	0	1,080
120	9	1,080	1	44	1,124	130	1,210
132	8	1,056	2	88	1,144*	260	1,316
144	7	1,008	3	132	1,140	390	1,398
156	5	780	5	220	1,000	650	1,430*

*Optimum

For Case I: French should adopt the following prices:
$$X - £30 \text{ per unit}$$
$$Y - £132 \text{ per unit}$$
These will give the highest overall benefit to French.

For Case II: French should adopt the following prices:
$$X - £36 \text{ per unit}$$
$$Y - £156 \text{ per unit}$$

These prices will give lower sales quantities and sales revenues in year I than will result from the case I prices. However, this will facilitate greater sales in year II which will outweigh the benefits previously foregone.

Note to student: The key feature of this rather unusual question is that the company is not 'producing to sell', in which case a comparison of marginal cost against marginal revenue would have been relevant. It is committed to produce a given number of units and to spend £2,000,000 in doing so.

18　Uncertainty and probability

INTRODUCTION

Complex problems in probability analysis require computer capacity and are outside the scope of current management accounting examinations.

A typical question will require the calculation of an expected outcome by the application of weightings to one or two variables. Occasionally a decision tree will be required, and an example is given in question 4 in this chapter. You should make yourself completely familiar with the method of constructing such a diagram.

The use of standard deviation as a measure of risk has not yet been called for in management accounting questions, but might be in the future.

STUDY REQUIREMENTS

Short-run decisions under uncertainty — risk analysis, decision trees and sensitivity analysis.

QUESTIONS

1   An engineering company has been offered a one-year contract to supply a motor car component XY at a fixed price of £8 per unit. Its normal capacity for this type of component is 25,000 units a year. The estimated costs to manufacture are shown below. These costs are considered to be firm except for the direct material price.

Variable costs per unit:

	£
Direct wages	1.50
Direct material	2.25
Direct expenses	0.65

Semi-variable costs per annum:

	Output levels		
	80%	100%	120%
	£	£	£
Indirect wages	15,400	16,000	23,100
Indirect materials	8,600	9,000	9,900
Indirect expenses	2,000	2,500	3,000

Fixed costs per annum:

	£
Supervisory salaries	10,000
Depreciation	4,000
Other overhead	16,000

(a)   Calculate the cost and profit per unit and total annual profit assuming that the customer's orders in the year total:
    20,000 components;
    25,000 components;
    30,000 components;
and that direct material is £2.25 per unit.

(b)   Calculate the estimated profit for the year if it is assumed that the probability of the total order is:
    0.3 for 20,000 components;
    0.6 for 25,000 components;
    0.1 for 30,000 components;
and that for direct material is:
    0.5 for £2.25 per unit;
    0.3 for £2.50 per unit;
    0.2 for £2.75 per unit;

(c)   State whether you would recommend the contract be accepted, giving brief reasons for your decision.   (30 marks)

2

(a) Allegro Finishes Ltd is about to launch an improved version of its major product — a pocket size chess computer — on to the market. Sales of the original model (at £65 per unit) have been at the rate of 50,000 per annum, but it is planned to withdraw this model and the company is now deciding on its production plans and pricing policy.

The standard variable cost of the new model will be £50, the same as that of the old, but the company intends to increase the selling price 'to recover the research and development expenditure that has been incurred'. The research and development costs of the improved model are estimated at £750,000 and the intention is that these should be written off over three years. Additionally annual fixed overheads of approximately £800,000 are allocated to this product line.

The sales director has estimated the maximum annual demand figures that would obtain at three selling prices:

Selling Price	Estimated maximum annual demand
£	(physical units)
70	75,000
80	60,000
90	40,000

Prepare a cost-volume-profit chart that would assist the management to choose a selling price and the level of output at which to operate. Identify the best price and the best level of output. Outline briefly any reservations that you have with this approach. *(5 marks)*

(b) With the facts as stated for part (a), assume that the sales director is considering a more sophisticated approach to the problem. He has estimated, for each selling price, an optimistic, a pessimistic and a most likely demand figure and associated probabilities for each of them. For the £90 price the estimates are:

	Annual demand	Probability of demand
Pessimistic	20,000	0.2
Most likely	35,000	0.7
Optimistic	40,000	0.1
		1.0

On the cost side, it is clear that the standard unit variable cost of £50 is an 'ideal' which has rarely been achieved in practice. An analysis of the past 20 months shows that the following pattern of variable cost variances (per unit of output) has arisen:

an adverse variance of around £10 arose on 4 occasions;
an adverse variance of around £5 arose on 14 occasions;
a variance of around £0 arose on 2 occasions.

There is no reason to think that the pattern for the improved model will differ significantly or that these variances are dependent upon the actual demand level.

From the above, calculate the expected annual profit for a selling price of £90. (6 marks)

(c)   A tabular summary of the result of an analysis of the data for the other two selling prices (£70 and £80) is as follows:

	£70	£80
Probability of a loss of £500,000 or more	0.02	0
Probability of a loss of £300,000 or more	0.07	0.05
Probability of a loss of £100,000 or more	0.61	0.08
Probability of break-even or worse	0.61	0.10
Probability of break-even or better	0.39	0.91
Probability of a profit of £100,000 or more	0.33	0.52
Probability of a profit of £300,000 or more	0.03	0.04
Probability of a profit of £500,000 or more	0	0.01
Expected value of profit (loss)	(£55,750)	£68,500

Compare your calculations in part (b) with the above figures and write a short memo to the sales director outlining your advice and commenting on the use of subjective discrete probability distributions in problems of this type.
(9 marks)

(d)   Assume that there is a 10% increase in the fixed overheads allocated to this product line and a decision to write off the research and development costs in one year instead of over three years. Indicate the general effect that this would have on your analysis of the problem. (2 marks)

(Total 22 marks)

3   For the past 20 years a charity organisation has held an annual dinner and dance with the primary intention of raising funds.

This year there is concern that an economic recession may adversely affect both the number of persons attending the function and the advertising space that will be sold in the programme published for the occasion.

Based on past experience and current prices and quotations, it is expected that the following costs and revenues will apply for the function:

Costs:	Dinner and dance:	Hire of premises	£ 700
		Band and entertainers	2,800
		Raffle prizes	800
		Photographer	200

Food at £12 per person (with a guarantee of 400 persons minimum)

	Programme:	A fixed cost of £2,000, plus £5 per page

Revenues: Dinner and dance: Price of tickets   £20 per person

Average revenue from:

	Raffle	£5 per person
	Photographs	£1 per person

Programme: Average revenue from advertising   £70 per page

A sub-committee, formed to examine more closely the likely outcome of the function, discovered the following from previous records and accounts:

No. of tickets sold	No. of past occasions
250 to 349	4
350 to 449	6
450 to 549	8
550 to 649	2
	20

No. of programme pages sold	No. of past occasions
24	4
32	8
40	6
48	2
	20

Several members of the sub-committee are in favour of using a market research consultant to carry out a quick enquiry into the likely number of tickets and the likely number of pages of advertising space that would be sold for this year's dinner and dance.

(a)   Calculate the expected value of the profit to be earned from the dinner and dance this year.

(b)   Recommend, with relevant supporting financial and cost data, whether or not the charity should spend £500 on the market research enquiry and indicate the possible benefits the enquiry could provide.

Note: All workings for tickets should be in steps of 100 tickets and for advertising in steps of 8 pages.
                                                                          (25 marks)

4   The Central Co Ltd has developed a new product and is currently considering the marketing and pricing policy it would employ. Specifically it is considering whether the sales price should be set at £15 per unit or at £24 per unit. Sales volumes at these two prices are shown in the following table:

Sales price £15 per unit		Sales price £24 per unit	
Forecast sales volume	Probability	Forecast sales volume	Probability
(000s)		(000s)	
20	0.1	8	0.1
30	0.6	16	0.3
40	0.3	20	0.3
		24	0.3

The fixed production costs of the venture will be £38,000.

The level of the advertising and publicity costs will depend on the sales price and the intended market. With a sales price of £15 per unit the advertising and publicity costs will amount to £12,000. With a sales price of £24 per unit these costs will total £122,000.

Labour and variable overhead costs will amount to £5 per unit produced. Each unit produced requires 2kg of raw material and the basic cost is expected to be £4 per kg. However, the suppliers of the raw materials are prepared to lower the price in return for a firm agreement to purchase a guaranteed minimum quantity. If Central Ltd contracts to purchase at least 40,000kg the price will be reduced to £3.75 per kg for all purchases. If Central contracts to purchase a minimum of 60,000kg the price will be reduced to £3.50 per kg for all purchases. It is only if Central Ltd guarantees either of the above minimum levels of purchase in advance that the appropriate reduced prices will be operative.

If Central Ltd were to enter into one of the agreements for the supply of raw material and find that it did not require to utilise the entire quantity of materials purchased, the excess could be sold. The sales price will depend upon the quantity offered for sale. If 16,000 kg or more are sold the sales price will be £2.90 per kg for all sales. If less than 16,000kg are offered the sales price will be only £2.40 per kg.

Irrespective of amount sold the costs incurred in selling the excess raw materials will be, per kg, as follows:

Packaging	£0.30
Delivery	£0.45
Insurance	£0.15

Central's management team feels that losses are undesirable while high expected money values are desirable. Therefore it is considering the utilisation of a formula which incorporates both aspects of the outcome to measure the desirability of each strategy. The formula is:

$$\text{'Desirability'} = L + 3E$$

where L = lowest outcome of the strategy
       E = expected monetary value of the strategy.

The marketing manager seeks the advice of you, the management accountant, in deciding the appropriate strategy. He says: 'We need to make two decisions now:

(i)   Which price per unit should be charged, £15 or £24?

(ii)   Should all purchases of raw materials be at the price of £4 per kg or should we enter into an agreement for a basic minimum quantity? If we enter into an agreement, what minimum level of purchases should we guarantee?

As you are the management accountant I expect you to provide me with some useful relevant figures.'

(a)   Provide statements which show the various expected outcomes of each of the choices open to Central Co Ltd.   *(12 marks)*

(b)   Advise on its best choice of strategies if Central Ltd's objective is:

       (i)   to maximise the expected monetary value of the outcomes;
       (ii)   to minimise the harm done to the firm if the worst outcome of each choice were to eventuate;
       (iii) to maximise the score on the above mentioned measure of 'desirability'.
                                                                              (9 marks)

(c)   Briefly comment on either:

       (i)   two other factors which may be relevant in reaching a decision, or
       (ii)   the decision criteria utilised in (b) above.   *(4 marks)*

                                                                        (Total 25 marks)

ANSWERS

1

(a)

COST AND PROFIT STATEMENT – COMPONENT XY

Capacity utilisation	80%		100%		120%	
Units	20,000		25,000		30,000	
	£	£ per unit	£	£ per unit	£	£ per unit
Variable costs:						
Direct materials	45,000	2.25	56,250	2.25	67,500	2.25
Direct wages	30,000	1.50	37,500	1.50	45,000	1.50
Direct expenses	13,000	0.65	16,250	0.65	19,500	0.65
	88,000	4.40	110,000	4.40	132,000	4.40
Semi-variable costs	26,000	1.30	27,500	1.10	36,000	1.20
Fixed costs	30,000	1.50	30,000	1.20	30,000	1.00
	144,000	7.20	167,500	6.70	198,000	6.60
Sales	160,000	8.00	200,000	8.00	240,000	8.00
Profit	16,000	0.80	32,500	1.30	42,000	1.40

(b)

Revised expected direct material cost

		£
0.5 × £2.25	=	1.125
0.3 × £2.50	=	0.750
0.2 × £2.75	=	0.550
		£2.425

Revised profit at each possible level of sales

$$£$$

20,000 components 16,000 − 20,000 × (2.425 − 2.25) = 12,500
25,000 components 32,500 − 25,000 × (2.425 − 2.25) = 28,125
30,000 components 42,000 − 30,000 × (2.425 − 2.25) = 36,750

Estimated profit for the year:
(0.3 × 12,500) + (0.6 × 28,125) + (0.1 × 36,750) = £24,300

(c) The profit estimate in part (b) has been constructed to incorporate both elements of uncertainty. These are independent variables, however, and it is conceivable that a total order for 20,000 units could be received and the price of materials would be £2.75 per unit. Even in this event there would be a profit of £0.30 per unit.

The most likely outcome appears to be an order for 25,000 units with a material price of £2.25 − the position shown in the middle section of the table in part (a).

As providing an addition to existing profits, the contract would be worthwhile, particularly if some of the £16,000 'other overhead' is an absorption of general fixed costs. The question to be asked is whether this 'capacity for this type of component' could be used more profitably on alternative work.

2

(a) Preliminary calculations:

	£70	£80	£90
Selling price	£70	£80	£90
Maximum demand	75,000	60,000	40,000
Maximum revenue	£5,250,000	£4,800,000	£3,600,000
Total variable cost	£3,750,000	£3,000,000	£2,000,000
Fixed costs	800,000	800,000	800,000
R & D costs	250,000	250,000	250,000
	£4,800,000	£4,050,000	£3,050,000
Estimated profit	£450,000	£750,000	£550,000

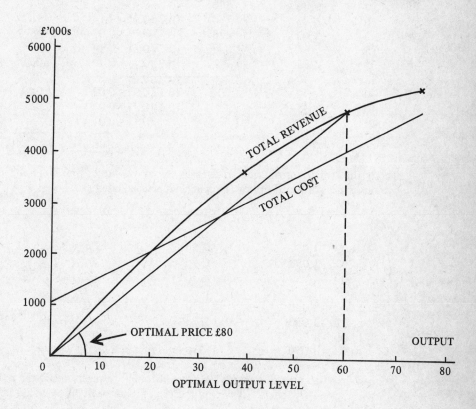

Although not readily identifiable owing to the small scale of the chart, it is at 60,000 units that the gap between the total cost line and the total revenue line is greatest. This coincides with the peak of the total revenue line, where it becomes parallel with the total cost line before curving downwards, i.e. at that point marginal revenue equals marginal cost.

Reservations about the approach arise from the fact that at least three figures are 'estimated' or 'approximate', i.e. research and development costs, fixed overheads and the maximum annual demand. Some form of probability estimation would be helpful. It is also noted that 60,000 units per annum is above the rate of production previously achieved.

(b)

CALCULATION OF EXPECTED PROFIT FOR A SELLING PRICE OF £90

Demand £000	Unit contribution	Total contribution	Probability	Expected total contribution
	£	£000		£000
20	30	600	(0.2)(0.2) = 0.04	24
20	35	700	(0.2)(0.7) = 0.14	98
20	40	800	(0.2)(0.1) = 0.02	16
35	30	1,050	(0.7)(0.2) = 0.14	147
35	35	1,225	(0.7)(0.7) = 0.49	600.25
35	40	1,400	(0.7)(0.1) = 0.07	98
40	30	1,200	(0.1)(0.2) = 0.02	24
40	35	1,400	(0.1)(0.7) = 0.07	98
40	40	1,600	(0.1)(0.1) = 0.01	16
			1.00	1,121.25

(c) From the 'total contribution' figures in the above table, the likelihood of various figures of profit or loss emerging can be calculated as follows:

	Profit (Loss)	Probability
	£000	
600 − 1,050	(450)	.04
700 − 1,050	(350)	.14
800 − 1,050	(250)	.02 } .34
1,050 − 1,050	0	.14
1,200 − 1,050	150	.02
1.225 − 1,050	175	.49 } .80
1,400 − 1,050	350	.14 (.07 + .07)
1,600 − 1,050	550	.01

		£70	£80	£90
Probability of a loss				
Greater than or equal to	£500,000	0.02	0	0
	£300,000	0.07	0.05	0.18
	£100,000	0.61	0.08	0.20
	0	0.61	0.10	0.34
Probability of a profit				
Greater than or equal to	0	0.39	0.91	0.80
	£100,000	0.33	0.52	0.66
	£300,000	0.03	0.04	0.15
	£500,000	0	0.01	0.01
Expected profit		Loss (£55,750)	£68,500	£71,250

To: Sales Director
From:
Subject: Price Review for Chess Computer (new model)

I have now analysed the information that you provided and from this I have prepared a table setting out the probability of achieving certain levels of profitability (and unprofitability) for the prices that we are considering. The table is attached to this memorandum.

The table shows that the £90 selling price has the largest expected profit, i.e. £71,250. It does not follow that £90 is the best price since an analysis of the table shows that it carries a probability of 0.34 of not making any profit. The company may well consider that this risk is too great, particularly when a comparison is made with the outcome of the analysis for the £80 price. A price of £80 yields a lower expected profit, £68,500, but the difference is not great when all the uncertainties are considered and there is a much lower probability (0.1) of not making any profit. There is a lower probability of a profit in excess of £300,000 but, on the evidence available and without knowledge of the company's attitude towards risk, I would consider that the price of £80 is the best of the alternatives under consideration.

It is inevitable that probability estimates shall be 'subjective', which means that they are difficult to substantiate and subject to bias. These dangers can be minimised by care in the selection of the experts who are asked to make the estimates, and by suitable estimating procedures – e.g. the Delphi method.

The use of 'discrete' rather than continuous probability distributions places some limitation on the usefulness of the results. Thus, for the £90 price, it has been calculated that there is a 14% chance of a loss of £350,000 and a 4% chance of a loss of £450,000; but this is rather different from the statement in the summary table that there is 18% 'probability of a loss greater than or equal to £300,000'.

Care is needed, therefore, when using statistics of this nature.

(d) If the additional fixed overhead is a genuine estimate of additional fixed costs incurred by reason of an increase in the volume of output of the product, then it should be considered as a relevant cost when the pricing decision is taken. If, however, the additional overhead follows from a revision of the company's overhead allocation practices and there is no suggestion that additional overhead has been caused by the new product, this should not affect the pricing decision.

Similar principles apply to the research and development expenditure. Although the company wishes to charge a price which will cover its research and development costs, such costs are 'sunk' costs and rationally the amount that has been spent should not be allowed to affect the pricing decision. It will affect the reported profits, however. The reported profits will thus be affected if the R and D costs are written off in a single year, but this should not rationally call for a change in the selling price unless the assumptions underlying the analysis are now invalid, e.g. if the decision to amortise the costs over one year follows from a change in the company's view of the future which affects the data relevant for the pricing decision.

3

(a)

Ticket sales (take mid-point)	Frequency	%	Income (£26 per person)	Food	Fixed	Profit (Loss)	X Frequency %
			£	£	£	£	
300	4	20	7,800	4,800	4,500	(1,500)	(300)
400	6	30	10,400	4,800	4,500	1,100	330
500	8	40	13,000	6,000	4,500	2,500	1,000
600	2	10	15,600	7,200	4,500	3,900	390
	20	100					1,420

The expected profit is £1,420 per annum for the dinner and dance.

Programme pages sold	Frequency	%	Income	Costs	Profit (Loss)	X Frequency %
			£	£	£	
24	4	20	1,680	2,120	(440)	(88)
32	8	40	2,240	2,160	80	32
40	6	30	2,800	2,200	600	180
48	2	10	3,360	2,240	1.120	112
	20	100				236

The expected profit on programme advertising is £236 per annum.
∴ Total expected profit is £1,420 + £236 = £1,656.

(b) Expected profit is a long-run concept, i.e. average annual profits for a dinner and dance which takes place every year will be £1,656. It does not mean

272

therefore that the dinner dance due to take place this year will produce profits of that magnitude.

At worst the position will be:

	£	£
Tickets sold 250 X 26		6,500
Costs − Food (minimum)	4,800	
− Other fixed	4,500	
		9,300
Loss on dinner dance		(2,800)
Programme loss		(440)
Total maximum loss		(3,240)

At best the position will be:

	£	£
Tickets sold 649 X 26		16,874
Costs − Food 649 X 12	7,788	
− Other fixed	4,500	
		12,288
Profit on dinner dance		4,586
Programme profit		1,120
Total maximum profit		5,706

Thus this year's dinner dance will produce a result between the extremes of a loss of £3,240 and a profit of £5,706.

To justify spending £500 to be more certain as to where in this range the result of this year's dinner dance will lie demands that the additional information shall have a value in excess of £500, which is possible only if it affects actions taken. For example, if £500 spent on research showed that dinner dance ticket sales and advertising pages sold would be at a minimum, resulting in a loss of £3,240, *and the function was therefore cancelled,* then £500 spent has prevented a loss of £3,240, and is therefore justified. If, however, policy dictates that a function *shall* be held each year, odd poor years are accepted and there would be little point in spending £500 to know what kind of year the current one will be.

However, if the committee will definitely take action on the information obtained from the consultant's enquiry, we need to look more closely at what that enquiry is likely to show. Using the figures from part (a), because it is only on these that we have probability distributions, there is a 20% chance that a ticket loss of £1,500 would be revealed; this could be combined with various probabilities relating to programme profits as follows:

Loss if 300 tickets sold	Profit (Loss) on programme	Total	Joint probability	
£	£	£		£
(1,500)	(440)	(1,940)	.04	(77.6)
(1,500)	80	(1,420)	.08	(113.6)
(1,500)	600	(900)	.06	(54.0)
(1,500)	1,120	(380)	.02	(7.6)
				252.8

So far as we can estimate, therefore, the enquiry would at best enable the committee to avoid a loss of £252.8. It is not worth spending £500 to obtain this information.

4 The decisions taken depend upon whether or not the new product has to be produced in advance before the sales volume is known; it is assumed that production can be adjusted to match demand.

(a) The choices open to Central Co are best set out in the decision tree below:

Sales (thousand units)

The costs and benefits are:

Selling price/unit		£15.00	or		£24.00
Materials cost/unit (2kg/unit)		£8.00	or £7.50 or		£7.00
Labour and variable overhead cost/unit			£5.00		
Fixed costs		£50,000	or		£160,000
Sale of excess materials	— proceeds	£2.90	or		£2.40
	— costs		£0.90		
	— net realisable value	£2.00	or		£1.50

The expected monetary values of the six courses of action, C to H, are tabulated:

	Sales revenue	Variable cost	Materials cost	Fixed cost	Profit (loss)	Probability	Expected outcome
	£000	£000	£000	£000	£000		£000
C	300	100	160	50	(10)	0.1	(1)
	450	150	240	50	10	0.6	6
	600	200	320	50	30	0.3	9
							14
D	300	100	150	50	0	0.1	0
	450	150	225	50	25	0.6	15
	600	200	300	50	50	0.3	15
							30
E	300	100	170*	50	(20)	0.1	(2)
	450	150	210	50	40	0.6	24
	600	200	280	50	70	0.3	21
							43
F	192	40	64	160	(72)	0.1	(7.2)
	384	80	128	160	16	0.3	4.8
	480	100	160	160	60	0.3	18.0
	576	120	192	160	104	0.3	31.2
							46.8
G	192	40	102*	160	(110)	0.1	(11.0)
	384	80	138*	160	6	0.3	1.8
	480	100	150	160	70	0.3	21.0
	576	120	180	160	116	0.3	34.8
							46.6
H	192	40	122*	160	(130)	0.1	(13.0)
	384	80	154*	160	(10)	0.3	(3.0)
	480	100	170*	160	50	0.3	15.0
	576	120	192*	160	104	0.3	31.2
							30.2

*These are net figures, purchase price less sale proceeds of excess.

275

(b) (i) From the previous table the strategy with the highest expected monetary value, £46,800, is that marked F. Set a sales price of £24 and make no contract for buying materials.

(ii) The strategy which has the least 'harmful' worst outcome is that marked D when, if sales are only 20,000 units, no loss is made. Set a sales price of £15 and contract to buy at least 40,000kg of materials.

(iii) The 'desirability' of each strategy is tabulated below:

Strategy	Expected monetary value	Lowest outcome	Desirability
	£000	£000	
C	14	(10)	32
D	30	0	90
E	43	(20)	109
F	46.8	(72)	68.4
G	46.6	(110)	29.8
H	30.2	(130)	(39.4)

On the basis of the above figures, strategy E has the greatest 'desirability'. Set a sales price of £15 and contract to buy at least 60,000kg of materials.

(c) (i) Other factors relevant in reaching a decision might include:

Competitors. If there are competitors for the market either now or in the near future it might be more important to maximise sales volume in the short term in order to maximise profit in the longer term.

Future. The above comment assumes that there may be long-term sales prospects which do not exist.

Labour. If labour is in short supply the cost of labour should include lost contribution from sales of existing products; if it is plentiful the opportunity cost of labour may be considerably less than that used.

Materials. If the supply is unreliable such supplies may be guaranteed by entering into a contract or else the company should set its sights on a lower sales volume.

(ii) The only right answer to a decision such as this is found with the benefit of hindsight; there is no right or wrong criterion. The expected values method shows what would occur on average if such a venture were repeated many times, which is not happening in this case. It ignores the risk, of each strategy, and ignores extreme values. The maximin or pessimists criterion concentrates solely on one, the worst, extreme value; one could just as easily use a maximax or minimax criterion. Which final criterion or combination is best for a particular organisation depends on that organisation's own attitude to risk. The third method used attempts to express this attitude to risk by combining both average and worst values. It would be difficult to assess the suitability of such a criterion, any final outcomes are likely to be confused by lack of accuracy in many of the original estimates.

19   Review of investment appraisal techniques

INTRODUCTION

The Institute of Cost and Management Accountants is the only professional body giving prominence in its management accounting syllabus to capital budgeting decisions and capital project evaluation. Questions on these subjects appear regularly, and may require either a brief essay or the application of a suitable evaluation technique to data provided.

Questions 1 and 2 in this chapter are of the essay type, while questions 3 to 5 indicate the style of the mathematical questions, which are seldom confined to the routine DCF evaluation of investments illustrated in most textbooks.

STUDY REQUIREMENTS

The capital budgeting decision
Project priority ranking criteria — payback, accounting rate of return, net present value, DCF yield
Project cost control and post-audit

QUESTIONS

1   Your company is reconsidering its methods of capital expenditure appraisal. At present only single value forecasts are prepared irrespective of the risk factors involved.

As management accountant prepare a paper for the board of directors explaining the various methods which the company could adopt to incorporate factors of risk into the appraisal process.   *(25 marks)*

2   (a)   The works manager has proposed that new equipment be installed to improve a manufacturing process. This equipment will reduce operating and maintenance costs and increase output. A sales forecast, however, indicates that no extra demand is anticipated until after 19X8.

Prepare notes to assist in evaluating this project listing the advantages and disadvantages of delaying investment in the circumstances given.

Note: It is now the end of 19X7.

(b)   If the project is implemented a post-completion audit will be required. Explain the purposes of this and indicate some of the problems likely to be encountered.   *(20 marks)*

3   A company wishes to decide when to replace the vehicles that it operates in its transport fleet.

The capital cost of a vehicle is £6,000.

Its estimated trade-in value is:

	£
If replaced after 3 years	1,000
If replaced after 4 years	700
If replaced after 5 years	300

Assume that corporation tax is 50% and that there are taxable profits to absorb capital allowances.

Tax allowance is 100% in the first year, and there is one year's delay in payment of tax and allowances.

The purchase and trade-in of vehicles is made at the beginning of a year.

The company's cost of capital for investment purposes is 15%.

Operating costs (excluding depreciation)

Year	Annual repairs and maintenance	Tyres	Fixed costs
	£	£	£
1	280	–	900
2	840	250	900
3	1,120	–	900
4	1,340	250	900
5	1,260	–	900

Fuel costs are estimated at £0.10 per mile.

Expected annual mileage is 25,000 miles.

Calculate which is the most economic option for the company, to replace its vehicles on a cycle of three, four or five years. *(25 marks)*

Present value of £1

The table shows the value today of £1 to be received or paid after a given number of years.

After n years	15%
1	0.87
2	0.76
3	0.66
4	0.57
5	0.50
6	0.43
7	0.38
8	0.33
9	0.28
10	0.25
11	0.21
12	0.19
13	0.16
14	0.14
15	0.12
16	0.11
17	0.09
18	0.08
19	0.07
20	0.06

4   A company is considering investing in a project with the following characteristics:

—   Equipment is to be purchased costing £70,000, payable at once and having a life of five years with no residual value. The equipment is used to produce one type of product whose sales are budgeted as follows:

Year to 30 June	Number of units
19X3	20
19X4	40
19X5	50
19X6	30
19X7	10
Total	150

—   The selling price of the units is to be £4,000 each.

—   Costs of units are:

Direct materials	£1,200 each
Variable production overhead	50% of direct wages
Variable selling and administration overhead	10% of selling price

—   Direct wages are paid at £3 per hour. The first unit to be produced is budgeted to take 1505.3 man-hours of work and an 80% learning curve applies to direct wages.

—   Fixed overhead relating to this project is £12,000 per annum.

—   The company requires a 12% DCF return on its investments.

(a)   Calculate whether or not the project meets the company's investment criterion, based on:

   (i)   the average direct wages rate for the whole quantity of units budgeted to be sold;
   (ii)   the direct labour times expected to be required in each individual year.

(b)   Comment briefly on the relative merits of bases (a) (i) and (a) (ii) above.

(25 marks)

Ignore the effects of tax and inflation.

Note: An 80% learning curve on ordinary graph paper would show the following relationship between the x axis (volume) and y axis (cumulative average cost of elements subject to the learning curve):

x	$y\%$	x	$y\%$
1	100	70	25.48
2	80	80	24.40
10	47.65	90	23.50
20	38.13	100	22.71
30	33.46	110	22.03
40	30.50	120	21.41
50	28.39	130	20.86
60	26.77	140	20.38
		150	19.93

5   A company is considering an overseas project which will involve the investment (in 19X0 money terms) of £1 million in plant, divided evenly over 19X1 and 19X2. This investment will yield a gross income of £800,000 per annum from 19X3 to 19X6 inclusive, but will incur costs of £200,000 per annum over the same period, both figures in 19X0 money terms.

Inflation for the period in question (with 19X0 as 100) is forecast as 20% per annum for plant and 10% per annum for income and costs. The projected local consumer price index, affecting income, plant investment and other costs, is an increase of 12% per annum. Taxation can be ignored.

(a)   Calculate for the project:

   (i)   the discounted cash flow (DCF) rate (internal rate of return) in real terms to the nearest whole number;
   (ii) the net present value (NPV) if the cost of capital is 10% real.

(b)   List any four tests of sensitivity analysis that could be applied to help management in its decision on this proposed investment.

(c)   (i)   Calculate, using a simulation method based on random numbers and working upwards cumulatively from the lowest levels of expenditure, income and costs at 00 to the highest levels at 99, the NPV of the project at 10% real if the random numbers appearing were:

	Random number
for plant	35
for income	06
for costs	93

An analysis of the possible levels of plant investment, income and costs shows the following:

Plant investment		Income		Costs	
Level in 19X0 money per annum	Probability of that level	Level in 19X0 money per level	Probability of that level	Level in 19X0 money per level	Probability of that level
£000		£000		£000	
450	0.10	650	0.10	170	0.10
500	0.50	700	0.15	185	0.20
550	0.30	750	0.25	200	0.40
600	0.07	800	0.35	215	0.20
650	0.03	850	0.15	230	0.10
	1.00		1.00		1.00

   (ii) Explain, very briefly, what advantages, if any, you see in this method of risk analysis (if a sufficiently large number of calculations were carried out) as compared with sensitivity analysis.   *(25 marks)*

ANSWERS

1

To: Board of Directors
From: Management Accountant
Subject: Introductory outline: provision for the risk factor in capital investment appraisal

(a)   *The need to make provision for the risk factor*

Hitherto decisions to adopt or reject investment projects have been made on the basis of *single value* forecasts. Investigations after the implementation of a project have frequently shown that these forecasts have not been achieved; indeed it is in the nature of forecasts to be imperfect, and there is a high possibility that the actual cash flows resulting from a decision will deviate from what is expected.

It is desirable therefore that we should take account of the possible effects of this uncertainty at the time a project is submitted for approval.

The purpose of this paper is to describe three possible techniques for doing this, without at this stage making any firm recommendation as to which should be adopted by this company. I have described these techniques as:

> sensitivity analysis;
> probability estimation;
> risk simulation.

(b)   *Sensitivity analysis*

Sensitivity analysis is not a method of quantifying risk but an attempt to identify which elements ('variables') in a forecast are most likely to affect the profit outcome.

In its simplest form it consists of:

(i)   breaking down the cash flow on a project into a number of major variables, such as initial outlay cost, production efficiency, wage rates, sales volume and selling price — though in practice there will be many more;

(ii)   taking each variable in turn and modifying it by a predetermined percentage upwards and downwards from the single-point estimate;

(iii)   recalculating the DCF rate of return on the project taking each new estimate in turn.

This procedure will show that the return achievable on the project is particularly sensitive to the accuracy of prediction of one or more key variables, and efforts can then be directed to improving the quality of those estimates.

The method does not show the likelihood of particular deviations occurring.

(c)   *Probability estimation*

Numerous procedures are available but the following is suggested for consideration. Taking *sales (units)* for example, assume that it is considered most unlikely that the figure will be less than two million or more than three million. This range of values is divided into sub-ranges and a judgement is made of the *probability* of actual sales falling within each sub-range.

Sub-range	Probability
(000s)	
2,001-2,200	0.1
2,201-2,400	0.4
2,401-2,600	0.2
2,601-2,800	0.2
2,801-3,000	0.1
	1.0

As 'probability' is a matter of opinion, several managers may submit their independent judgements and a consensus be reached.

The difficulty in using such forecasts is that the definition of sub-ranges would not be the same for all variables. The weighted average for each variable could be used in calculating a DCF rate of return, but a range of probable DCF rates could not be obtained.

(d)   *Risk simulation*

This last problem could be overcome by what is in practice a rather simpler procedure — to ask each estimator to carry out a three-point probability estimation using predetermined probability percentages that were common to all variables and equidistant from the mean; e.g. if the most likely figure of sales is 2,400, there is a 10% chance that it might be above 2,800 and a 10% chance that it might be below 2,200. From data in this form it is possible to create a probability distribution curve for each variable each year. A package computer program can then be used to take a number of random samples from the various probability curves and to combine them into a DCF probability distribution for the project as a whole. This will indicate the degree of risk that the rate of return on the project will incur at various levels.

(e)   In conclusion I should point out that none of these methods can dictate the correct decision on a project, but any of them can assist the board in evaluating the uncertainties in the project under review.

2

(a)   *Advantages and disadvantages of delaying investment in the new equipment*

Advantages

(i)   It is not clear to what extent the reductions in costs are reductions in

285

unit costs caused by an increase in output. If this is so, it is significant that an increase in output is needed only to satisfy sales in 19X9.

Sales prospects are more predictable in the short term than in the long term because of the uncertainty of economic trends and of the actions of competitors, and unforeseen events over the next six months could drastically change the outlook for 19X9. A more reliable estimate should be possible at the end of 19X8.

(ii) During the period when increased output was not needed, it is possible that the cost savings would be more than offset by the financing costs of the investment.

(iii) It is possible that the available finance could be put to more profitable uses during 19X8.

(iv) It is possible that further technological innovations will improve the design of the equipment during 19X8.

Disadvantages

(i) The purchase price of the quipment is almost certain to rise in the not too distant future and it could well be that a substantial saving can be made by purchasing now rather than later.

(ii) Even though the general level of turnover is not thought likely to increase this year, there may be week by week fluctuations in demand and the availability of reserve productive capacity would make it possible to meet such demands without overtime working.

(iii) The new equipment should be less likely to break down and disrupt output.

(b) *The post-completion audit*

Capital investment projects are authorised when management is convinced that the company will benefit from them. It is likely, however, that what actually happens will differ from what had been forecast because of bias in the preparation of forecasts, the uncertainties inherent in any forecast, or the specification of the project (intentionally or otherwise) had been modified during the course of implementation.

A post-completion audit will bring to light these various influences, enable revised operating plans to be made, improve the quality of future forecasts and act as an inducement to take care when presenting estimates.

The problems encountered in a post-completion audit are those of identifying and explaining deviations from estimate under three headings:

(i) Those attributable to specification changes introduced subsequent to the approval of the plan. If, for example, a new foundry was authorised to make crankcase castings but, by board decision, it was switched to the production of connecting rods and other ancillary equipment, it is virtually impossible to identify what actual operating costs might have been under the original plan,

(ii)   Those attributable to factors external to the project, such as changes in operator bonus rate, changes in sales demand and loss of production due to strikes, disrupted supplies or faulty materials,

(iii) Those that could have been but were not controlled by the project managers.

3   Preliminary notes

(i)   The shortest period over which cycles of 3, 4 and 5 years co-incide is 60 years. Bearing in mind, however, that after 20 years the discounted value of any amount is insignificant, comparisons are made over 20 years (21 years for the three-year cycle).

(ii)   Fixed costs, fuel costs and tyre costs are common to all the alternatives, and are ignored. The omission of tyre costs is open to doubt because it is not clear when tyres would be replaced during the second five-year cycle; but it is assumed that tyre wear is directly related to annual mileage.

(iii) There are alternative ways of setting out the solution to this problem, but the simplest is probably the condensed form used in the model answer to this question issued by the professional body concerned.

Capital costs

(a)   3-year replacement (7 cycles = 21 years)

	£			£
Cost of vehicle	6,000	yrs 0, 3, 6, 9, 12, 15, 18	2.76	16,560
Tax saving	(3,000)	yrs 2, 5, 8, 11, 14, 17, 20	2.09	(6,270)
Residual value	(1,000)	yrs 3, 6, 9, 12, 15, 18, 21	1.82	(1,820)
Tax on residual value	500	yrs 5, 8, 11, 14, 17, 20, 23	1.37	685
				9,155

(b)   4-year replacement (5 cycles = 20 years)

	£			£
Cost of vehicle	6,000	yrs 0, 4, 8, 12, 16	2.20	13,200
Tax saving	(3,000)	yrs 2, 6, 10, 14, 18	1.66	(4,980)
Residual value	(700)	yrs 4, 8, 12, 16, 20	1.26	(882)
Tax on residual value	350	yrs 6, 10, 14, 18, 22	0.95	333
				7,671

(c)   5-year replacement (4 cycles = 20 years)

	£			£
Cost of vehicle	6,000	yrs 0, 5, 10, 15	1.87	11,220
Tax saving	(3,000)	yrs 2, 7, 12, 17	1.42	(4,260)
Residual value	(300)	yrs 5, 10, 15, 20	0.93	(279)
Tax on residual value	150	yrs 7, 12, 17, 22	0.71	107
				6,788

Operating costs

(a)   3-year replacement (7 cycles = 21 years)

Costs	Tax saved	Net			£
280	–	280	years 1, 4, 7, 10, 13, 16, 19	2.54	711
840	(140)	700	years 2, 5, 8, 11, 14, 17, 20	2.09	1,463
1,120	(420)	700	years 3, 6, 9, 12, 15, 18, 21	1.82	1,274
	(560)	(560)	years 4, 7, 10, 13, 16, 19, 22	1.59	(890)
					2,558

(b)   4-year replacement (5 cycles = 20 years)

Costs	Tax saved	Net			£
280	–	280	years 1, 5, 9, 13, 17	1.90	532
840	(140)	700	years 2, 6, 10, 14, 18	1.66	1,162
1,120	(420)	700	years 3, 7, 11, 15, 19	1.44	1,008
1,340	(560)	780	years 4, 8, 12, 16, 20	1.26	983
	(670)	(670)	years 5, 9, 13, 17, 21	1.09	(730)
					2,955

(c)   5-year replacement (4 cycles = 20 years)

Costs	Tax saved	Net			£
280	–	280	years 1, 6, 11, 16	1.62	454
840	(140)	700	years 2, 7, 12, 17	1.42	994
1,120	(420)	700	years 3, 8, 13, 18	1.23	861
1,340	(560)	780	years 4, 9, 14, 19	1.06	827
1,260	(670)	590	years 5, 10, 15, 20	.93	549
	(630)	(630)	years 6, 11, 16, 21	.81	(510)
					3,175

Summary

Replacement period in years	Capital costs	Operating costs	Total
	£	£	£
3	9,155	2,558	11,713
4	7,671	2,955	10,626
5	6,788	3,175	9,963

Conclusion: The vehicles should be replaced at five-year intervals.

Note: An alternative answer would be to calculate the present value in perpetuity of each alternative.

4

(a)   (i)   To produce the 150 total number of units, the average direct labour hours will be 1,505.3 × 19.93% (from the table provided), i.e. 300 hours approx.

288

The direct labour cost per unit will on average be 300 × £3 = £900; the variable production overheads per unit will be 50% × £900 = £450.

The relevant cash flows will therefore be:

Year	1	2	3	4	5
Units	20	40	50	30	10
	£	£	£	£	£
Sales value	80,000	160,000	200,000	120,000	40,000
Direct material	24,000	48,000	60,000	36,000	12,000
Variable selling and administration	8,000	16,000	20,000	12,000	4,000
Fixed overhead	12,000	12,000	12,000	12,000	12,000
	44,000	76,000	92,000	60,000	28,000
Margin	36,000	84,000	108,000	60,000	12,000
Labour and production overhead	27,000	54,000	67,500	40,500	13,500
Operating cash flow	9,000	30,000	40,500	19,500	(1,500)
12% discount factors	.89	.80	.71	.64	.57
Discounted cash flow	8,010	24,000	28,755	12,480	(855)

	£72,390
Less purchase of equipment	70,000
Net present value	2,390

On this basis the project meets the company's investment criterion.

(ii) Working for learning curve impact:

Year	Units	Cumulative units	Cumulative hrs @ 1505.3	% factor	Hours	Incremental hours	@ £4.50
							£
1	20	20	30,106	38.13	11,479	11,479	51,655
2	40	60	90,318	26.77	24,178	12,699	57,145
3	50	110	165,583	22.03	36,478	12,300	55,350
4	30	140	210,742	20.38	42,949	6,471	29,120
5	10	150	225,795	19.93	45,000	2,051	9,230
						45,000	202,500

Year	1 £	2 £	3 £	4 £	5 £	
Margin from workings for (a) (i)	36,000	84,000	108,000	60,000	12,000	
Direct labour and variable production overhead	51,655	57,145	55,350	29,120	9,230	
	(15,655)	26,855	52,650	30,880	2,770	97,500
12% discount factors	.89	.80	.71	.64	.57	
Discounted cash flow	(13,933)	21,484	37,382	19,763	1,579	

$$£66,275$$

Equipment		70,000
Net present value		(3,725)

On this basis, the project does not meet the company's investment criterion.

(b) Method (a) (i) is incorrect, because although on average the direct labour hours will be 300 per unit, longer times will be needed in the earlier years of the project, and shorter times in the later years. Method (a) (i) therefore does not give a correct statement of labour-related costs (and therefore of cash flows) over the various years of the project.

5

(a) In part (a) the examiner asks for a yield in real terms and a net present value using a real 10% as the discount rate. Since the cash flows are given in 19X0 money terms the inflation rates given in the question would not appear to be required and the calculation would be:

	£000	10%		30%	
19X1	(500)	.91	(455)	.77	(385)
19X2	(500)	.83	(415)	.59	(295)
19X3	600	.75	450	.46	276
19X4	600	.68	408	.35	210
19X5	600	.62	372	.27	162
19X6	600	.56	336	.21	126
	1,400		NPV 696		94

This indicates an NPV at 10% of £696,000 and a DCF yield or internal rate of return in excess of 30%.

Having made the above statement, which is correct on the face of the information given, the student must attempt to identify why home and 'local' inflation rates have been provided.

If inflation overseas is running at a lower rate than at home, this will tend to cause the foreign exchange rate to move against the home currency, and vice versa. If therefore investment and income have occurred in local currency but have been converted into home currency at a constant rate, the statement of cash flows in terms of home currency will be incorrect and should be adjusted. In simplistic terms the adjusting indices will be as follows:

Year	Plant			Income and costs		
	Home rate	Local rate	Index	Home rate	Local rate	Index
19X0	100	100	1.00	100	100	1.00
19X1	120	112	1.07	110	112	0.98
19X2	144	125	1.15	121	125	0.97
19X3				133	140	0.95
19X4				146	157	0.93
19X5				161	176	0.915
19X6				177	197	0.90

Applying these indices to the original £500 and £600 cash flows would give the following results:

Year	Modified cash flows	10%		Trial at 29%	
	£000		£000		£000
19X1	(535)	.91	(487)	.775	(415)
19X2	(575)	.83	(477)	.600	(345)
19X3	570	.75	428	.466	266
19X4	558	.68	379	.361	201
19X5	549	.62	340	.280	154
19X6	540	.56	302	.217	117
NPV			485		(22)

This gives a revised indication of NPV at 10% of £485,000, and a DCF yield or internal rate of return just below 29%.

(b) Sensitivity analysis is the process of testing the variation in project acceptability in response to variation in selected project variables. A listing only is asked for in the question.

(i) Effect of delays in bringing the project to production, e.g. construction over three years instead of two years.
(ii) Effect of escalation in plant costs.
(iii) Effect of variation in the commercial life of the entire project.
(iv) Effect of cost inflation which does not result in a corresponding income increase.

(c) (i) It must be assumed that the 'random number' indicators correspond to cumulative probabilities, e.g.:

Plant investment

Amount £000	Cumulative probability	Random numbers
450	0.10	00 – 09
500	0.60	10 – 59
550	0.90	60 – 89
600	0.97	90 – 96
650	1.00	97 – 99

Using this interpretation:

		£
Plant investment	RN 35	500,000
Income	RN 06	650,000
Costs	RN 93	230,000
		420,000

The net present value at 10% using the above data and adjusting by the differential inflation indices would be:

Year	Cash flow £000		10% factor	Discounted cash flow £000
19X1	500 × 1.07	= (535)	.91	(487)
19X2	500 × 1.15	= (575)	.83	(477)
19X3	420 × 0.95	= 399	.75	299
19X4	420 × 0.93	= 391	.68	266
19X5	420 × 0.915	= 384	.62	238
19X6	420 × 0.90	= 378	.56	212
			NPV	51

(c) (ii) If the suggested procedure is repeated many times a distribution of internal rates of return for the project can be computed, thus providing management with additional guidance in decision making. The distiribution of each variable must be known in order that random samples can be selected from each, and the values combined to produce an internal rate of return. Such an internal rate of return is a project simulation whereas sensitivity analysis is selective in identifying the impact on project return of change in a single variable.

Note: This answer is not the only solution, owing to the confusion caused by the question using a constant real cost of capital in conjunction with different rates of inflation. In practice this is impossible.

20 Divisional performance measurement

INTRODUCTION

A 'division' for the purpose of this chapter is a profit centre, in the sense that the manager is fully responsible for the profitability of the activities he controls. He will have a substantial degree of authority to decide what his operations will be, and also how he carries them out. The assets employed in the division will either be controlled by him directly or administered centrally on his behalf. In either case the primary measure of divisional performance will be the rate of return achieved on divisional capital employed. Changes in this rate will be investigated by the use of subsidiary ratios and statistical performance indicators in the same way as for an independent business, though it must be emphasised that a division can never be entirely independent. It is a substantially self-contained part of a larger whole, the interests of which may require some central intervention in the division's affairs.

In some cases a division will be charged interest on its capital employed, and will then be judged on the amount of 'residual income' achieved after satisfying that cost of capital.

The majority of examination questions on divisional performance require narrative answers (possibly referring to a simple example) dealing with particular difficulties in defining divisional profit or capital employed; but one comprehensive arithmetical question has been included as question 3 in this chapter.

Because divisions are profit centres, the procedures for inter-firm comparison can be applied to them, and an example of this is provided in question 6.

STUDY REQUIREMENTS

Financial planning and control in divisionalised companies
Inter-firm comparisons and intra-group comparisons between subsidiaries

QUESTIONS

1   Cobbold Ltd, a long-established, highly centralised, company, has grown to the extent that its chief executive, despite having a good supporting team, is finding difficulty in keeping up with the many decisions of importance.

Consideration is therefore being given to reorganising the company into profit centres. These would be product divisions, headed by a divisional managing director, who would be responsible for all the division's activities relating to its products.

Explain in outline:

(a)   the types of decision area that should be transferred to the new divisional managing directors if such a reorganisation is to achieve its objectives;

(b)   the types of decision area that might reasonably be retained at company head office;

(c)   the management accounting problems that might be expected to arise in introducing effective profit centres.

(20 marks)

2   Divisionalisation is a common form of organisational arrangement but there is some diversity of opinion as to the best measure of divisional performance.

Discuss this topic and describe and compare the main performance measures that have been suggested.

(17 marks)

3   A group of companies is divided into ten operating divisions, each of which is autonomous. The cost of capital for the group is 12% per annum and it is currently earning 15% on its capital employed.

In the ROCE calculation, return is equated with net profit and capital employed is the figure at the beginning of the financial year. All fixed assets are depreciated on a straight-line basis. Investments in new projects include incremental working capital. Projects sold or withdrawn from operation are treated as consisting of fixed assets only.

If no new capital expenditure transactions take place the position of four of the divisions would be:

Division	Capital employed as at 1 January 19X0	Budgeted for 19X0	
		Net profit	Sales
	£000	£000	£000
P	320	80	800
Q	450	150	1,400
R	280	84	700
S	200	26	200

The following transactions are proposed:

Division P: Investment of £100,000 to yield sales of £150,000 per annum and net profit of £20,000 per annum.

Division Q: Sale for £75,000 of a project that is budgeted to yield a net profit of £15,000 in 19X0. The original equipment cost £600,000 seven years ago with an expected life of eight years.

Division R: (i) Sale of product line at book value. The original equipment cost £60,000 two years ago with an expected life of three years. This line is budgeted to yield a net profit of £20,000 in 19X0, combined with

(ii) replacement of (i) above by investing £100,000 in a new product to yield £30,000 per annum.

Division S: Investment of £80,000 in a project to yield sales of £36,000 per annum and a net profit of £11,200 per annum.

Note: In connection with each of the above transactions, you are to assume that the sale and/or investment would be completed by 1 January 19X0 so as to be included in the relevant ROCE calculations for the year 19X0. Ignore taxation and inflation and assume that actual results are as budgeted.

(a) On the assumption that each transaction goes ahead:

(i) Calculate the new ROCE for each division for the year ending 31 December 19X0.

(ii) Identify those divisional managers whose bonuses will be higher if they receive annual bonuses directly related to the level of their respect ROCE.

(iii) State in respect of each division whether the group's interests will be favourably or adversely affected by the proposed transactions. Explain briefly why in each case. *(10 marks)*

(b) Identify, with brief reasons, which proposals the group would approve if its new capital expenditure were limited to £200,000 for the four divisions. *(4 marks)*

(c) (i) Compare the old results of division P and division S, both of which are in the same type of business, and briefly advise the divisional manager of division S how he might improve his performance based on the data concerning division P.

(ii) Comment briefly on how the new project for division S fits in with the advice given in (c) (i) above. *(5 marks)*

(d) Calculate the lowest price at which the equipment should be sold by division Q if the transaction proposed is to break-even financially for the group. *(3 marks)*

(e) (i) Explain briefly the concept of 'residual income' in the context of performance evaluation.

   (ii) Calculate the residual income for each division for 19X0 on the assumption that each transaction goes ahead. *(3 marks)*

(Total 25 marks)

4   The finance director of Jackson Brothers plc is considering a change in the procedures for evaluating divisional performance. Instead of merely charging interest on intra-company cash borrowing, he is considering the charging of interest on the company's total investment in each division.

Comment on this proposal and discuss the difficulties and advantages of such a system.

(6 marks)

5   At a recent meeting of the board of the Alpha Omega Group, the group finance director proposed that all properties owned by operating companies should be transferred to a newly formed group property company and that the properties should be leased back to the operating companies at a rental of 10% of their value as assessed by professional valuers.

AB Ltd, one of the operating companies, currently owns a factory that was valued at £150,000 ten years ago when the company was acquired by the Alpha Omega Group. The company expects the factory to be valued at £300,000 now.

In calculating its profits hitherto, it has been charging depreciation on a straight-line basis of 1½% per annum on the value ten years ago of this factory.

In the year just ended, AB Ltd's sales were £1,100,000, its profits were £91,000 and its return on capital employed (ROCE) was 26%.

(a)   Calculate the change in AB Ltd's ROCE that would result from acceptance of the group's proposal if all other relevant factors did not change.

(b)   Discuss briefly the extent to which the results of the above proposed transaction cast doubt on the validity of the use of ROCE as a means of measuring company performance within the group.

(20 marks)

6   As management accountant for a group of four similar companies you have recently introduced an interfirm comparison scheme. A summary of basic information received from each company for the period under review is given below:

	Companies			
	A	B	C	D
	£000	£000	£000	£000
Operating profit	221	209	315	162
Net current assets	520	385	525	315
Fixed assets	930	715	975	585
Sales	2,470	1,980	2,925	1,665
Production cost	1,605	1,228	1,784	1,016
Selling cost	370	317	497	300
Administration cost	274	226	329	187

(a) Present the information to management in such a way as to compare clearly the results achieved by each company with those of the rest of the group.

(b) Write a short constructive report to the directors of company A, setting out the possible reasons for the differences in their results as compared with the rest of the group.

(30 marks)

ANSWERS

1

(a)   The objective would seem to be to improve decision making by two means:

–   by restructuring the organisation to allow product group specialisations;
–   by delegating certain decision areas.

These decision areas for transfer would include:

(i)   product decisions — introduction, withdrawal, etc, and all matters relating to marketing mix — pricing, promotion, etc;

(ii)   plant replacement and disinvestment (with some constraints);

(iii)   stock-carrying decisions;

(iv)   employment decisions within the product group except perhaps those at the highest level;

(v)   short-term financing arrangements, although this will depend upon the degree of autonomy given to the product groups;

(vi)   short-term operational decisions of all kinds — subcontracting, rerouting of products, direction of marketing effort.

It is not suggested, of course, that product group managing directors would personally make all the decisions mentioned. However, they would have ultimate control over the decision process, and over managers at varying levels in the product group hierarchy.

(b)   The type of decision area retained at head office will be heavily influenced by the degree of autonomy given to the product groups. It is clearly implied that the product groups will be responsible for production, marketing, etc, but there are service areas to be considered, as well as influences that will permeate all product groups, e.g. financing. The head office will in all probability retain the following decision areas:

(i)   company financing decisions; for example, it may be considered important that company borrowing powers and commitments are carefully controlled, and certainly dividend policy, affecting the flow of funds available from retentions, is a company and not a product group matter;

(ii)   appointment of top personnel, although one would of course expect the product group managing director to be involved as well;

(iii)   company sourcing decisions; where more than one product group used the same raw material, component, etc, corporate interests may be best served by making this a head office activity;

(iv)   arbitration decisions if transfer pricing between groups is involved;

(v)   final decisions on major capital expenditure programmes in the product groups;

(vi)   decisions on matters to benefit the company rather than an individual product group, e.g. taxation, leasing negotiations, computer applications, etc;

(vii) decisions on product group closure, sale, etc.

(c)   The key word in this section seems to be 'introducing', in that there are a number of problems to be settled at the inception of profit centre control on a product group basis. These will include:

(i)   How, and by whom, will profit targets be established for the product group?

(ii)   If significant inter-product group trading occurs, a price determination mechanism is required. Such prices will affect the reported results and apparent success of two profit centres.

(iii)   At what level will profit centre results be controlled? If the answer is to be at the 'below the line' point, problems arise in making cost apportionments when sharing company cost between all profit centres.

(iv)   A behavioural problem may exist in that the top management of each profit centre is being encouraged to think of its own product group as a separate firm and to manage it accordingly. At the same time they must be asked to recognise that they will not be able to take unrestricted action in maximising profit centre profits. The company-wide view must be taken into account.

2   The purpose of divisionalisation, as contrasted with any other form of decentralisation, is to delegate profit responsibility. The scope of this delegation varies from business to business, and will influence the nature of the main measure of divisional performance. The three measures commonly used are:

> divisional profit;
> rate of return on divisional capital employed;
> residual income.

(a)   *Divisional profit.* The profit achieved would be compared against a budget or target and variances in volume, prices and rate of expenditure would be brought under review. It is likely, since a division is not a completely independent business, that some costs will be charged to the division in respect of goods or services provided by other segments of the enterprise. Some of these will be requisitioned as required by the divisional manager and will be charged at 'arm's length' prices. Others, however, will be apportionments of cost over which the divisional manager may have no control in the short term. For the purpose of judging the manager's personal achievement, a 'controllable profit' figure may be used prior to charging these non-controllable costs.

(b) *Rate of return on divisional capital employed.* This is the more appropriate measure when divisional management can influence significantly the level of divisional investment — whether in stocks, debtors or fixed assets. There are problems, however, in deciding

   (i) what assets should be included in divisional capital employed, e.g. whether the figure should be confined to those assets which are under the direct control of the divisional manager or should be extended to apportionments of central assets in various categories;

   (ii) at what value the assets should be included in the statement of capital employed.

   Since this is an internal measure, the precise definition of capital (or of profit) might not be regarded as of overriding importance provided target rates of return were set on a comparable basis. The weakness of this contention becomes apparent however when there is need to compare the rates of return achieved by different divisions having different capital structures.

(c) *Residual income.* Divisional residual income is divisional profit less an imputed interest charge on the net assets employed by the division. The rate of 'interest' will normally be the required pre-tax rate of return of the enterprise as a whole, so that any residual income will indicate earnings in excess of a normal rate of return.

   It is argued that since the capital employed has already yielded the return required, the success of the division can be judged from the absolute amount of the residual income, without further regard to the amount of capital used in achieving it.

   The following example illustrates the point:

	Division X	Division Y
Divisional capital employed	£10,000	£35,000
Divisional profit	£1,750	£4,200
Rate of return on capital	17½%	12%
If enterprise cost of capital is 8%:		
Divisional profit as above	£1,750	£4,200
Capital charge	800	2,800
Residual income	950	1,400
If enterprise cost of capital is 15%:		
Divisional profit	£1,750	£4,200
Capital charge	1,500	5,250
Residual income	250	(1,050)

Thus on the basis of divisional profit division Y earns more than division X, and would be said to have the better performance. But division Y employs considerably more capital. On the basis of return on capital employed, division X is the more successful.

If however the company's required rate of return is only 8%, division Y (having satisfied the rate of return requirement) is the more successful division, yielding a residual income of £1,400 compared with £950 only from division X.

3

(a) (i)

	Division			
	P	Q	R	S
	£000	£000	£000	£000
Profit				
Original 19X0 budget	80	150	84	26
Proposals:				
Additions to profit	20		30	11.2
Reductions of profit		15	20	
Revised profit	100	135	94	37.2
Capital employed				
Original 1980 budget	320	450	280	200
Proposals:				
Additions to C/E	100		100	80
Reductions of C/E		75	20	
Revised capital employed	420	375	360	280
ROCE	23.8%	36%	26.1%	13.3%

(ii) ROCE on original budget 25% 33% 30% 13%

Therefore the divisional managers of Q and S will benefit from increased bonus payments in 19X0.

(iii) The group's cost of capital is stated to be 12% and this is therefore the 'hurdle' rate for investment and divestment decisions in the divisions. the 12% rate would preferably be used as a discount rate to be applied to the incremental cash flows. This is not possible in this question since the inclusion of working capital in the investments makes it impossible to establish depreciation figures and therefore cash flows. As a result the ROCE approach to this part of the question will have to be taken using 19X0 figures, even though it is appreciated that ROCE will tend to increase year by year since depreciation reduces the investment base.

	P £000	Q £000	R £000	S £000
Incremental or (lost) profit	20	(15)	10	11.2
Incremental or (lost) C/E	100	(75)	80	80
ROCE for proposal	20%	(20%)	12½%	14%
ROCE for original budget	25%	33%	30%	13%
Group cost of capital	12%	12%	12%	12%

Thus in every case the ROCE for the proposal exceeds the group cost of capital. This means that the proposals for divisions P, R and S are favourable to the group interest, despite the fact that it has already been shown in part (a)(i) that divisional ROCE for P and R will deteriorate. The proposal for division Q should not be undertaken since it deprives the group of a return in excess of the group cost of capital. However, there is the unanswered question of what return may be earned on the reinvestment of the sales proceeds of £75,000.

(b) As suggested under (a)(iii), the 12% cost of capital should be used as a discount rate, and the proposal for division Q eliminated from the range of possibilities. Available new investment funds £200,000.

Competing projects:

	Finance required	ROCE	Residual income
Division P	£100,000	20%	£8,000
R	£100,000 (net)	12½%	£400
S	£80,000	14%	£1,600

The board would therefore choose the projects in divisions P and S, as having the highest ROCE figures and the highest aggregate residual income.

(c) (i) The term 'old results' is taken to mean the 19X0 budget on the assumption that none of the proposals is to be implemented.

Division

	P	S
ROCE	25%	13%
Profit/sales	10%	13%
Capital turnover rate	2.5	1
Hence:	2.5 × 10% = 25%	1 × 13% = 13%

The profit/sales % in division S compares favourably with that of division P. This suggests that division S's problems may not be cost inefficiency, low product volume, etc. The real problem seems to be the turnover of capital employed. If this figure could be raised to 2 for example, ROCE would become 26%. Whilst additional volume would tend to increase both the profit/sales % and the capital turnover rate (and therefore ROCE), it may pay the divisional manager in S to question asset utilisation, stock levels, credit control, etc to see if the same level and profitability of sales is possible on a lower level of net asset investment.

(ii) The proposal in division S was:

ROCE £11,200/£80,000 = 14%
Profit/sales % £11,200/£36,000 = 31%
Capital turnover, etc £36,000/£80,000 = 0.45

It is evident therefore that whilst the proposal offers a ROCE marginally in excess of the 12% cost of capital, it does so by margin profitability, since the capital turnover rate is less than half the existing one. In this sense then it is not consistent with the advice given in (c)(i).

(d) In part (a)(iii) it was suggested that the divestment decision should be made incrementally. Because of this view the proposal for division Q was rejected, since by depriving the division of £75,000 income from the sale of a project the division was also deprived of £15,000 profits — a return of 20%, considerably in excess of the 12% cost of capital. The decision changes therefore when the rising disposal value makes the potential profit equal to 12% of that disposal value:

i.e. £15,000 is to equal 12%, break-even disposal value is £125,000

(e) (i) The concept of residual income attempts to give recognition to the investment base. In this way comparisons of residual income are valid in that a financing cost has already been taken out of profits made.

(ii)

	Division			
	P	Q	R	S
	£000	£000	£000	£000
Profit forecast	100	135	94	37.2
Cost of capital	50.4	45	43.2	33.6
Residual income	49.6	90	50.8	3.6

Note: The above calculations could have been made using the return on capital employed figure of 15%.

4   The finance director's proposal is that divisional performance shall be judged by reference to a division's residual income — where residual income is period profit less an interest charge for the company's investment in the division. The aim is to charge a division for the funds which it uses and thus to encourage divisional managers to have regard to the cost of finance in their decision making. The method is more appropriate for divisions which have a significant degree of control over the level of investment, i.e. it is more appropriate for profit centres that are also investment centres than for organisations where investment decisions are taken centrally.

The status of divisions in Jackson Brothers plc in this respect is not stated; but the system in current use requires managers to consider the cost of finance since they are charged interest on borrowing and they earn interest on loans. This system could however lead to disputes on the matter of remittances to head office, since presumably head office will periodically siphon off surplus cash. The proposal under consideration may be considered as a means of avoiding such difficulties. Residual income however has its own difficulties.

Since residual income is *divisional profit* less an imputed *interest charge* on *divisional assets*, it is appropriate to consider the difficulties for each of these component parts.

Divisional profit

Divisional profit will be calculated whether or not an interest charge is introduced. There will be measurement problems (such as the need to deal with joint costs) but these should have been faced — and satisfactorily answered — at an earlier stage. It is generally agreed that a distinction should be made between items that are controllable by the divisional management and those that are not controllable. It may be thought appropriate to include some or all of the non-controllable items in the divisional profit and loss account but these should be introduced after a controllable profit figure has been calculated.

Divisional assets

There can be considerable difficulties in identifying and valuing a division's investment in its assets. The main problems are:

(i)   Should the division's assets be reduced by its liabilities to give a net asset figure?
(ii) Should fixed assets be valued at original cost, current net book value or at an appraised value?
(iii) How should assets shared by more than one division be dealt with?
(iv) Should the investment base be taken at the beginning of the accounting period, at the period end or at some intermediate date?

These are the same problems as arise when a divisional rate of return is to be calculated.

Interest charge

It is usually proposed that the interest rate to be used for calculating the interest charge is the company's cost of capital rate which it uses in its investment decisions. A possible difficulty with the use of this rate (and with residual income itself) has been discussed by Amey. Amey claims that an emphasis on a division's residual income could lead the divisional manager to make erroneous operating decisions because the imputed interest charge at the cost of capital rate is not relevant for such decisions.

5

(a)   The present book value of the factory would be:

$$£150,000 - (10 \times 1\tfrac{1}{2}\% \times £150,000) = £127,500$$

As we are told that profits of £91,000 represent a rate of return of 26% on capital employed, the total book value of the capital employed by AB Ltd must be:

$$£91,000/0.26 \qquad = £350,000$$

The value of net assets other than the
factory would therefore be: £222,500

As a result of the group's proposal, the declared profit of AB Ltd would be:

	£
Existing profits	91,000
Add depreciation charge, no longer	
made (1½% × £150,000)	2,250
Deduct rent (10% × £300,000)	(30,000)
Adjusted profit	63,250

The new rate of return on capital employed would therefore be £63,250/ £222,500 = 28.43%, 2.43 percentage points higher than the rate of return currently calculated.

(b) In assessing the performance of an individual company, the only requirement relating to the valuation of assets and the calculation of profit is that both target (or budget) and actual figures shall be calculated on the same basis.

If the performance of a company is to be compared with that of other companies, either within or outside the group, it is essential that the 'actual' figures of all of them shall be on a common basis. In particular:

(i) It is not valid to compare rates of return on capital employed when similar assets in different companies were acquired at different prices (and thus give rise to different depreciation charges) for reasons not connected with operating requirements. A common solution to this difficulty is to revalue the assets of all companies at a common, normally a current, price level.

(ii) It is not valid to compare rates of return on capital employed when some companies occupy purchased premises and others are renting the premises they use. A common solution is to delete the value of premises from the figure of capital employed, and to charge the profit and loss account with an economic rental for the premises occupied.

The group in this question therefore has proposed a correct solution to one of the problems of inter-company comparison, and at the same time has created a property-holding company from the results of which the benefit of property investment can be judged.

6

(a) From the following table, the results achieved by each company can be compared with those of other companies in the group. Because in part (b) a comparison is required between the results of company A and those of the 'rest of the group', the combined results of companies B, C and D have been shown in the last column of the table.

ABCD Group Limited   *Year ended*

Comparative ratios

		A	B	C	D	B, C & D combined
Return on capital employed	(%)	15.2	19.0	21.0	18.0	19.6
Sales to capital employed	(times)	1.7	1.8	1.95	1.85	1.9
Profit to sales	(%)	8.9	10.6	10.8	9.7	10.4
Costs (% of sales):						
Production		65.0	62.0	61.0	61.0	61.3
Selling		15.0	16.0	17.0	18.0	17.0
Administration		11.1	11.4	11.2	11.3	11.3
Total		91.1	89.4	89.2	90.3	89.6
Assets (per £ of sales):						
Current	(£)	0.21	0.19	0.18	0.19	0.19
Fixed	(£)	0.38	0.36	0.33	0.35	0.35
Total	(£)	0.59	0.55	0.51	0.54	0.54

(b) To: Board of Directors, A Ltd   Date . . . . . .
From: Group Management Accountant

Company performance for year ended . . . . . .

The enclosed statement summarises the main financial ratios for your company for the year just ended, and compares them with those for other companies in the group.

You will see that the company's rate of return on capital employed is lower than that of any other company.

This has occurred because not only is your profit per £1 sales lower than that of other companies but also you are achieving less sales value per £1 of capital employed.

Looking first at the company's cost structure:

(i)   Administration costs represent a lower proportion of sales value (11.1%) than in any other company. One would not expect, however, that administration costs would vary in proportion to sales value. Most such costs are fixed in amount. The fact is that the administration costs of company A, at £274,000, are the second highest in the group. It would be worth investigating whether economies could be achieved.

(ii)   Selling costs again represent only 15% of sales value, as compared with an average of 17% for the other three companies. This is a favourable feature of the results, but at the same time could provide the starting point for investigating whether a relatively small increase in sales promotion activities might give rise to proportionately higher increases in sales and profit earned.

(iii) Production costs, at 65% of sales value, are excessively high in relation to those of the other three similar companies. Among the reasons for this might be:

— failure to increase your selling prices in line with cost increases;
— an unsatisfactory product mix, perhaps due to badly directed selling efforts;
— the inclusion in sales of transfers to other companies at prices below the outside market price;
— inefficient buying at uneconomic prices, either this year or in previous years with excess quantities brought forward in opening stocks;
— inefficient manufacturing techniques or performance.

More detailed comparisons with other companies, perhaps by direct discussion with them, might be helpful.

Turning now to the capital turnover ratio, I have already suggested that the sales value achieved might be improved by changes in prices or products, or by more efficient use of materials and manpower. With regard to your investment in assets, I have calculated in addition to the ratios displayed that your total asset structure comprises 64% fixed assets and 36% current assets, compared with a 65/35% split in all other companies. Overall this difference is not significant; but it will be worthwhile to make a more detailed breakdown so as to ensure that the mix of assets (e.g. stocks and debtors less creditors within the total current assets) does not show wide deviations from that in other companies.

21 Transfer pricing

INTRODUCTION

Where goods or services are transferred between divisions in an enterprise, it is important that so far as possible transfer prices shall be set in such a way as to ensure:

— incentive to the manager of the supplying division;
— goal congruence between divisional and organisational objectives; the managers of the divisions concerned should be able to rely on transfer prices to guide them in making volume decisions that will be in the interest of the enterprise as a whole;
— autonomy for divisional managers, i.e. the minimum of central staff involvement in transfer price fixing.

Where a competitive open market price exists, this forms the ideal basis for transfer pricing; otherwise alternative means of fixing transfer prices will have to be found.

Question 1 in this chapter calls for discussion of alternative methods. Questions 2 to 4 deal with the practical application of transfer pricing procedures.

STUDY REQUIREMENTS

Interdivisional transfer pricing
Revision of pricing policy and contribution theory

QUESTIONS

1   A company operates four factories. Each makes components which are incorporated into the products sold by one or more of the other factories. To encourage a competitive environment the directors have decided that each factory should become a separate profit centre. This will necessitate the use of transfer prices for the inter-factory components.

(a)   Describe three different methods of establishing the transfer prices.

(b)   State which method you would recommend for the company described, giving reasons for your choice.

(c)   Prepare for the one method chosen a policy statement outlining how the pricing system would be operated among the different factories.   *(20 marks)*

2   An industrial group of companies includes two divisions, A and B. The output of division A is product A, two units of which are used by division B for every one of its product B. Division B has first call on division A's output but there is a separate market outside the group for the balance of division A's output. All the output of division B is sold outside the group.

The maximum capacity of division A is 140,000 units of A and that of division B is 50,000 units of B per annum. Each division maintains a stable level of stocks throughout the year.

The group would like to examine the results of using different bases of transfer pricing under different scenarios (i.e. situations that could be expected to arise).

The bases of transfer pricing are:

Absorbed standard cost	AS
Market price	MP
Variable cost plus a lump sum of 80% of division A's fixed cost.	VC

The scenarios are:

	Product A		Product B	
Scenario number	Market price (per unit) £	Total demand 000s	Market price (per unit) £	Total demand 000s
15	30	100	100	40
23	25	70	90	30
29	35	130	90	30

Costs per unit are:

	Product A	Product B	
Variable cost	£20	£12	(exclusive of 2 units of product A)
Fixed cost	£5	£18	
Budgeted volume in units per annum	100,000	40,000	

(a) Calculate the profits shown by division A and by division B for the following seven situations:

Scenario	Basis of transfer pricing		
15	MP	VC	–
23	–	VC	AS
29	MP	VC	AS

(b) Assume that division B receives an overseas order for 20,000 units of B that will in no way influence its other clientele. As manager of division B state, with supporting calculations, whether you would recommend acceptance of the order in the following two situations:

Scenario	Price per unit (ex factory)	Basis of transfer pricing
(i) 23	£55	AS
(ii) 29	£65	MP

(c) If you were managing director of the whole group state, with very brief reasons, whether you would recommend acceptance of the orders in (i) and (ii) above.

(30 marks)

3

(a) Quoin Ltd, an abrasives manufacturer, has two divisions. Division M manufactures abrasive grain, an intermediate product, which it can sell either to division D (where it is incorporated into coated grain final products) or on the open market (where there is perfect competition). In order to maintain a sufficient element of divisional autonomy division D is allowed to buy abrasive grain in the open market if it so wishes. There are no extra costs of buying or selling in the open market as compared with buying and selling between the divisions.

State and explain the optimal transfer pricing policy which will maximise the profits of Quoin Ltd as a whole, showing how this profit would accrue to the two divisions. *(15 marks)*

(b) Son of Quion Ltd has three divisions. Division S supplies a special grain to divisions X and Y (in lots of 100 tons), which each utilises in the preparation of its own final products. There is no other market for the special grain.

Division S has the following cost structure:

Tonnage produced	400	500	600	700	800	900	1,000
Total cost (£000)	400	420	450	485	525	585	665

Divisions X and Y can generate total net revenues (after meeting their own respective independent processing costs) as follows, in relation to the tonnage of special grain processed:

Division X

Tonnage processed	100	200	300	400
Total net revenues (£000)	120	180	220	240

Division Y

Tonnage processed	100	200	300	400	500	600
Total net revenues (£000)	120	240	360	420	460	480

Show the price at which the special grain should be transferred from division S to divisions X and Y, stating your reasons. *(10 marks)*

(Total 25 marks)

4   The Philadelphia Company has two divisions, A and B. For one of the company's products division A produces a major sub-assembly and division B incorporates this sub-assembly into the final product. There is a market for both the sub-assembly and the final product, and the divisions have been delegated profit responsibility. The transfer price for the sub-assembly has been set at long-run average market price.

The following data are available to each division:

	£
Estimated selling price for final product	300
Long-run average selling price for intermediate product	200
Outlay cost for completion in division B	150
Outlay cost in division A	120

The manager of division B has made the following calculation:

	£	£
Selling price – final product		300
Transferred-in cost (market)	200	
Outlay cost for completion	150	350
Contribution (loss) on product		£(50)

(a)   Should transfers be made to division B if there is no excess capacity in division A? Is market price the correct transfer price? *(7 marks)*

(b)   Assume that division A's maximum capacity for this product is 1,000 units per month and sales to the intermediate market are presently 800 units. Should 200 units be transferred to division B? At what relevant transfer price? Assume for a variety of reasons that A will maintain the £200 selling price indefinitely, i.e. A is not considering cutting the price to outsiders regardless of the presence of idle capacity. *(5 marks)*

(c) Suppose A quoted a transfer price of £150. What would be the contribution to the firm as a whole if the transfer were made? As manager of B, would you be inclined to buy at £150? *(5 marks)*

(d) The manager of division A has the option of:

> cutting the external price to £195 with the certainty that external sales will rise to 1,000 units;
> maintaining the outside price of £200 for the 800 units, and transferring the 200 units to B at a price that would produce the same total contribution for A.

State the minimum transfer price that should be used, and demonstrate whether it leads to the most desirable decision for the company as a whole. *(8 marks)*

(Total 25 marks)

ANSWERS

1

(a) *Alternative methods of transfer pricing*

    (i)   **At market prices.** The price would be that at which an outside competitor would be prepared to supply. Provided the supplier factory is able to produce the components at a variable cost which is lower than the competitive price it is in the company's interest that it should be given the order. There may be instances where none of the company's factories is technically equipped to compete economically, in which case the work should be ordered outside.

    (ii)   **At 'cost plus'.** The price would include not only 'full cost' but an added profit margin. This is a fair basis for the supplying factory but, unless exceptions are made, it could result in the buying factory paying more than a fair market price.

Where cost is an element in arriving at a price, such cost may be *actual* or *standard*. Standards are preferable as unpredictable month-by-month fluctuations are avoided and there is also a fairer sharing of the *inefficiency factor*. No factory operates to perfection and the buyer should be prepared to pay a reasonable amount towards the difficulties and lapses from perfection inherent in manufacture, but he should not be charged with additional cost arising from exceptional carelessness or lack of control. Standard costs provide an excellent basis as they are usually based on *good attainable performance* and include only reasonable allowances for lapses from perfection.

A modification of 'full cost' often encountered in practice is to exclude from the cost figure those selling and administration costs which are specific to external sales but are not necessary to the achievement of internal sales. At the extreme, this may be equivalent to transferring at manufacturing cost; it is sometimes listed as a separate method.

    (iii)   **At negotiated price.** Where competitive prices are not available, prices could be negotiated between the factories concerned. These would be regarded as commercially based and would be in lieu of market prices. Not being linked with some firm base they could be unrealistic.

(b) *Preferred method*

As indicated above, the preferred method when it can be used is the open market price, which gives the following advantages:

    (i)   It offers a fair reward to the supplying factory as well as an incentive to produce efficiently.

    (ii)   It leaves the buying factory in the same position as it would have been if the associated factory had not existed.

(iii) It cannot lead to controversy as to the efficiency or inefficiency of the manufacturing unit.

(iv) Executive time is not devoted to the bargaining process.

If however the components transferred are destined purely for incorporation into the company's end product and no outside market for them exists, there will be no market price.

Under such circumstances, goal congruence is best achieved by making the transfers at marginal cost. This however provides no incentive to the transferor division, and two main alternative solutions to the problem are suggested:

— to transfer at full cost (plus profit if desired) but to declare to the buying division the marginal cost content of that price;
— to transfer at marginal cost, but to allow the selling division to make periodic lump-sum charges to cover its fixed costs and profit mark-up (i.e. to have a 'two-part tariff').

(c) *Policy statement for transfers at market price*

(i) Inter-factory sales will be effected at market price.

(ii) No factory will be obliged to accept an order from an associated factory at market price if the former is not equipped to manufacture at a cost which at least allows a reasonable contribution towards its fixed costs, or if the acceptance of such an order would result in more profitable work being displaced.

(iii) Where a factory is prepared to supply components at market price, the buying factory will be obliged to buy therefrom unless it can be established that there are reasons to doubt that quality or delivery will be satisfactory.

(iv) Where it is not reasonably possible to obtain an outside quotation for a component the transfer price will be full standard cost plus 10% profit.

(v) Difficulties arising concerning inter-factory pricing will be referred to the chief accountant who will give a ruling based on the overriding company interest.

2

(a) It is assumed in the following calculations that the 'total demand' for product A is inclusive of quantities transferred to division B.

Scenario 15

Transfers at market price of £30 per unit.

		Division A	Division B
		£000	£000
External sales	(20,000 × £30)	600	(40,000 × £100)4,000
Transfers to Division B	(80,000 × £30)	2,400	
	100,000	3,000	4,000
Variable costs	(100,000 × £20)	2,000	(40,000 × £12) 480
Transferred cost		–	2,400
Fixed cost		500	720
		2,500	3,600
Profit		500	400

900

Transfers at variable cost. This, in fact, is the variable cost of £20 per unit plus a lump sum amounting to 80% of £500,000, i.e. £400,000.

	Division A	Division B
	£000	£000
External sales	600	4,000
Transfers to division B:		
Variable cost (80,000 × £20) 1,600		
Fixed cost 400		
	2,000	
	2,600	4,000
Variable costs	2,000	480
Transferred cost	–	2,000
Fixed cost	500	720
	2,500	3,200
Profit	100	800

900

Scenario 23

Transfers at variable cost. See note under Scenario 15.

		Division A		Division B	
		£000		£000	
External sales	(10,000 × £25)	250	(30,000 × £90)	2,700	
Transfers to					
Division B:					
Variable					
cost	(60,000 × £20)	1,200			
Fixed cost		400			
		1,600			
	70,000	1,850		2,700	
Variable costs (70,000 × £20)		1,400	(30,000 × £12)	360	
Transferred cost		—		1,600	
Fixed cost		500		720	
		1,900		2,680	
Profit (loss)		(50)		20	
			(30)		

Transfers at absorbed standard cost, i.e. variable cost £20 plus fixed cost £5 = £25 per unit.

		Division A	Division B
		£000	£000
External sales		250	2,700
Transfers to			
division B	(60,000 × £25)	1,500	
		1,750	2,700
Variable costs		1,400	360
Transferred cost		—	1,500
Fixed cost		500	720
		1,900	2,580
Profit (loss)		(150)	120
			(30)

Scenario 29

Transfers at market price of £35 per unit

		Division A		Division B
		£000		£000
External sales	(70,000 × £35)	2,450	(30,000 × £90)	2,700
Transfers to				
division B	(60,000 × £35)	2,100		—
	130,000	4,550		2,700
Variable costs	(130,000 × £20)	2,600	(30,000 × £12)	360
Transferred cost		—		2,100
Fixed cost		500		720
		3,100		3,180
Profit (loss)		1,450		(480)

970

Transfers at variable cost

		Division A	Division B
		£000	£000
External sales		2,450	2,700
Transfers to			
division B:			
Var. cost	(60,000 × £20)	1,200	
Fixed cost		400	
		1,600	
		4,050	2,700
Variable costs		2,600	360
Transferred cost		—	1,600
Fixed cost		500	720
		3,100	2,680
Profit		950	20

970

318

Transfers at absorbed standard cost

	Division A	Division B
	£000	£000
External sales	2,450	2,700
Transfers to		
division B (60,000 × £25)	1,500	–
	3,950	2,700
Variable costs	2,600	360
Transferred cost	–	1,500
Fixed cost	500	720
	3,100	2,580
Profit	850	120

970

(b) At whatever price product A is transferred, the manager of division B will regard it as a variable cost in his division. He will add his own variable cost of £12 per unit in arriving at the total marginal cost for comparison with the special order price.

Scenario 23

	£
Transfer price absorbed standard cost	25

	£
∴ Divisional marginal cost:	
2 units @ £25	50
Conversion cost	12
	62

∴ The divisional manager in B would not recommend sale at an ex-factory price of £55.

Scenario 29

Transfer price: market price £35.

	£
∴ Divisional marginal cost:	
2 units @ £35	70
Conversion cost	12
	82

∴ Again, the divisional manager in B would not recommend sale at an ex-factory price of £65,

(c) The managing director of the group would have knowledge of the true variable costs in division A (£20 per unit of product A) and would use these in arriving at a decision that would be in the interest of the group as a whole.

Scenario 23

	£
Variable cost in division A £20 × 2	40
Variable cost in division B	12
	52

The managing director would therefore recommend acceptance since a group contribution of £55 minus £52 = £3 would be earned.

Scenario 29

This scenario has division A operating at maximum capacity. Therefore the undertaking of the additional order will mean that some other contribution is lost.

Units normally sold from:

	Division A		Division B
	£		£
Variable cost	20	2 × 20 =	40
		Conversion	12
	20		52
Market price	35		90
Contribution	15		38

The extra units must therefore better the £30 contribution from normal division A units under Scenario 29 (2 × £15 = £30).

	£
Variable cost in division B	52
Price	65
Contribution	13

The managing director would therefore not recommend acceptance.

3

(a) The optimal transfer pricing policy in these circumstances will be the open market price.

The optimal policy will be designed to encourage the divisional managers to make decisions beneficial to the company as a whole. Divisional autonomy is required to encourage the managers to maximise the performance of their divisions by awareness of their own responsibilities and of local market conditions. Division M must be encouraged to produce and sell the abrasive grain to division D. It will be prepared to do this only if the returns from sale to D are at least equal to the returns from sale to the open market. Division

D, on the other hand, will be prepared to buy the grain from division M only if the price is not in excess of the open market price. Thus the only price that will motivate both divisions to deal internally will be the open market price.

The profits of the company will be divided as follows:

		£
Cost of manufacture	Division M (say)	10
Further costs	Division D (say)	10
Open market price	grain (say)	15
	final product (say)	30

Let us compare three transfer prices: £12, £15, £17:

£12	Division M will sell externally	– profit	5
	Division D will buy externally	– profit	5
			10

£15	Division M will sell internally	– profit	5
	Division D will buy internally	– profit	5
			10

£17	Division M will sell externally	– profit	5
	Division D will buy externally	– profit	5
			10

Thus, providing there is a market for the intermediary product, which under perfect competition there will be, the only price that encourages transfer internally is the open market price. Profits will be shared between the divisions as if they were buying from and selling to the open market, thereby making them indifferent between internal and external transactions. Perfect competition entails that the company can sell all it wishes at the open market price. Thus no transfer price below this is possible for division M to be prepared to sell internally and division D will not pay more than the open market price. In perfect competition for both intermediary and final products the overall profits of the company will be unaffected by the transfer price.

(b)

Profit matrix

Division X processing

Division Y processing		100	200	300	400
	100	X	X	(60)	(60)
	200	X	20	10	30
	300	80	120	130	115
	400	120	150	155	135
	500	130	155	155	115
	600	115	135	115	55

Profit is maximised under three possibilities:

X	200	with	Y	500
X	300	with	Y	400
X	300	with	Y	500

The transfer price should be set with the aim of arriving at one of these situations.

Once the price is set S will wish to produce at a level that maximises its contribution and X and Y will wish to do the same. In these situations the limiting condition is when marginal cost equals marginal revenue, i.e. production will be undertaken providing there is a positive contribution from each marginal unit produced. The marginal revenue/cost tables are as follows:

Marginal revenues (£000)

Level	0-100	100-200	200-300	300-400	400-500	500-600
X	120	60	40	20	–	–
Y	120	120	120	60	40	20

Marginal costs (£000)

Level	400-500	500-600	600-700	700-800	800-900	900-1000
S	20	30	35	40	60	80

The marginal revenue will equal the marginal cost to X and Y at the required levels if the transfer price is £400 per ton and this will equate marginal cost to marginal revenue for S at the 700-800 level. This figure is then the limiting price per ton, but there remains the possibility of a number of non-optimal outcomes when S produces in excess of the requirements of X and Y. If the divisions are to be considered autonomous they must be encouraged to produce at a level that will be optimal without doubt. A price of just under £400 per ton will encourage the following:

S to produce at 700
X to be willing to process at 300, Y at 500

Although S's production does not fulfil the requirements of both X and Y the restriction will operate to optimal positions.

Thus if S is to decide independently on a production level in advance a transfer price of between £350 and £400 is recommended to result in a production level of 700 tons. However, if S is to be willing to produce according to the orders of X and Y divisions a transfer price of £400 is recommended as by this means a production level of 800 is available which could also be optimal.

4

(a) An outlay cost approach shows a positive contribution for the firm as a whole:

	£	£
Selling price — final product	–	300
Outlay cost in division A	120	
Outlay cost in division B	150	270
Contribution		30

However, if there is no excess capacity in division A, any transfer will result in diverting product from the market for the intermediate product. Sales in that market result in a greater contribution for the firm as a whole.

	£
Selling price — intermediate product	200
Outlay cost in division A	120
Contribution	80

Therefore transfers should not be made to division B, where division A has no spare capacity. Market price is the transfer price which leads to the correct decision, i.e. do not transfer to division B unless there are extenuating circumstances regarding the necessity for continuing to market the final product. B must either drop the product or must reduce costs.

(b) If A has excess capacity, and there is no intermediate external demand for more than 800 units at £200, the minimum transfer price that should be used is the outlay cost to division A of £120. At this price B would buy because a contribution of £30 per unit would be generated.

(c) Division B would show zero contribution, but the firm as a whole would generate a contribution of £30 per unit on the 200 units transferred. Any price between £120 and £150 would induce the transfer that would be desirable from the viewpoint of the firm as a whole. A motivational problem often arises regarding how to split the £30 contribution between division A and B. Unless the price were below £150, B would have little incentive to buy.

Tutorial note

The transfer price that may appear optimal as an economic analysis may be totally unacceptable from the viewpoint of preserving autonomy of the managers and evaluating the performance of the divisions as economic units. For instance, consider the simplest case discussed above, where there is idle capacity and the £200 intermediate price is to be maintained. That A should sell to B at £120, the variable cost of A, may be desirable from the viewpoint of B and the firm as a whole regarding this particular decision. However, the manager of A is likely to be unhappy because he will earn nothing and his autonomy is being eroded. He can rightly maintain that he is contributing to the earning of income on the final product, so he deserves a portion of the total firm contribution of £30 per unit. But how much? This is a major unanswered question in practice. The price can be negotiated upward to somewhere between £120 and £150 so that some 'equitable' split is achieved. A dual transfer pricing scheme has also been suggested whereby the supplier gets credit for the full intermediate market price and the buyer is charged only with variable or incremental cost. In any event, when there is heavy interdependence between divisions some system of subsidies may be needed to deal with the three problems of goal congruence, incentive and preservation of autonomy. Where heavy subsidies are needed a question can be raised as to whether the existing degree of decentralisation is optimal .

(d)   £

Potential contribution from external intermediate
sale is 1,000 X (£195 − £120)   75,000
Contribution through keeping price at £200
is 800 X £80   64,000

Foregone contribution by transferring 200 units   £11,000

Opportunity cost per unit by transfer $= \dfrac{£11,000}{200} = £55$

Transfer price = £120 + £55 = £175

An alternative approach to obtaining the same answer is to recognise that the outlay cost is the same for all 1,000 units in question. Therefore the total revenue desired by A would be the same for selling outside or inside. Let X equal the transfer price of indifference:

$$1,000 \, (£195) \quad = \quad 800 \, (£200) + 200 \times X$$

$$X \quad = \quad £175$$

The £175 price will lead to the correct decision. B will not buy because its total costs of £175 + £150 will exceed its prospective selling price of £300. A will then sell 1,000 units at £195 to the outside; A and the firm will have a contribution margin of £75,000. Otherwise the firm would have a contribution of £64,000 plus £6,000 (200 units of final product X £30) = £70,000.

Index

References in roman type are to questions, and those in *italic* to answers.